KING SOLOMON'S
EMPIRE

In their introduction to *King Solomon's Empire*, Archie and Margaret Roy state that Solomon is often avoided on the basis that fewer books have been written about him in comparison to the many books about his father, David.

They have given us a widely researched, comprehensive, yet very readable study on this amazing biblical character, the Scriptures attributed to his authorship, and what can be learned from various historical sources, as well as the personality and psychological aspects of this most fascinating man. His God-given gift of astounding wisdom, his great wealth, and the creation of a powerful but peaceful empire is contrasted with his overindulgence, materially and sexually, as he allowed the idolatry of his many foreign wives to take root in the kingdom, leading to its breakup following his death.

His unwillingness to apply to himself the wisdom for which he was held in world-renown is fully exposed. I like the various New Testament references, such as in the description of the laver of bronze in Solomon's Temple with its lily fretwork around the rim being connected to Jesus saying, "Look at the lilies and how they grow. They don't work or make their clothing, yet Solomon in all his glory was not dressed as beautifully as they are" (Luke 12:27). A very interesting and enlightening read!

Randall Staley, Founder | Transformation in Christ | London, England

I enjoyed *King Solomon's Empire*. Archie and Margaret Roy have done a great job in providing a comprehensive picture of his life. With Solomon, we are inclined to focus on three main subjects at first glance: the temple, his wisdom, and his one thousand wives and concubines. We tend not to get a sense of the essence of Solomon's character and what he stood for. There is so much more to Solomon's story. The writers have embarked on a quest to give us a more rounded measure of the man and ruler.

Archie and Margaret Roy take us on a journey through Solomon's Temple. They carefully cover the practical aspects of the temple, how it intertwined with daily life, Solomon's instruction from his father David, and the king ultimately going above and beyond with regard to grandeur. The writers draw us into the biblical significance, a picture of a heavenly reality, and also reveal the other influences which Solomon allowed. They ultimately show how it all ties into the undeniable truth that God is on the throne. In essence, the writers are correct when they explain that the presence of God in the temple was the apex of Solomon's reign.

Finally, as we read of the end of Solomon and of his ongoing legacy, it is hard to understand such a fall. The writers take us through Solomon's wisdom and his Song and Proverbs and finish this off with the *how* of Solomon's fall. They then describe the impact of his falling away and show the long-term consequences of the splitting of the kingdoms and the resultant exile. They also guide readers through some modern-day aspects of Solomon's influence, especially on Israel as a state since 1948.

The writers conclude with this great truth: Christ changes us and is the perfect Friend.

Pastor Martin Tatton | Calvary Glasgow City Church | Glasgow, Scotland

Archie Roy is a thinker. This is not a shallow book of mere religious history, but a carefully and prayerfully thought-out map that will help the reader understand not only the many mysteries of Solomon as a biblical writer, king, and philosopher, but of his spiritual world influence both for good and for ill.

Students often ask why Solomon is referred to as the "wisest man who ever lived" yet manifests such folly. Archie doesn't skirt this important question and goes in depth to unpack the spiritual, emotional, psychological, and occult roots that contribute to this complicated portrait. But Archie goes even further: he gives us a detailed map of how Solomon's legacy has formed and deformed a wide variety of important current events and human contemporary struggles such as the national identity of modern Israeli warfare and the sexual revolution. He also uncovers how King Solomon's kingdom and its legacy foreshadow both the end-of-this-age kingdom of the Antichrist as well as the true Messiah's rule.

If you are hungry for a demanding yet readable study of the life and mystery of King Solomon, this book by Dr. Archie Roy is like no other I know of in offering clear answers, raising vital and intriguing questions, and bringing satisfactory conclusions to the many mysterious contradictions of King Solomon.

Clay McLean, President | Nightlight, Inc. | McLean Ministries | Hickory, North Carolina

Invited by the authors to read and give comment on the manuscript was not only a privilege but also an opportunity to indulge myself in Old Testament study, which has always been of special interest to me. The topic of King Solomon intrigued me and led me to ask the question, why Solomon? Searching for an answer, it became clear to me that (apart from the Bible) out of the abundance of books written about Old Testament Scriptures—such as the history, theology, book commentaries, and biographical studies of Old Testament characters—specific material in comparison on the life of King Solomon was limited in number and in scope. I, therefore, have to applaud Dr Roy for his keen initiative to embark upon this somewhat rather neglected subject and to endeavor to contribute a piece of scholarly work that is long overdue on the life, times, successes, failures, warnings, richness, and positive contributions of King Solomon, the third monarch who ruled over the United Kingdom of Israel.

Reflecting on the text, I liked the way the book had been arranged. Two of the four sections (1 and 3) offer great insight about Solomon's early life, rise to kingship, his gifts, relationships, and later, sadly, his tragic personal decline and that of the nation due to his many wrong decisions as a result of pride and disobedience to God's commands and instructions. The author does a thorough job in revealing Solomon's strengths and weaknesses by hitting the mark square on—"warts and all." When reading these chapters, one could not come away without a deeper insight and appreciation of Solomon the man, his culture and the atmosphere of the times in which he lived and reigned. "Sitz im Leben" (Setting in Life) is most important to me as I am always enriched when I can read a text in context, which helps me grasp the value and the richness of the story. Dr. Roy has, in my view, achieved this! He is to be commended for the depth of research that he has put into this excellent scholarly work.

Adding wonderfully to the book is the contribution (Section 2) of Dr. Roy's wife, Margaret, as she focuses on Solomon's writings: Song of Solomon, Ecclesiastes, and Proverbs. After reading the weighty historical part of Section 1, I appreciated being led to reflect on aspects of the richness and brilliance of Solomon's writings. These convey the extent of the king's gift and anointing from

God and, together with the addition of reflective comment by Margaret, brought life to the sayings, thus conveying the enduring value that they are to many readers. This was something that I liked in the book. It gave me an opportunity to think and reflect but also to appreciate the incredible truths that Solomon sought to impart for the enrichment and betterment of life and faith.

All in all, this book, in my opinion, contains a masterly grasp of the essence of Solomon, third king of Israel. It contains the story of a man's call to be king, his successes and failures; but above all, it gives valuable lessons, challenges, and warnings to anyone called into national and/or spiritual leadership. Dr. and Mrs. Roy have presented a valuable contribution in this book to the world of Old Testament scholarship. Personally, I have been deeply blessed by reading this book and would have no hesitation in recommending it to any generally interested reader of Old Testament. In addition, it would be an extremely worthwhile acquisition for the serious student wishing a more detailed study.

The book's closing section, aptly named "Is There Anything New Under The Sun?," leaves open some questions for the reader to wrestle with and to prayerfully seek answers for themselves! For myself, no bad thing in itself!

Rev. Morris M. Dutch, Minister | Church of Scotland

ARCHIE W. N. ROY PHD
AND MARGARET P. ROY

KING SOLOMON'S
EMPIRE

The Rise, Fall, and

Modern-Day Influence

of an Iron-Age Ruler

AMBASSADOR INTERNATIONAL
GREENVILLE, SOUTH CAROLINA & BELFAST, NORTHERN IRELAND

www.ambassador-international.com

King Solomon's Empire

The Rise, Fall, and Modern-Day Influence of an Iron-Age Ruler

Hardcover ISBN: 978-1-64960-342-5
Paperback ISBN: 978-1-64960-341-8
eISBN: 978-1-64960-359-3

Cover Design by Hannah Linder Designs
Interior Design by Dentelle Design
Edited by Katie Cruice Smith

Scripture taken from Scripture the New King James Version®. Copyright © 1982 by Thomas Nelson. Used by permission. All rights reserved.

AMBASSADOR INTERNATIONAL
Emerald House
411 University Ridge, Suite B14
Greenville, SC 29601
United States
www.ambassador-international.com

AMBASSADOR BOOKS
The Mount
2 Woodstock Link
Belfast, BT6 8DD
Northern Ireland, United Kingdom
www.ambassadormedia.co.uk

The colophon is a trademark of Ambassador, a Christian publishing company.

For

Frances H. Roy, née Hall

1926-2021

TABLE OF CONTENTS

Hold Thou Thy cross before my closing eyes
Shine through the gloom and point me to the skies
Heaven's morning breaks, and earth's vain shadows flee
In life, in death, o Lord, abide with me.

—H. F. Lyte, 1847

That which has been is *what will be, that which* is *done is what will be done, and* there is *nothing new under the sun.*

—Ecclesiastes 1:9

ACKNOWLEDGMENTS

Our heartfelt thanks go to those whose conversations and insights helped shape this endeavor. When we met up with him at the wonderful Blue Ridge Assembly in Black Mountain, North Carolina, Clay McLean, in particular, helped us to identify a few of the significant themes contained herein, such as the oblique observations made by Asaph on Solomon and his times. Orthopedic surgeon, Dr. Kenneth David-West's lectures on the Song of Solomon at Victory Bible College in 2013-2014 first opened Margaret's eyes to its real meaning—that there was more to it than the allegorical view preached most often in churches. Our thanks also go to our publisher at Ambassador International, Sam Lowry, and his team, as well as to our editors, Katie Cruice Smith of Ambassador International and Allie D. Zitvogel of Anderson University, South Carolina, and to librarians at the University of Glasgow's main library who helped us track down some of the more obscure Solomon-related references.

INTRODUCTION

Of all the people in the Bible who are studied, Solomon is often the one most avoided. We say *avoided* rather than overlooked. His was hardly a life one could overlook; it is more a case that certain aspects of his life cause most commentators to shy away from him. In contrast to his father, King David, there are very few books about Solomon and very few sermons, despite the fact that he is recorded as the author of three Old Testament works. We have heard scores of sermons about David. We have heard none concerning his son.

One of the reasons, we believe, is the seeming conflictual information in Scripture as to his character, his pursuits, his impact, and his legacy. He built the Jewish kingdom up until it was the most powerful Iron Age kingdom in the Middle East, yet his strategies for achieving this led to the kingdom's rapid decline after his death both spiritually and geopolitically. Solomon created a glorious temple to Yahweh; yet all too soon, it became infiltrated by pagan religious worship, and the temple itself was finally destroyed.

The king is recorded as possessing seven hundred wives and three hundred concubines, and yet the same record only mentions one son and two daughters by name with the inference that there were other unnamed daughters. Would there not have been many hundreds of children, if not thousands? Why is even the number of them omitted from Scripture?

Furthermore, Solomon is a king who is recorded as having been devoted to his God, Yahweh, but in later life, he turned away and worshipped idols. He was given wisdom by God, and we see him exercising this wisdom even up to the end of his life when he either penned or was the inspiration for Ecclesiastes.

21

Yet in a number of respects, he can be said to have acted very foolishly. These spiritual conundrums combined with profound questions as to his character and personality are perhaps the main reasons why most commentators and preachers avoid him unless they are writing specifically about the books of Kings or Chronicles, neither of which Solomon wrote.

He is also just so hard to categorize. He was not like his father, David, who, after all, was much more transparent. He is also unlike any of the other kings after him. Solomon is unique, and he has been uniquely baffling. The character and appearance of Solomon's reign were so magnificent that almost a thousand years later, Jesus alludes to it all when He teaches about physical possessions and worry during His Sermon on the Mount (recorded in Matthew's gospel). He points out the wildflowers (they were not necessarily lilies) and says that although they do not labor or spin, they are beautifully clothed by God, more so "than Solomon in all his glory" (Matt. 6:29). He is neither saying that it was good that Solomon was so splendidly dressed or that it was sinful. He is merely saying that it was so. The wildflowers are remarkable because they are more beautiful; they are created and blessed by God. They surpass even the greatness of Solomon's appearance. But how great was Solomon in all his glory? What would it have looked like? Why was he remembered so clearly after all the time which had elapsed? Surely, these things are worth finding out.

Some commentators split Solomon's reign into two almost equal halves. In his first twenty or so years in power, he behaved wisely and creatively. He worshipped Yahweh, and he built up the kingdom while guaranteeing international peace. The second half of his reign, however, was characterized by folly, idolatry, and self-indulgence. Is this accurate? We believe that there *was* a profound change in the character of his reign and that it can only be understood when we consider the man's personality. What was his family of origin like, and what personality dynamics drove the king and the decisions he made? These questions have received very little attention, but we believe there is enough evidence in the biblical material to give these questions some proper consideration.

Sometimes, we have quoted from *Midrasham* and other extra-biblical sources, usually at the start of chapters. *Midrasham* are parables and imaginative ideas written out through many centuries by rabbis who wanted to teach lessons—for instance, that wrong decisions have consequences. Like the parables taught by Jesus, they are not meant to be taken literally. At the same time, they concern truth and should, therefore, not be dismissed.

PART I

A TIME TO BUILD

BY: ARCHIE W. N. ROY

WHEN A WILDLIFE PHOTOGRAPHER SETS out with a team to track and film a rare animal these days, it is often done for television. A whole series will unfold on the screen in due course, spread over several weeks' duration. Until the last episode, however, the dramatic question to keep the viewers watching is whether the team will be successful. This question is made up of several others to do with what that success means. Will the team find the animal at all? If they do, how good will the footage actually be?

The snow leopard, for instance, is very rare and very elusive. It is no small thing to set out to photograph it in its natural habitat. Initially, the team are beset with difficulties. The rain, humidity, mud, bugs in the food, and so on take their toll on a team who must endure weeks of trekking and camping out at night. Because the cats prefer an inhospitable, mountainous terrain, vehicles can only take the photographers and their crew part of the way. Their first nights in the camp are not auspicious. The remote cameras do not catch anything to do with the leopard. Small rodents trigger one or two of the cameras when the team sleeps fitfully. There is nothing to see night after night. Sheer tenacity finally overturns the lack of success, and a remote camera initially captures something of the majestic beast—a hind leg passing by—not much but still proof that the animal is there. It is the encouragement they needed so badly.

We all know how the series ends. The snow leopards are filmed at dusk, when they are most active, high up on a rocky cliff face. Their cubs come into view as well and then disappear again. We did not expect the leopards to look quite as they do with their bright blue eyes. Their fur blends in so well with their environment; it is only with the benefit of telescopic lenses that anything can be viewed at all. It is a wonderful culmination to the journey of discovery. A trip well worth the undertaking.

Hunting for the majestic and elusive King Solomon is a bit like hunting for the snow leopard. Perhaps this is why there are so few biographies of him. For a start, as is the case of Jesus, there is not one physical description of Solomon in Scripture. We do not know what he looked like. Also, it is difficult to capture him in other ways. We will find, for instance, that there is very little direct speech attributed to him in Scripture. He speaks through his writings, but it would help if we had more examples of conversations which record what he said. We know what the Queen of Sheba actually said, word for word, to Solomon but we do not know what he said to her! For some reason, what he said has been obscured. We know what King David said to Solomon, but we do not know what Solomon said, if anything. Why is that?

I believe that God has chosen to protect Solomon. We are only allowed to know so much about him. We may be able to photograph a hind leg passing by. We may capture some movement of the king when he is most active at dusk. It may become as if he is finally and fully going to come into view, and we will now see him in all his glory. But the moment does not come. He has disappeared again. We have seen shadows and a brief glimpse of spellbinding detail, but what exactly was it that we saw? Was the camera on?

The shape this biography of King Solomon has taken has been determined by the nature of the man himself and the life he lived. His trajectory is not straightforward. In fact, whether one considers him to have been a good king or a bad one depends very much on where you focus. We have felt it necessary to divide our biography of King Solomon into two parts and then divide these with a consideration of the writings commonly ascribed to him. In this first part of his biography, the king's journey takes him from being a background figure in his family to the throne of Israel, and from there to the mountain of the Lord's house, spoken of by the prophets of Israel both before and after Solomon's reign. Solomon built a temple for God, and God manifested His presence there. This is the apex of Solomon's life as king of Israel. God's presence in His temple promises so much. Out of Zion, God's law would go forth, and there would be peace. All would sit under their vines and fig trees, and no one would make them afraid. Solomon was so successful relatively early on in his reign that Asaph and the other temple priests, prophets, and musicians of Solomon's time would have thought that Israel had arrived.

Yet the prophet Micah was prophesying about the mountain of the Lord's house long after Solomon's reign, not before it. Two hundred years later, when

Micah lived, things were much worse for the Jewish people. Now, Jerusalem was in grave danger. Micah was prophesying destruction for Jerusalem, albeit with the promise of a final, lasting peace in a new age. What happened to the promise of peace with Solomon, and why did it become just a glimpse of something much greater still to come? Solomon ascended the mountain but somehow descended it afterward. This is his trajectory. For some reason or reasons, he was unable to remain close to God. What was it in his character which caused him to slide? This first part of our biography will focus on the king's upward journey to the mountain of Zion and the temple he built there. This then leads on to a consideration of the inspired Scriptures ascribed to the king.

Why does God protect King Solomon from full scrutiny? I believe it is primarily because, as he says, He loved Solomon. He knows what Solomon could have been—someone even greater than he was. But over and above that, He loved him. Further, more detail about the king would not be to our benefit. We are given enough for instruction and guidance, no more. What we have is sufficient. We will find, as we investigate the great king, that there is still plenty to discover. The journey is well worth setting out on. There are fascinating things in store, many of them neglected for too long. We will spend enough time on the journey to give Solomon every possible opportunity to come into view.

CHAPTER 1
SOLOMON'S FAMILY OF ORIGIN

"To everything there is a season, A time for every purpose under heaven:
A time to be born, And a time to die."

—Ecclesiastes 3:1-2a

Although King David had many wives and concubines, we do not know the exact number of either. Even when it comes to his wives, some are unnamed. However, all seem to have borne him children, with the exception of Michal, King Saul's daughter, who was childless. We do know that David had at least nineteen sons.

Apart from Michal, seven wives are also named. Ahinoam, the Yizre'elite, gave him a son, whom they named Amnon. He was the heir-apparent until he was assassinated by Absalom, David's son by Maacah, an Aramean princess of the royal house of Geshur in Syria. In turn, Absalom was killed in battle by David's army commander, Joab, a turn of events that greatly distressed the king.

David married Abigail, the former wife of Nabal, and they had a son called Chileab. He also married Haggith; and their son, Adonijah, the second heir-apparent, was killed ex-judicially by Solomon, whose mother was Bathsheba. David and Bathsheba, the former wife of Uriah of the Hittites, had three other sons called Shammua, Shobab, and Nathan. David married Abital, and their son was Shephatiah. He also married Eglah. Their son was Ithream.

The Bible lists at least nine other sons of David by name but does not relay who their respective mothers were; instead, Scripture focuses on where they were born (e.g. 1 Chronicles 3:4-9). It also indicates that there were a number of concubines. There also may have been other wives in addition to those listed.

Solomon was born around 992 B.C. His half-brother Adonijah was about ten years old at that time, while Absalom was about twelve years old and Amnon about thirteen. Amnon, Adonijah, and Absalom were born in Hebron between 1005 and 1002 B.C. during David's war against Saul (2 Samuel 3:2-4). Unlike David and some of Solomon's brothers, we are not given any detail at all as to what Solomon looked like. We are also given no detail at all about what his wives and concubines looked like or their relationships with him. Did he love them? Did any of them love him?

The mystery about Solomon grows even more when we realize that almost no conversation between him and another individual is recorded. This includes, for instance, Hiram in Tyre and the Queen of Sheba; but *her* words to *him* are recorded at length.[1] Why is that? The sole exceptions to this omission of direct speech from Solomon are his conversation with Yahweh in a dream and one occasion when he spoke directly to his mother concerning Abishag.

The story of Solomon's birth is unique in Scripture if we compare it to the other kings recorded as ruling over Israel as a unified kingdom and also all the kings who ruled subsequently over the two separated kingdoms of Israel in the North and Judah in the South. It is also unique when we compare it to all his siblings, especially to his older sibling (David and Bathsheba's first child), who died unnamed. He is given the name Solomon (המלש) immediately by his parents—the name meaning *peace*. But soon after, he is given a second name by the prophet Nathan. He is called Yedidyah (הידידי). It is also recorded that "the Lord loved him" (2 Sam. 12:24-25). Why the additional, special name?

The Divine choice or election of Saul and David as kings over Israel is arguably more obvious in Scripture, which also records God's absolute turning away from Saul (e.g. 1 Sam. 10 and 15-16). However, the use of a second name and the subsequent affirmation is not so clear-cut. In fact, the affirmation underlines the

---

1   The quotation in 2 Chronicles 8:11 is not an exception, since it is not clear whom Solomon is addressing. It appears to be a court audience.

second name, which literally means "beloved of the Lord." Presumably, Nathan gave Solomon the second name at the Lord's behest.

The additional naming or renaming of a Jewish king was highly unusual, and there are no further examples in Scripture of God renaming any. There are many examples, though, of the pagan renaming of kings in the ancient Middle East in order to legitimize usurpers of the throne or kings who were not in the direct line. The last king of Judah, Mathaniah, was renamed Zedekiah (literally, "the Lord helped me to get my right") by Nebuchadnezzar. Mathaniah was not the legitimate king.

Isaac Kalimi draws on a substantial number of sources to argue that Yedidyah is a royal or regal name.[2] It is also a theophoric name: the name contains the name of God. God's purpose was to reveal that the baby had His blessing, in contrast to the unnamed, illegitimate child, who was now dead. God was also revealing that despite the curse on David's house, Solomon would, nevertheless, live and succeed through God's blessing. "Now therefore, the sword shall never depart from your house, because you have despised Me" (2 Sam. 12:10). The name also affirms Solomon's right to rule, despite not being first in line to the throne. Some viewed him as a usurper, but his second name said that the Lord still preferred him; He chose him as David's legitimate heir, and Solomon was not a usurper. When he was older, Solomon inferred back to his name as God's promise at birth to him: "Now therefore, *as* the LORD lives, who has confirmed me and set me on the throne of David my father, and who has established a house for me, as He promised, Adonijah shall be put to death today!" (1 Kings 2:24).

Once he ascended the throne of Israel as Solomon, or "Prince of Peace," neither Solomon nor anyone else referred to the king as Yedidyah. The theophoric name had served its purpose. He was chosen to be king from before he was born, and he had now taken his appointed place on his father's throne. Among all the Israelite kings, Solomon was uniquely favored by God. Even after half a millennium had passed, the governor of Persian Judea, Nehemiah, reflected back

---

2   Isaac Kalimi, "Love of God and *Apologia* for a King," *Journal of Ancient Near Eastern Religions 17*, No. 1, (2017), 28-63, *doi:* https://doi.org/10.1163/15692124-12341285.

on this as he and his work party repaired the walls of Solomon's ruined capital city, the king's many sins notwithstanding. "Did not Solomon king of Israel sin by these things? Yet among many nations there was no king like him, who was beloved of his God; and God made him king over all Israel. Nevertheless pagan women caused even him to sin" (Neh. 13:26).

CHAPTER 2

THE END OF KING DAVID'S REIGN

"As the Lord has been with my lord the king, even so may He be with Solomon, and make his throne greater than the throne of my lord King David."

—1 Kings 1:37

David was about seventy years old when his reign came to an end. The book of 2 Samuel narrates how he could not get warm while lying in bed, and so his advisors brought him a young virgin named Abishag to warm him up. It is likely that she functioned as a quasi-nurse. Orthodox Jewish understanding of Scripture states that David did not have sexual intercourse with her—not because he could not but because of his love for Solomon's mother, Bathsheba (e.g. see Israel Drazin's *The Authentic King Solomon*). The reality, though, may have more to do with David's old age. He is described as a man whose strength and virility were passing away.

The Bible shows that David had built up a state which had become akin to an empire, albeit one which was more limited in territory than that of the twin empires north and south of Israel—the kingdom of Hattusa (the Hittites) now gone from the scene and Egypt. His Judean tribal kingdom had grown into a national one through his alliance with Israel and was then developed further into a consolidated, territorial state. This led to frequent warfare with the Philistines, and although David could not conquer them, he was able to isolate them to the coastline west of his kingdom.

David was able to take things further. Having subdued the Philistines, he rotated his military focus to the east and conquered Edom, Moab, and Ammon, thereby creating a multinational state. These nations were dealt with in various ways. Moab became a vassal state; Edom was brought in as a province; and Ammon was annexed outright. David was creating a state which had never existed before in the Middle East. Finally, he forged the empire, which Solomon would develop further by expanding across the northeast, defeating the Syrian-Aramean kingdom of Zobah and making it a tributary state (which his son Solomon would lose control over).

Historians such as Abraham Malamat conclude that David created an empire and that Solomon extended it by treaty over a much bigger territory, turning the united monarchy of Israel-Judah into an imperial state with himself at its center, reigning as emperor.[3] However, there had been carnage within David's household during the second half of David's reign after his adultery with Bathsheba and his murder of her husband, Uriah, the Hittite. At this time, Adonijah[4] was his eldest living son because his elder sons, Amnon and Absalom, were both dead. Scripture recounts how Amnon deceived and raped his half-sister Tamar. Her brother Absalom took her into his home and looked after her, waiting two years before assassinating Amnon in revenge since their father David, although angered by the incident, could not bring himself to punish his firstborn son.[5]

Absalom was another of his father's favorites. According to 2 Samuel 14:27, he had three sons and one daughter, whom he named Tamar in memory of his beloved sister. After murdering Amnon, Absalom fled to his grandfather, the king of Geshur, until finally returning to Jerusalem some three years later. He was not reconciled to his father, though; and after seeing David's weakness in old age and his abnegation of judicial power, Absalom instigated a major

---

3   Abraham Malamat, "The Kingdom of David & Solomon in Its Contact with Egypt and Aram Naharaim," *The Biblical Archaeologist* 21, No. 4 (1958), 96–102, doi: https://doi.org/10.2307/3209177.
4   The meaning of the name is "Yah is my Lord."
5   This detail is included in the Dead Sea Scrolls narrative but not in the Hebrew text.

rebellion and declared himself king. Also perceiving David's weakness, most of the people sided with Absalom, and David fled for his life. Finally, David's troops went head to head with Absalom's army at a site known as Ephraim's Wood. David's army commander, Joab, caught Absalom, who had become entangled in the overhanging boughs of a tree, and killed him, against David's orders not to harm his son. Then, David mourned for the son who would surely have killed him.

As David's health and strength began to fail even more rapidly after losing his son, Adonijah now assumed he could be king. "Then Adonijah the son of Haggith exalted himself, saying, 'I will be king'; and he prepared for himself chariots and horsemen, and fifty men to run before him. (And his father had not rebuked him at any time by saying, 'Why have you done so?'" (1 Kings 1:5-6).

Therefore, David encouraged the people to see Adonijah as the crown prince without having the idea fixed in his mind. As with Absalom, David was acquiescent and did not see rebellion or the longer-term maneuvering and striving for power. He was blind to his sons' characters and ambitions. Adonijah also had enough strength of will to sway some of David's key loyalists at court, particularly Joab, David's military commander, who had been questioning David's judgment for some time. In fact, Joab had to deal with many matters of state as David's focus as king and supreme judge in the kingdom had waned.

Adonijah selected those from the military command and the priesthood who would be on-side and organized his own coronation outside Jerusalem, away from any opposing factions, with the plan then being to return to the capital and either seek David's approval or to eliminate him along with Solomon. The coronation was an unconstitutional *coup d'état*. Adonijah invited all of David's sons to the event with the sole exception of Solomon. They assembled at a sacred spring known as *Ein Rogel*, the serpent or dragon well. And there they sacrificed a large number of animals on a rocky plateau called the serpent-stone or *Zoheleth*. The roasted flesh was eaten in a meal, which served as a covenant ritual. As they ate, they all said, "*Long* live King Adonijah" (1 Kings 1:25), the king to reign after David passed away, one way or another.

The prophet Nathan knew that this sequence of events had to be thwarted. Its success would lead to the execution of Solomon, his mother, and possibly himself, since he also had not been invited to the ceremony. He quickly informed Bathsheba, who went in to the king and said, "'My lord, you swore by the LORD your God to your maidservant, *saying, Assuredly Solomon your son shall reign after me, and he shall sit on my throne.*' So now, look! Adonijah has become king; and now, my lord the king, you do not know about *it*'" (1 Kings 1:17-18). She then implored David to announce to Israel who was to succeed him as king.

The old man was able to summon up the mental energy required. He said, "'Just as I swore to you by the LORD God of Israel, saying, *Assuredly Solomon your son shall be king after me, and he shall sit on my throne in my place*, so I certainly will do this day'" (1 Kings 1:30). He commanded everything which needed to take effect immediately; and so a procession including Solomon, priests, the ark of the covenant,[6] and royal guards was assembled and made its way to Gihon, a spring which rises from an underground cave and is associated to this day with Jewish ritual purity ceremonies.

There in a place which looks down the Kidron brook and over to a series of mountains, the highest of which is the Mount of Olives, Solomon was proclaimed and anointed king of Israel. The shofars were sounded, and Solomon returned to Jerusalem to be enthroned on David's throne in the hall of ceremonies. For the remainder of David's days, Solomon ruled as *Nagid,* or prince of Israel and Judah, invested with the judicial and punitive powers of the king.

The anointing of Solomon by Zadok the priest had taken place just two-thirds of a mile from where the serpent-stone congregation had gathered further down the Kidron, and they were so perplexed by the sounds of rejoicing that they stopped eating their feast. When they realized that Solomon had been anointed king with David's approval, they scattered in every direction, realizing that being named as one present at Adonijah's celebrations signified their opposition to the king. But the most fearful of all was Adonijah. He fled to an altar and grabbed

---

6   The presence of the Ark can be inferred from the priest Zadok taking the anointing oil from the tabernacle in 1 Kings 1:39.

hold of its corners, claiming refuge and begging to be spared. He would not move from it until he knew that Solomon would pardon him. Solomon was told of it, and he realized that only a murder accusation was a sufficient reason to remove Adonijah by force.

CHAPTER 3

SOLOMON TAKES THE THRONE AND CONSOLIDATES POWER

I say that every prince must desire to be considered merciful and not cruel.
He must however take care not to misuse this mercifulness. . . . Men have less
scruple in offending one who makes himself loved than one who makes himself
feared; for love is held by a chain of obligation which,
men being selfish, is broken whenever it serves their purpose;
but fear is maintained by a dread of punishment which never fails.

—*The Prince* by Niccolò Machiavelli

On the very day Solomon sat on his throne for the first time, he faced a major dilemma involving his family and the nation. If he did not punish Adonijah in some way, he would be seen by the people as weak, and he might precipitate a civil war. But if he removed him and killed or imprisoned him, he would be seen as tyrannical on his first day in power. Given that first impressions really count, the people would fear and probably distrust him from there on in. Solomon uttered his first judgment as king: "If he proves himself a worthy man, not one hair of him shall fall to the earth; but if wickedness is found in him, he shall die." So King Solomon sent them to bring him down from the altar. And he came and fell down before King Solomon; and Solomon said to him, 'Go to your house'" (1 Kings 1:52-53).

It is an interesting exercise to analyze the pronouncement and its associated commands. The first part describes the possibility of a clean

39

slate in the future. It is about future actions, which signify a right attitude generally and toward the king. The second part is also about the future and outlines the king's absolute and definite will. He is able to punish and has the will to execute the prince. Solomon used a category of wickedness, which is only future-oriented because he was not king at the time when Adonijah sought the throne. But now that he *was* king, he would execute the prince if he set himself against him. Solomon also required Adonijah to bow before him in an act of obeisance, which also signified to his erstwhile followers that the Adonijah faction was dissolved. His command, "Go to thine house," signifies that both Adonijah and his belongings were protected by him, but the sentence also carried a whiff of contempt. Solomon had found his solution to the dilemma, apparently without difficulty. It was a balancing of gentleness, firmness, and contempt all clearly communicated.

The commentator Steven Weitzman compares this first recorded act of wisdom to the cold logic of Machiavelli.[7] A ruler should *appear* to be virtuous, but *being* virtuous is unimportant. Adonijah survived in the short-term because of Solomon's political astuteness but only for a few weeks. Yet we do not actually know what was going through Solomon's mind. He achieved something on day one by cutting through the dilemma, and he dismissed his brother in peace. Whether this hid an intention to kill him later, we do not know. In the end, it was Adonijah who precipitated a disastrous turn of events.

About a month later, Adonijah was seen to renew hostilities but in a much more covert way than before. His goal, though, was, perhaps, the same: to become ruler of Israel.[8] Adonijah deceived Bathsheba into asking Solomon to allow him to marry Abishag, his father's concubine, under the pretense of love and possibly as some sort of compensation. Solomon was aware that a ruler's concubines pass on to the next ruler and that *he,* therefore, had ownership over Abishag. If his brother took the woman, it would amount to a claim to the throne by his elder brother. On

---

7   Steven Weitzman, *Solomon: The Lure of Wisdom* (New Haven: Yale University Press, 2011).
8   There is an alternative explanation that Adonijah really had fallen in love with Abishag. He was so in love that he was blind to how his attempt to have her would be perceived by the king.

the other hand, to refuse the request but take no punitive action would enable the ongoing conspiracy to gain ground on the basis that Adonijah had been refused a personal request, which the king's mother had supported. Solomon would be perceived as very harsh. He had denied his older brother a woman he loved, even after he had taken the crown from his head. Solomon would be denigrated; rebellion would be encouraged; and Joab would bring the army in to depose and kill the king.

In quick order, King Solomon assassinated Adonijah for sedition; David's army commander, Joab, who was conspiring with Adonijah; and Shimei "by the hand of Benaiah," commander of David's eleventh rotational army division. Solomon now appeared to be justified in killing his older brother. If only his older brother had "sat still," as Dale Ralph Davis puts it.[9] But he moved and lost his life.

For multiple reasons, Solomon also now moved to fulfill his father's orders that Joab should be killed, not because of the slain Absalom but because of the current conspiracy against Solomon and also because of Joab's earlier killing of two army officers, Abner and Amasa. These actions by Joab had been against the social conventions of warfare and peace during that time. Joab had "shed the blood of war in peacetime" (1 Kings 2:5). The instruction by David to kill Joab was not so much a desire for revenge but, as Friedrich Thieberger puts it, a desire to restore the balance of justice and the good name of the crown.[10] Because he was convicted of murder, Joab was killed at the altar he fled to and refused to leave. He was replaced by Benaiah.

Solomon ruled the unified kingdom between 970 and 931 B.C. This unified empire was held aloft by the king, and as soon as he passed away, his kingdom did, too. His energy, confidence, and style held it high. Yet commentators, such as Thieberger, point out that in contrast to the lives of Saul and David, Scripture never mentions a single friend or confidant, not even an advisor. Why would

---

9   Dale Ralph Davis, *1 Kings: The Wisdom and the Folly (Focus on the Bible)* (Fearn, Scotland: Christian Focus, 2000).

10   The Austrian philosopher Friedrich Thieberger (1888–1958) taught Franz Kafka Hebrew between 1914 and 1917; they had met in a Prague bookstore in late 1912. His cited comment is to be found in his book, *King Solomon* (1947).

a man blessed with such wisdom require one? His God-given wisdom was sufficient to enable him to maintain the empire, define its borders, govern its spiritual life, and manage the economy and its international trade agreements.

As we review Solomon's life as king, though, we will also see that in his character, wisdom was juxtaposed with passion. He was a man who loved. What did Solomon love? Early on, we see he had a love for Yahweh (1 Kings 3:3). But he also loved women, wealth, banqueting, and aesthetics. He loved the splendor of royal power and the projection of it. Reigning alone, Solomon's inner loneliness compelled him to find comfort in the arms of a thousand women. Many of these women pulled him away from governing the empire's spiritual life. His love for them led him and his nation astray.

SOLOMON'S CONSOLIDATION OF POWER

When David demanded that he use force, Solomon was ruthless in establishing his rulership but also deliberated very carefully. He only carried out David's order to kill Joab, David's nephew and brutal military commander, when further offenses precipitated it. We see from this that the young King Solomon was not influenced by fear. He was not unduly concerned about the families of Abner and Amasa exercising their right to retaliate against Solomon and his family after Joab had slain the men to maintain his military position.[11] He did not immediately kill Joab to cut off the danger of being a victim of vengeance.

He also delayed killing Adonijah until it was clear that the man was not going to stop pursuing the throne. Solomon also delayed killing Shimei, a man who had stood against David and cursed him in public. David believed that this curse would carry on down the generations, affecting Solomon. It would only be canceled when the utterer of it died. Solomon merely asked Shimei, a Benjaminite, to relocate to and remain in Jerusalem so that he could be kept under observation. Realizing he has been let off lightly, Shimei obeyed for three years but then left Jerusalem to chase after two of his runaway slaves, presumably Philistine slaves, who got as far as Gath, thirty-four miles away. When Shimei brought them back,

---

11   The Iron Age law of blood for blood, the right of retaliation or vengeance.

Solomon executed him on the basis that he disobeyed the king's order for him to remain in the capital. The execution may or may not have been legal, but the actual deliberation by Solomon was complicated. There was, in all likelihood, another conspiracy going on between Shimei and the Philistine king, who was seeking independence after the deaths of David and Joab. The escaped slaves were possibly just a set-up and an excuse for Shimei to make the trip. By killing Shimei, Solomon hoped to thwart a Philistine rebellion. And so, Solomon's kingdom was established.

We should take account of the fact that Solomon had executed a series of extrajudicial killings. Ancient Jewish law required a trial by an assembly or court and the agreement of witnesses.[12] But Solomon, like many absolute monarchs, has his enemies killed without due process. Commentator Henri Gaubert likens Solomon to a wily, patient cat waiting for the mice to come out of their holes.[13] As soon as they did, he would strike. This served as an early sign of darker things to come. He did not spare his enemies for long, and he used careful moral and religious arguments as to why they should be killed, regardless of the law—dragging Joab from the altar being a particular case in point. While appearing virtuous, Solomon showed by his actions and his rationalizing for the public that he was a dangerous man.

At the same time, we can see that at this early stage, Solomon refrained from a wider killing spree. He spared Abiathar, the priest from Shiloh who was about to anoint Adonijah. Surely, he was the next name on Solomon's hit list. Abiathar was allowed to continue in service of the Ark as he was under David but was then exiled to Anathoth, a Levitical town about three miles from Jerusalem. Solomon removed him as high priest serving the Ark and replaced him with Zadok. With Abiathar out of the way, Solomon gained control of the priesthood as well as the temple building project.

What was happening in Solomon's own family at the start of his reign? Solomon was about twenty years old when he came to power, while his son

---

12   See Numbers 35:24, 30.
13   Henri Gaubert, *Solomon the Magnificent* (Roxbury: Hastings House, 1970).

Rehoboam was an infant.[14] It seems clear that Solomon only had one wife at the time of his coronation, the Ammonite princess, Naamah. The marriage may have been a political act by David in line with his thinking about Solomon's future. The Ammonite conquest was David's last, and their territory, with all its conquered and plundered cities, was now at his kingdom's furthest reach. The Ammonite gods were Chemosh, a war god, and Molech, who was worshiped through human sacrifice. Charles Chavel and others note the brutal war against the Ammonites and the measures David placed them under, such as forced labor after victory was won.[15] David also gave him a wife from the people his army was besieging when he had Uriah killed in the battle. They had been besieging Rabbah, the Ammonite royal city, for two years, which lay twenty miles east of the Jordan River.

We will see in the next chapter that this royal marriage would be soon followed by another. It would be a marriage tied in with a political alliance, rather than a marriage from a conquered people group. One princess would soon be followed by another, and in this, Solomon follows in the footsteps of his father David. As we know however, he then goes much further into marital territory entered by only a very few rulers in history.

---

14   We see in 2 Chronicles 12:13 that Rehoboam was forty-one years old when he came to power; his father, Solomon, had reigned for forty years.

15   Charles B. Chavel, "David's War against the Ammonites: A Note in Biblical Exegesis," *The Jewish Quarterly Review New Series* 30, No. 3 (1940), 257-261, doi: https://doi.org/10.2307/1452367.

CHAPTER 4

SOLOMON'S RELATIONSHIP WITH A WEAKENED EGYPT

The daughter of Pharaoh appeared before Solomon, and said unto him, "It is good to worship the gods like my father and all the kings of Egypt who were before my father." And Solomon answered and said unto her, "They call gods the things which have been made by the hands of the worker in metal, and the carpenter, and the potter, and the painter, and the hewer in stone, and the sculptor; these are not gods, but the work of the hand of man . . . But we worship none else than the Holy God of Israel . . . "

And one day she beautified and scented herself for him, and she behaved herself haughtily towards him, and treated him disdainfully. And he said unto her, "What shall I do? Thou hast made thy face evil towards me, and thy regard towards me is not as it was formerly, and thy beautiful form is not as enticing as usual. Ask me, and I will give thee whatsoever thou wishest, and I will perform it for thee, so that thou mayest make thy face (or, attitude) gracious towards me as formerly"; but she held her peace and answered him never a word. And he repeated to her the words that he would do whatsoever she wished, and she said unto him, "Swear to me by the God of Israel that thou wilt not play me false." And he swore to her that he would give her whatsoever she asked for, and that he would do for her everything that she told him. And she tied a scarlet thread on the middle of the door of [the house of] her gods, and she brought three locusts and set them in the house of her gods. And she said unto Solomon, "Come to me without breaking the scarlet thread, bend thyself and kill these locusts before me and pull out their necks"; and he did so. And she said unto him, "I will henceforward do thy will, for thou hast sacrificed to my gods and hast worshipped them." Now he had done thus because of his oath, so that he might not break his oath which she had made him to swear, even though he knew that it was an offence (or sin) to enter into the house of her gods.[16]

Historians, such as Friedrich Thieberger, point out that at the start of Solomon's reign, Egypt was an empire which had shrunk back from its previous expansion across the Middle East. Its northern zenith, or reach, many generations before Solomon was its border with the Hittite Empire; but by 1250 B.C., its northern border had retreated to just north of Damascus. As their empire weakened further in the late Bronze Age, the Egyptians retreated back to Sinai, at the same time losing control of a lot of territory to the Philistine invaders from the Aegean. When Solomon ascended the throne of Israel-Judah, Egypt had reunited after civil unrest and disruption but was still quite reduced. Solomon seized on this opportunity. Even one of Pharaoh's daughters became Solomon's wife, a sign that a weak pharaoh perceived Solomon as at least a ruler of equal status. A result of this marriage, and the Israel-Egypt treaty associated with it, was a joint military venture, led by Egypt, against the Philistines followed by greatly increased trade between Solomon's kingdom and Egypt (1 Kings 10:28-29).

No historical or archaeological records have come to light so far which confirm and specify the identity of Pharaoh's daughter or her father. However, the rulers of Egypt, with their timelines, are well-documented, and we can compare them to Solomon's timeline. Doing this, and given the lack of contrary evidence, we can infer that Solomon's wife was the daughter of the second-to-last pharaoh of the twenty-first dynasty who ruled from about 986 to 967 B.C. His title was Siamun, or Son of Amun, the Egyptian creator-god. He was a weak pharaoh in terms of royal and political power, ruling at the end of a weak dynasty and "in

---

16   E. A. W. Budge, Chapter 64 in *The Kebra Nagast: The Glory of the Kings* (New York, NY: Cosimo Classics, 1922).

much reduced circumstances."[17] It is interesting that God states His opposition to the deity Pharaoh worshipped in the book of Jeremiah: "'Behold, I will bring punishment on Amon of No, and Pharaoh and Egypt, with their gods and their kings—Pharaoh and those who trust in him'" (Jer. 46:25).

Siamun was mainly concerned with domestic matters, and like Solomon, he was a builder. He developed the Amun temple at Tanis and built another temple to the god in Memphis. However, it turned out that when Solomon came to power, he and Solomon both had the same immediate financial and foreign policy objective—the destruction of Gezer, the Philistine fortress city fifteen miles west of Jerusalem. Solomon achieved something his father had failed to achieve in several campaigns (e.g. 1 Chron. 14:16). He also achieved security on his western border and a fortress standing against any invasion from the Mediterranean coastline. If he could successfully attack it, Siamun would remove a hostile customs post on the trade route between Egypt, Israel, and Syria. Pharaoh was fed up with draconian Philistine taxation on his caravans. Since Philistine weaponry was superior to Israelite weaponry, largely consisting of bronze and wood, Solomon could not attack successfully, but Egypt could with a chariot force.

This Siamun did. He waged a limited war against the Philistines, captured the Gezer fortress, and then gave it to Solomon as a dowry when he married Pharaoh's daughter (1 Kings 9:16). He was not interested in holding the territory. It was sufficient for him to benefit financially from the trade routes now under more benign management from Jerusalem. The territorial gift consolidated the deal. Being on a major trade route connecting Egypt with Damascus, it was highly desirable. Solomon was careful to build it up as a fortress city and, in due course, finished his Egyptian wife's palace there. Archaeologists discovered evidence of such a palace in 2016.[18] In a strange example of Solomon's doublemindedness, the Bible recounts, "Now Solomon brought the daughter of Pharaoh up from the City

---

17   Michael Rice, *Who's Who in Ancient Egypt* (London: Routledge, 1999).
18   Daryl Worthington, "'Solomon's Palace' Discovered in Gezer, Israel," New Historian. com, September 3, 2016, https://www.newhistorian.com/2016/09/03/solomons-palace-discovered-gezer-israel.

of David to the house he had built for her, for he said, 'My wife shall not dwell in the house of David king of Israel, because *the places* to which the ark of the Lord has come are holy'" (2 Chron. 8:11).

Solomon seems to have taken advantage of Egypt's post-imperial weakness and united himself with its royal house at a time when, unusually, Egypt saw an advantage in the arrangement. It would not normally ally itself to any foreign power in this way, either before or after its weak and obscure twenty-first dynasty. By giving Solomon his daughter and territory, Pharaoh recognized formally that Solomon's kingdom was a greater power than Egypt. Solomon had also struck the deal while it was possible to do so. In 943 B.C., the expansionist Shoshenq I of Egypt's new Libyan twenty-second dynasty (i.e. Shishak in 1 Kings 14 and 2 Chronicles 12) became pharaoh. He was greatly in favor of weakening and splitting up the Jewish empire. Ruling until 922 B.C., he gave sanctuary to Solomon's opponents; and five years after the king's death, he invaded his son Rehoboam's southern state, Judah, unopposed, entered Jerusalem, and carried off its golden treasures. The biblical account of the invasion is confirmed in the Shoshenq I temple victory reliefs at Karnack, which list 150 captured enemy towns.

Solomon was already married to a pagan wife, but 1 Kings recounts that very early in his reign, just after his extrajudicial killings, Solomon married the daughter of Pharaoh. This contravened at least two Mosaic laws: not to marry a non-Jew (Deut. 7:3) and not to let a first- or second-generation Egyptian into the assembly (Deut. 23:8). The Bible does not comment directly on the marriage. Rather, it mentions five times in 1 Kings the Mosaic law as if to say, "Take note." It does, of course, mention the negative effects on Solomon of the multiple marriages and other unions with concubines. And there is no evidence at all that Pharaoh's daughter converted to Judaism.

Thieberger and other scholars state unequivocally that Solomon's model for the state of Israel was Egypt. Through his wife, he discovered the splendor of Egyptian court life with its intricate ceremonies and its enchanting, irresistible displays. He also took on board Egypt's ideas of political and military organization. For instance, all citizens had the right to appeal directly to the king. Also, although most Egyptians were monogamous, a pharaoh and even the higher nobles would have multiple wives, and in the case of some of the Egyptian dynasties, a royal court would include a harem. These wives would be present to give heirs to pharaoh but would also establish loyalties between the king and regional nobles as well as foreign rulers. Further, Solomon's use of slave labor was very symptomatic of the Egyptian-forced labor practices; their temples and pyramids would never have been built without it.

In terms of court life, Solomon also drew from Egypt when it came to reciprocal giving of gifts at court with foreign visiting monarchs, such as the Queen of Sheba, or with trade delegations. Sometimes, these were the same thing. This would include the trading of compliments and the agreement of alliances. Out of etiquette, though, each ruler accepted the other's offerings as gifts. In the commercial world, the Egyptians had financed some of their huge building projects, such as the Temple of Karnak, largely from international trade. When Solomon started his international trading with Ophir, he was simply restarting and developing earlier trading ventures the Egyptians had made when they had been more expansionist. His imports were similar to theirs: gold, sandalwood, incense, and so on. His purpose was effectively the same as Egypt: the financing of vast building projects and a filling up of the state coffers.

Solomon also drew in a very practical way from Egypt when it came to his military review and his transformation of Israelite forces. He moved quickly to create an iron-armored chariot force, along with a support system for it: stables, barracks, job roles such as grooms, instructors, handlers, drivers, and specialized mobile projectile troops. He may have bought most or all of the hardware and horses from Egypt. This was transformation in a number of respects. Solomon's military was now as good as anything outside his realm. With his chariot force, he also had a permanent standing army whose effectiveness was reliable. He was a "prince of peace" with an army permanently on a war footing.

Spiritually, Israel was monotheistic, and so the people's mindset was radically different from the Egyptian polytheistic one. This was despite the fact that Israel had lived in Egypt for four hundred years. The Egyptian gods with animal heads were peculiar to Egypt and did not expand their territory into other people's hearts and minds. But under Solomon, the focus on monotheism would change.

The curve of Solomon's reign was predicted well in advance. The book of 1 Samuel records God's commentary to the prophet. In effect, He is saying that if Israel is given a king, the inevitable outcome will be a rule characterized by oppressive autocracy. To start with, the desire is rebellion against God and a negation of their calling to be "a holy people to the LORD your God" (Deut. 14:21). If His people want a king as other nations have, then the rule will be as autocratic as that suffered by those nations. In emulating Pharaoh, Solomon became rather like Pharaoh, especially in his later years in power. While the king's clever foreign policies gave them peace on their borders, Solomon's subjects became rather like the slaves their predecessors were in Egypt.

Finally, it is worth pointing out that around Solomon's kingdom, it was not just Egypt that languished in a weakened state. The other powerful kingdoms did not pose an immediate threat either. The Hittite empire in the North had collapsed because of civil war following external warfare. The Philistines living on the eastern seaboard had been weakened by David's wars against them, while Egypt was also hostile toward them. To the east, Assyria and Babylonia were experiencing massive contraction and life in an unstable dark age, after their initial expansions and before their resurgence post-Solomon. Modern theories about this focus on evidence of long-term crop failures and famine caused by climatic changes (a long-term drought affecting the Tigris and Euphrates rivers) and the effects of military defeats by hostile nomadic Aramean tribes.[19] Solomon, therefore, took the throne at a very propitious, fortunate time. There were perceived threats beyond Solomon's borders from small Aramean and

---

19   Steven W. Holloway, "Assyria and Babylonia in the Tenth Century BCE," in *The Age of Solomon: Scholarship at the Turn of the Millennium* (Harrisonburg: James Madison University, 1997).

neo-Hittite kingdoms but no immediate threat from any powerful neighbor. Assyria had retreated to east of the Habur River, close to the border now between Syria and Iraq. It was intact, though, as a political and military entity, and long after Solomon's time, it would invade and destroy the northern kingdom of Israel. Throughout Solomon's reign, however, no significant invasion would threaten his kingdom at any of his borders.

CHAPTER 5

SOLOMON'S DREAM AT GIBEON: A NEW WISDOM

"At Gibeon the Lord appeared to Solomon in a dream by night;
and God said, 'Ask! What shall I give you?'"

—1 Kings 3:5

We saw earlier that as a young king, Solomon was astute. He also loved Yahweh (1 Kings 3:3). There was a change in him, though, at the high place called Gibeon when he encountered Yahweh directly. After his Gibeon encounter, his wisdom was seen to be unprecedented in Israel and without equal across the known world. People remembered it long after his death. It is even remembered in the modern era. But Solomon was still capable of a more Machiavellian rule.

The book of 1 Kings suggests that Solomon placed so much priority on marrying Pharaoh's daughter that the event preceded his request for wisdom at the "great high place" at Gibeon. It is likely that Solomon journeyed to Gibeon because it was the most important and largest high place in Israel. Its remains can be found just six miles northwest of Jerusalem. Solomon went there to sacrifice a thousand burnt offerings to the God he acknowledged. Did he do this because he suddenly felt overwhelmed by his fast-paced geopolitics as well as his efforts to secure the throne? The text reveals that the following occurred there:

At Gibeon the Lord appeared to Solomon in a dream by night; and God said, "Ask! What shall I give you?"

And Solomon said: "You have shown great mercy to Your servant David my father, because he walked before You in truth, in righteousness, and in uprightness of heart with You; You have continued this great kindness for him, and You have given him a son to sit on his throne, as *it is* this day. Now, O Lord my God, You have made Your servant king instead of my father David, but I *am* a little child; I do not know *how* to go out or come in. And Your servant *is* in the midst of Your people whom You have chosen, a great people, too numerous to be numbered or counted. Therefore give to Your servant an understanding heart to judge Your people, that I may discern between good and evil. For who is able to judge this great people of Yours?"

The speech pleased the Lord, that Solomon had asked this thing. Then God said to him: "Because you have asked this thing, and have not asked long life for yourself, nor have asked riches for yourself, nor have asked the life of your enemies, but have asked for yourself understanding to discern justice, behold, I have done according to your words; see, I have given you a wise and understanding heart, so that there has not been anyone like you before you, nor shall any like you arise after you. And I have also given you what you have not asked: both riches and honor, so that there shall not be anyone like you among the kings all your days. So if you walk in My ways, to keep My statutes and My commandments, as your father David walked, then I will lengthen your days."

Then Solomon awoke; and indeed it had been a dream (1 Kings 3:5-15).

In my earlier book, *The God of Dreams,* I look in some detail at this dream and how best to understand it. We can say that early on in his reign, Solomon was focused on his people and was aware that he was not up to the task of ruling wisely. He acknowledged that God had already delivered on His earlier promises to Israel, since the king, standing on the high place, saw the land promised and delivered to his people now spread out before him. In the dream, God gave the king a blank check, which was also a test: what do you want to have? The king responded honestly and wisely, so God granted him some unconditional promises—wisdom, wealth, and honor were already his. He followed this with a conditional promise. If the king remained close to God, he would reign into old age. Solomon woke up and was surprised to find that his all-too-real audience with God had occurred in a dream. He returned to Jerusalem filled with joy and gave a feast for his entire royal court.

The book of 1 Kings also reveals that on his return to Jerusalem from Gibeon, Solomon stood before the ark of the covenant to offer up burnt offerings and peace offerings. In doing so, he emulated the actions of his father, David, who did likewise after he had brought the ark into the tabernacle, a sacred tent that he had erected for it (1 Chron. 16:2). For Solomon, it was a choice to continue to remain in God's presence. The ark had long associations for Israel with God's miraculous interventions. The Jordan river had parted when the ark was brought up to it, and the walls of Jericho had fallen after the priests had carried the ark around the city seven times. Scripture does not record any of Solomon's prayers before God at this stage, but for Solomon, the ark was a place of meeting with God as it had been for Joshua and Moses.

Solomon had faith and also an intentional approach to dreaming. He had delayed his sojourn at Gibeon in order to hear from God through a dream. Yahweh responded to his faith. Did Solomon's approach influence the Greeks and the Romans later on? The ancient Greeks would tarry overnight at their temples to Aesculapius, their god of medicine, which were often built in secluded places far into the countryside. They believed that in their dreams, Aesculapius would give them information as to the medicines and surgical procedures which would lead to the curing of their maladies.

In any case, we know that Solomon was genuine in his request for wisdom—so much so that God was pleased with the request and responded in all generosity to it. We will see next that one of the immediate effects of Solomon's transformation through his God-given wisdom was its display in his Hall of Justice in Jerusalem which stood in front of Solomon's royal palace, according to 1 Kings 7. Solomon was able to deal effectively with the most intractable and confounding legal cases brought before him by his people. His judicial displays of wisdom were so unusual and unparalleled by others—sages, priests, and kings—that all the surrounding nations heard about it. Their rulers decided it was well worth their while to pay the king a visit.

CHAPTER 6
THE JUDGMENT OF SOLOMON

"The Queen of Sheba asked: 'What are the seven that issue and nine that enter,
the two that offer drink, and the one that drinks?' Solomon answered: '
The seven that issue are the seven days of menstrual impurity. The nine that
enter are the nine months of pregnancy. The two that offer drink are the breasts,
and the child is the one who drinks.'"

—Midrash: Proverbs 1[20]

The book of 1 Kings describes Solomon as wise almost twenty times, detailing his building of the temple and other major constructions. But the same chapters also contain examples of his decisions that were not wise. Scripture juxtaposes the wisdom with behavior that lacked it. Solomon did not always apply his wisdom. His marriage to Pharaoh's daughter, for instance, followed by many other marriages to pagan women, led to his apostasy.

However, the first clear example of his new level of wisdom had to do with a court case brought before him. Two prostitutes who lived in the same house were before him with a baby, and each said the baby was hers (1 Kings 3). Initially, there were two babies, each belonging to one of the women, but one of them rolled over onto her baby in the night and crushed him to death. Each said that the live baby was hers. The claim was made that the unwitting killer got up in the night and switched the babies around so that

---

20   Bernard H. Melhman and Seth M. Limmer, *Medieval Midrash: The House for Inspired Innovation* (Boston: Brill Reference Library of Judaism, 2017).

she was with the other woman's live baby when morning came. There were no witnesses.

Solomon summarized the intractable situation for the court and then moved to the following judgment:

> Then the king said, "Bring me a sword." So they brought a sword before the king. And the king said, "Divide the living child in two, and give half to one, and half to the other." Then the woman whose son *was* living spoke to the king, for she yearned with compassion for her son; and she said, "O my lord, give her the living child, and by no means kill him!" But the other said, "Let him be neither mine nor yours, *but* divide *him*." So the king answered and said, "Give the first woman the living child, and by no means kill him; she *is* his mother" (1 Kings 3:24-27).

The king used a device to stir up the true mother's love for her baby and also stirred up the other woman's spite and antipathy. The events astounded the people: "They feared the king, for they saw that the wisdom of God *was* in him to administer justice" (1 Kings 3:28b). In his commentary on 1 Kings, Dale Ralph Davis points out that the judgment is clear evidence that Solomon had been given what he sought—he was able to govern his people wisely and his heart could discern between right and wrong. Davis also asserts that there is a glimpse of the future Messianic King in Solomon's judicial process: "But with righteousness He shall judge the poor, And decide with equity for the meek of the earth" (Isa. 11:4a).[21]

THE QUEEN OF SHEBA

Scripture describes the visit made to Solomon by the Queen of Sheba, who had heard of his wisdom and renown across the then-known world and came to test him with riddles and questions (1 Kings 10:1).[22] These were not frivolous; they came from burdens that she was carrying "in her heart" (2 Chron. 9:1). She

---

21   Dale Ralph Davis, *1 Kings: The Wisdom and the Folly* (Fearn: Christian Focus, 2008).
22   The NKJV describes it as fame caused by the Name of the Lord.

arrived at his court with a retinue of servants and camels bearing huge quantities of spices, along with 120 talents of gold. The interaction is described in this way:

> So Solomon answered all her questions; there was nothing so difficult for the king that he could not explain *it* to her. And when the queen of Sheba had seen all the wisdom of Solomon, the house that he had built, the food on his table, the seating of his servants, the service of his waiters and their apparel, his cupbearers, and his entryway by which he went up to the house of the LORD, there was no more spirit in her. Then she said to the king: "It was a true report which I heard in my own land about your words and your wisdom. However, I did not believe the words until I came and saw with my own eyes; and indeed the half was not told me. Your wisdom and prosperity exceed the fame of which I heard. Now King Solomon gave the queen of Sheba all she desired, whatever she asked, besides what Solomon had given her according to the royal generosity. So she turned and went to her own country, she and her servants (1 Kings 10:3-7, 13).

We do not know her name and cannot be certain as to the exact location of her country, although scholars tend to agree that it was located in modern-day Yemen. If she had ambitions other than those listed, we cannot define those either. They probably included trade agreements, and we can infer they were agreed, given that he gave her all that she wanted. She was generally impressed by his palace complex and his lavish hospitality. She was probably a sun-worshipper, which is probably why the text does not say she was impressed with the temple. We are given no examples of the wisdom which impressed the queen, but she is presented as an example of many rulers who behaved in the same way. She is merely one of them. Many powerful rulers came from far away to seek an audience with the wise man, and they were awed by both his wisdom and his imposing and dazzling possessions.

CHAPTER 7

THE WISDOM OF SOLOMON

When Solomon was flying on his magic carpet, he saw some ants in a valley and swooping down, he said to their queen, "I want to ask you a question." The ant replied, "it is not becoming for the interrogated to be below and the interrogator to be above." So Solomon brought her up, out of the valley. The ant then said, "it is not fitting for the interrogator to be upon a throne and the interrogated to be on the ground." So Solomon placed her on his hand and asked her, "is there anyone on earth greater than me?" "I am much greater," replied the ant. "Otherwise God would not have sent you to place me on your hand." Greatly angered, Solomon threw her down and said, "Dost thou know who I am? I am Solomon, the son of David!" The ant replied, "I know thou art created of a corrupted drop, therefore thou ought not to be proud." Filled with shame, Solomon fell on his face.[23]

What was Solomon's wisdom? Given to him as a supernatural gift, we have to acknowledge at the start that it is perhaps impossible to define. It is also something which made Solomon unique among humanity at the time.[24] God points out that it would set Solomon apart from all those before him and all those after him. There would be sages and experts afterward, of course, but they would not have the same wisdom as Solomon. They would strive toward it—and they would learn by experience and study—but they would never reach it. And the level of expertise or wisdom that they *would* reach would have been achieved

---

23   Melhman and Limmer, "Solomon and the Ant."
24   1 Kings 3:12

by human means and over a long period of human striving. In contrast, Solomon's wisdom was there in an instant, a God-given attribute and something which pointed forward in time to the wisdom of Jesus.

One main aspect of Solomon's wisdom was insight into the nature of reality, and he demonstrated this by creating riddles and proverbs. A proverb (or *mashal* in Hebrew) is an analogy which reveals a truth applicable to the human psyche, human behavior, or to the natural world. The wise live in harmony with wisdom, but the foolish follow their own plans and collide with wisdom on the way to their own destruction. When you read one of Solomon's proverbs for the first time, you know that it is innately true. It is wise because it reveals a truth often overlooked. "'He who corrects a scoffer gets shame for himself, And he who rebukes a wicked *man only* harms himself. Do not correct a scoffer, lest he hate you; Rebuke a wise *man*, and he will love you'" (Prov. 9:7-8).

For Solomon, there were eight types of fool, and most of those were unteachable.[25] The types included those governed by narcissism, brutality, insanity, or stupidity. The ignorant, though, could be taught. There was only one type of wise person— someone who sought out wisdom; the natural, created order of things ordained by God; and refrained from anything which would cast wisdom aside—wild, sexual promiscuity; laziness; addiction; and gossip.

Solomon was intrigued by the mysteries of nature and of human sexuality and often contemplated them. The book of 1 Kings recounts that Solomon wrote down three thousand proverbs, many of which are now lost, and he composed 1,005 songs. Again, the majority of these songs are lost to us, unless like the Hittite library buried underneath Hattusa, they suddenly come to light in the form of clay inscriptions or even scroll manuscripts.

At times, Solomon's wisdom reflected God's wisdom. A couple of examples can be given from Proverbs 25, a section of the book explicitly ascribed to Solomon. "Do not exalt yourself in the presence of the king, And do not stand in the place of the great; For *it is* better that he say to you, 'Come up here,' Than

25   Rami M. Shapiro, *The Divine Feminine in Biblical Wisdom Literature* (Woodstock: SkyLight Paths, 2013).

that you should be put lower in the presence of the prince, Whom your eyes have seen" (Prov. 25:6-7).

This was also a saying of Jesus on a Sabbath when he dined in a chief Pharisee's house, the context being his observation of the diners taking the most desired seats. Many of those present would know that Jesus was drawing directly from and expanding Solomon's saying.

> So He told a parable to those who were invited, when He noted how they chose the best places, saying to them: "When you are invited by anyone to a wedding feast, do not sit down in the best place, lest one more honorable than you be invited by him; and he who invited you and him come and say to you, 'Give place to this man,' and then you begin with shame to take the lowest place. But when you are invited, go and sit down in the lowest place, so that when he who invited you comes he may say to you, 'Friend, go up higher.' Then you will have glory in the presence of those who sit at the table with you. For whoever exalts himself will be humbled, and he who humbles himself will be exalted" (Luke 14:7-11).

Another example comes just slightly later in Solomon's Proverbs: "If your enemy is hungry, give him bread to eat; And if he is thirsty, give him water to drink; For so you will heap coals of fire on his head, And the LORD will reward you" (Prov. 25:21-22). This wisdom is mirrored in Luke, and there is a similar passage in Matthew 5: "'But I say to you who hear: Love your enemies, do good to those who hate you, bless those who curse you, and pray for those who spitefully use you . . . But love your enemies, do good, and lend, hoping for nothing in return" (Luke 6:27-28, 35a).

At times, Jesus amplified the wisdom initially put forward by Solomon, even referring directly back to him in relation to the theme expounded. A good example of this comes from Proverbs 27, where Solomon said, "Do not boast about tomorrow, For you do not know what a day may bring forth" (Prov. 27:1). Jesus expanded on this by reiterating the futility of a false focus on tomorrow but changed the emphasis toward needless anxiety:

Consider the lilies, how they grow: they neither toil nor spin; and yet I say to you, even Solomon in all his glory was not arrayed like one of these. If then God so clothes the grass, which today is in the field and tomorrow is thrown into the oven, how much more *will He clothe* you, O *you* of little faith? "And do not seek what you should eat or what you should drink, nor have an anxious mind. For all these things the nations of the world seek after, and your Father knows that you need these things. But seek the kingdom of God, and all these things shall be added to you. "Do not fear, little flock, for it is your Father's good pleasure to give you the kingdom. Sell what you have and give alms; provide yourselves money bags which do not grow old, a treasure in the heavens that does not fail, where no thief approaches nor moth destroys. For where your treasure is, there your heart will be also" (Luke 12:27-34).

Solomon also had practical wisdom. This had to do with resourcefulness and skill. Solomon's wisdom gave him considerable mental agility as a genius administrator and organizer. He used wisdom to solve difficult problems and to switch effortlessly between very different matters of state (i.e. across what would usually be entirely different political and administrative departments or areas of interest). He used his wisdom to rule over and across all internal and international matters, creating order through a year-by-year process of conceiving, planning, and organizing.

Solomon's efforts led to the development of a well-fortified network of trade routes, protected by garrisons stretching from Palmyra in the far northeast of his kingdom down to the Red Sea. But beyond that, the king focused on world trade. With assistance from the Phoenicians, around 950 B.C., he constructed a major seaport and navy at Ezion-geber where no town had ever existed, near modern-day Eilat, well away from any competing ports located along the Mediterranean coastline. From there, his navy explored and traded, bringing back vast amounts of gold, silver, and ivory from Ophir, as well as livestock, such as apes and exotic birds like peacocks and parrots. It is likely that Ophir was located in southern India in Tamil territory: Hebrew and classical Tamil words for apes, ivory, and peacocks are very similar and suggest that the Hebrew terms are borrowed from the Tamil language.[26] At the same time, though, Solomon's merchant navy was also trading with countries such as Sheba, a country whose territory is now probably in modern-day Yemen.

Ezion-geber also had a major industrial zone containing ironworks and large smelting works for copper. These industries used copper ore mined over a large area, stretching right up to the Dead Sea. Solomon used the copper objects—such as idols, figurines, fish hooks and pots—in the international trade for far more valuable imports: gold, silver, elephant tusk, ivory from Africa, precious stones, exotic animals such as monkeys and baboons, red sandalwood from India for the temple's and his palace's staircase, musicians' harps, and so on.[27]

Archaeologists have disputed exactly where the remains of Solomon's seaport are to be found, but the most likely location is the island just within the Egyptian border, modern-day Jezirat Faraun. Its position and shape is very like Tyre before its development; it is probable that Solomon's Phoenician advisers would have recommended the site to him.[28] Jezirat Faraun and Eilat, about seven miles northeast of the island, were probably two aspects of the same enterprise: the former being Solomon's seaport and the latter consisting of factories, warehouses, and his *caravanserai terminus*. When the king toured these two sites, they were recorded as separate locations.[29] Both had fortifications built to keep the Edomites under subjugation. Solomon constructed a twenty-five-foot-high city wall with three gates and guard posts around the more northern location. It is a certainty that much of the industry and the supplies for it were organized through a system of slavery. The area had once been part of Edom, and the conquered people were conscripted by Solomon into the workforce.[30] This labor force was insufficient, and Solomon supplemented it with enforced

---

26   For instance, the word *parrot* is "thukki" in Hebrew and "thogkai" in classical Tamil (see *Smith's Bible Dictionary*).

27   2 Chronicles 9:10-11; 1 Kings 10:22

28   Alexander Flinder, "Jezirat Faraun: Is this Solomon's Seaport?," Bible.ca, https://www.bible.ca/archeology/bible-archeology-exodus-kadesh-barnea-ezion-geber-jezirat-faraun-is-this-solomons-seaport-alexander-flinder-1989ad.htm (accessed July 3, 2019).

29   2 Chronicles 8:17

30   See 1 Kings 9:21

Israelite labor. In the burning heat and in such an inhospitable terrain, the death toll would have been considerable. Added to this, the Phoenicians also chose the site because of the fierce wind, which blew across it and which could be used to power the furnaces using wind chargers for momentum exchange. The working conditions would have been extremely unhealthy.

After Solomon's time and after the reigns of several other kings of Judah, the Edomites retook the area and rebuilt the port and its industrial complex for themselves. Evidence from archaeological digs in the area suggests, though, that before that, Pharaoh Sheshonk destroyed the port, along with Solomon's fleet in his campaign against Rehoboam. Solomon's trade route down through the eastern half of the Red Sea had depended on his alliance with Egypt. The agreement dissolved on his death, and so the whole trade and military complex became an immediate target for Pharaoh.

Domestically, Solomon re-divided the unified kingdom of Israel and Judah into twelve administrative areas, plus the Jerusalem and Hebron area, ruled directly by Solomon with no other administrative head. The twelve other areas all had district heads dependent entirely on Solomon; two of them were married to Solomon's daughters. The boundaries of the twelve areas were very different from, but not completely non-overlapping with, the traditional areas occupied by the twelve tribes of Israel under the judges and King David. This was Solomon's attempt to create a unified kingdom, which disempowered any of its tribes who might seek to dwell in the past or break away. As he applied his post-Iron Age wisdom, therefore, to the remodeling of his kingdom, Solomon became almost akin to much more recent autocratic emperors and monarchs. His efforts did create a functioning and successful kingdom, which lasted throughout his lifetime. But he either did not foresee the negative effects his reformations were having, or he *was* aware of them, ignored them, and did not care what their consequences would be after he was gone.

Unlike his father, Solomon needed to tax each area heavily to supply the central power in Jerusalem and sustain the luxurious opulence of his kingdom. Taxation levels increased as time went by, and forced labor was part of the requirement. Each area was also responsible for all the royal court's food supply for one month. This rankled greatly with the northern tribes of Israel, since apart from anything else, Jerusalem and Hebron were exempted from the taxation system.

Yet it did not start out like that. Initially, Solomon's administrative reconstruction and geographical expansion of David's kingdom brought peace and joy to the people. There was both internal peace and international peace with the countries beyond Israel's expanded borders. God's promises to Israel were fulfilled, and this itself is a sign that He will fulfill all His promises to both Israel and the Church in the future. "Judah and Israel *were* as numerous as the sand by the sea in multitude, eating and drinking and rejoicing. So Solomon reigned over all kingdoms from the River *to* the land of the Philistines, as far as the border of Egypt" (1 Kings 4:20-21a).

CHAPTER 8

SOLOMON AS THE IDEAL KING

They had ... hair hanging down and were clothed in garments of Tyrian purple.
They had also dust of gold every day sprinkled on their hair, so that their heads
sparkled with the reflection of the sunbeams from the gold. The king himself
rode upon a chariot in the midst of these men, who were still in armour, and
had their bows fitted to them. He had on a white garment; and used to take his
progress out of the city in the morning. There was a certain place about fifty
furlongs[31] distant from Jerusalem, which is called Etham, very pleasant it is in
fine gardens, and abounding in rivulets of water.

—*Antiquities of the Jews*, Flavius Josephus.

The Bible initially portrays Solomon as a ruler who rises to an apotheosis, both for himself as a ruler and for his people, who enjoyed an unparalleled time of peace and stability. The king was wise, just, and law-abiding (for the most part), at least for a time. He feared Yahweh and was able to function as an ideal king. K. I. Parker brings it all together like this: "Solomon is able to render justice by using his wisdom to comply with the law."[32] When he was at Gibeon, Solomon asked God in a dream for wisdom and discernment so that he could rule his people effectively. God granted Solomon wisdom, but there

---

31 Approximately six miles.
32 K. I. Parker, "Solomon as Philosopher King? The Nexus of Law and Wisdom in 1 Kings 1-11," in *Journal for the Study of the Old Testament*, Vol. 17, No. 53 (1992), https://doi.org/10.1177/030908929201705305.

was the added proviso that he would only be able to continue ruling well if he continued to obey Yahweh by walking in His ways.

> At Gibeon the LORD appeared to Solomon in a dream by night; and God said, "Ask what I shall give you?" And Solomon said: "You have shown great mercy to your servant David my father, because he walked before you in truth, in righteousness, and in uprightness of heart with You; You have continued this great kindness for him, and you have given him a son to sit on his throne, as *it is* this day. Now, O Lord my God, You have made your servant king instead of my father David, but I *am* a little child; I do not know *how* to go out or come in. And Your servant *is* in the midst of Your people whom You have chosen, a great people, too numerous to be numbered or counted. Therefore give to Your servant an understanding heart to judge Your people, that I may discern between good and evil. For who is able to judge this great people of Yours?" The speech pleased the Lord, that Solomon had asked this thing. Then God said to him: "Because you have asked this thing, and have not asked long life for yourself, nor have asked riches for yourself, nor have asked the life of your enemies, but have asked for yourself understanding to discern justice, behold, I have done according to your words; see, I have given you a wise and understanding heart, so that there has not been anyone like you before you, nor shall any like you arise after you. And I have also given you what you have not asked: both riches and honor, so that there shall not be anyone like you among the kings all your days. So if you walk in My ways, to keep My statutes and My commandments, as your father David walked, then I will lengthen your days." Then Solomon awoke; and indeed it had been a dream. And he came to Jerusalem and stood before the ark of the covenant of the Lord, offered up burnt offerings, offered peace offerings, and made a feast for all his servants (1 Kings 3:5-15).

Immediately after this theophany, Solomon demonstrated this new wisdom in action in his dealings with the two prostitutes fighting over a baby. He demonstrated wisdom combined with justice. He was able to discern who the baby's mother was, who the liar was, and how to dispense justice. Because his wisdom is God-given, it is difficult, probably impossible, to characterize exactly. No writer of Scripture attempts to do that. Instead, the biblical account shows us this practical example of his wisdom. We see the wisdom in action, but it is impossible to explain—so much so that no one has managed to do that. Modern explanations based on the king's reading of the women's behavior in court or the baby's appearance are spurious because Solomon was not using any observational, philosophical, or psychological ruse or procedure. His wisdom was in contrast to all these since it originated from a supernatural gift. Whatever its nature, the wisdom was incisive, revelatory, and very wide-ranging.

Later, he was shown to be the ideal Jewish king when he was recorded as having extended Israel's territory over the complete geographical area promised to his forebearer Abraham—from the Euphrates to the border of Egypt (1 Kings 4:21). He was also able to do this peacefully, albeit by using diplomacy and marriage alliances to capitalize on his father's earlier military victories. "On the same day the Lord made a covenant with Abram, saying: 'To your descendants I have given this land, from the river of Egypt to the great river, the River Euphrates'" (Gen. 15:18).

Solomon was also able to work to fulfill the prophecy by the court prophet, Nathan, to David regarding the construction of the temple in Jerusalem. He was just and wise, given that the contract with Hiram and the peace treaty which ensued enabled everything to be brought about to successful completion. Hiram fully recognized Solomon's wisdom and praised the fact that God had given David a wise son to rule over Israel.

Solomon also exercised wisdom and justice in the actual construction process: "Then King Solomon raised up a labor force out of all Israel; and the labor force was thirty thousand men. And he sent them to Lebanon, ten thousand a month in shifts: they were one month in Lebanon *and* two months at home" (1 Kings 5:13-14). That is to say, the laborers only worked a third of the time and were free to rest and go about their usual domestic and working activities two months in every three. They would be recharged enough to always give of their very best efforts. Solomon used his own wisdom to manage the labor force, rather than drawing (for this specific project) from the Egyptian model of slave labor.

He also fully obeyed the law, or Torah, regarding the construction methods. For instance, he banned the use of iron tools in full compliance with the law (1 Kings 6:7; Deut. 27:5). It is likely that the ban on the use of iron was to separate the construction of a holy temple from the use of the metal to construct implements of warfare. He is also portrayed as obeying instructions given by God in advance. The dimensions of the temple were communicated to Solomon by David, who stated that he had been given them by God.

The biblical record shows Solomon to be a ruler who balanced his many passions across his rulership. He was greatly impassioned by art and luxury, but he also valued order at home and abroad. He loved peace, and there would have been a sense of stability and serenity in his court of justice. Without military, political, or priestly advisors, he and his clear reasoning ruled across all the dimensions of the state: legal, economic, trade, military, ecclesiastical, building construction, and international relations. Prophets such as Nathan were only around for the first few years of Solomon's reign, and when they passed away, no successors came to the fore.

Solomon ruled passionately and energetically for most of his reign. As Thieberger put it, he ruled "in his unapproachable glory and inconceivable wealth."[33] He became a potentate on an even grander scale than the pharaohs or the Assyrian rulers still to arise. Like them, however, a formidable network of fortifications built throughout his realm bolstered his rule.

---

33   Thieberger, ibid, 232.

CHAPTER 9

THE BUILDING OF THE
TEMPLE AND THE KINGDOM

"To everything there is a season, A time for every purpose under heaven . . .
And a time to build up."

—Ecclesiastes 3:1, 3b

From the start of Solomon's reign, the king departed from the typical focus of Iron Age kings. Although he had inherited a formidable war machine and although he continued to build it up with the creation of chariot cities and better fortresses at strategic locations, he used none of this apparatus of war in expansionist campaigns. Instead, he identified the building of the temple as his primary enterprise, along with several other major building projects. He enlisted large sections of the working population to these ends. The two purposes were unified in his thinking: to build and protect the temple, he must also develop his military power.

Solomon took for himself the promise Yahweh gave to David through the prophet Nathan. Solomon believed that the promise was about him. He was the seed who would build Yahweh's temple. This belief drove the first part of the king's reign: "'When your days are fulfilled and you rest with your fathers, I will set up your seed after you, who will come from your body, and I will establish his kingdom. He shall build a house for My name, and I will establish the throne of his kingdom forever. I will be his Father, and he shall be My son'" (2 Sam. 7:2-14a).

But there was also a third consideration. Solomon's first act of foreign policy was aimed at Egypt, and he used his ambassadors to obtain a comprehensive peace treaty, which probably included, along with mutually beneficial trade agreements, an Egyptian insistence that he purchase Egyptian military technology (1 Kings 3:1). From the side of Pharaoh, this agreement was welcome. Libyans were threatening to take over his kingdom, and his agreement with Solomon bolstered his position, delaying the ending of his dynasty until after the death of his successor in 943 B.C. And as part of all this, one of Pharaoh's daughters became Solomon's principal wife.

Why was this treaty necessary? Egypt was not a threat to Solomon and had been in long-term decline throughout its weak twenty-first dynasty; surely, he could supersede Egyptian military technology through wisdom or espionage. Yet he had his reasons. As well as building up trade and prosperity, these also had to do with internal security. Solomon found that he had inherited a number of enemies in exile in Egypt such as the Edomite prince, Hadad (1 Kings 11:17, 19-22). His treaty wrong-footed them and prevented any alliance with Egypt, which would be hostile to Solomon.

To construct the temple, Solomon also entered into a collaborative trade treaty with Hiram, king of Phoenicia, whose throne was in Tyre. A record of Solomon's intentions is found in 2 Chronicles.

> Then Solomon determined to build a temple for the name of the LORD, and a royal house for himself. Solomon selected seventy thousand men to bear burdens, eighty thousand to quarry *stone* in the mountains, and three thousand six hundred to oversee them. Then Solomon sent to Hiram king of Tyre, saying: As you have dealt with David my father, and sent him cedars to build himself a house to dwell in, *so deal with me.* Behold, I am building a temple for the name of the LORD my God" (2 Chron. 2:1-4a).

The agreement benefited both rulers with Hiram extending his sphere of influence, gaining access to Israelite ports and annual imports from Israel of major quantities of wheat and oil. He gained land from Israel and twenty villages across a strip of land bordering his kingdom, but only for a period of time; it was finally returned to Solomon.[34]

Phoenician women became Solomon's wives, and one of these was Hiram's daughter, another political marriage. This is alluded to in the wedding song included in Psalm 45:

> So the King will greatly desire your beauty; Because He *is* your LORD, worship Him. And the daughter of Tyre *will come* with a gift; The rich among the people will seek your favor. The royal daughter *is* all glorious within *the palace*; Her clothing *is* woven with gold. She shall be brought to the King in robes of many colors; The virgins, her companions who follow her, shall be brought to You. With gladness and rejoicing they shall be brought; They shall enter the King's palace (Psalm 45:11-15).

CONSTRUCTION OF THE KINGDOM

Solomon inherited a lot of ideas and personnel from David for the secular and spiritual aspects of his kingdom. David's officials were taken on by Solomon and developed further into a functioning civil service. For instance, Adoniram remained minister of finance and head of taxation, and later, he also became head of forced labor.[35] Jehoshaphat remained chancellor,[36] but the position of secretary of state was taken from Seraiah and given to two brothers, Elihoreph and Ahijah.[37] The complexity of Solomon's foreign policy probably required this duplication.

Solomon also consolidated the priestly class as royal appointees. The high priests were, in effect, officials of the king. New officials appeared as well, people who were not needed by David. Ahishar became chief of staff and head over the royal household,[38] a role required by the king's expanding collection of domestic buildings, state property, and in due course, hundreds of wives and concubines. Ahishar was the first incumbent in this role, and it is interesting

---

34   Thieberger, ibid, 145-146.
35   2 Samuel 20:24; 1 Kings 4:6
36   2 Samuel 8:16; 2 Samuel 20:24; 1 Kings 4:3
37   1 Kings 4:3
38   1 Kings 4:6

to see that the role continued on. Hundreds of years later, Shebna was chief of staff to King Hezekiah of Judah.[39] There was also a new minister for internal affairs. Solomon wanted someone to administer a decentralized network of district commissioners or overseers responsible for regional taxation and the provisioning of military forces stationed in their areas. Azariah, a son of David's prophet Nathan, acquired this role. The tribal exception was Judah. It was unlisted in the names of tribal or regional commissioners in 1 Kings 4. In fact, Solomon was governor of Judah, and its taxation income went straight to him at Jerusalem to supplement all his other income sources.

Solomon created internal divisions or districts and regional governors over them within his united kingdom, which did not correspond to the tribal divisions. His reasoning, most likely, was that he wanted all Israelites to identify with his kingdom rather than their tribal affiliations. At the same time, though, his massive construction projects throughout his kingdom required taxation, and Solomon instituted systems which included forced labor for Israelites and slavery for non-Jews. The result of this was that after the king's death, the despairing northern tribes revolted anyway; Solomon's administrative procedures could not prevent the rebellion.

The nation at peace under Solomon was a substantial state, a "minor imperial power," to quote Carol Meyers.[40] This is clear from the 1 Kings 4 account and also from the narrative provided by the historian Josephus. For instance, Josephus recounted that just one regional governor—Gabrius—ruling over Gilead and Gaulanitis, the former Amorite territory, was responsible for "sixty great and fenced cities."[41] Each would have had high bronze gates, substantial surrounding walls, and watchtower fortifications.

Solomon also refortified the capital. In building up Jerusalem's walls,[42] he sought to expedite his father's prayer as recorded in Psalm 51: "Do good

39   Isaiah 22:15
40   Carol Meyers, "Israelite Empire: in Defense of King Solomon," *Michigan Quarterly Review*, 22, No. 3 (1983).
41   Josephus, "Chapter 2," in *Antiquities of the Jews*, Book VIII, 196, in *The Complete Works of Flavius Josephus.*
42   1 Kings 3:1

in your good pleasure to Zion; build the walls of Jerusalem" (v.18). Josephus also recounts that Israelite land and the crops it provided greatly increased in worth. Farmers could attend to it without the interference and distraction of war.

Solomon also concerned himself with the roads. Josephus records that the king "laid a causeway of black stone along the road that led to Jerusalem."[43] This was to make travel easier but also to demonstrate his wealth and domestic power. We do not know what the black stone was, but it may have been obsidian or black basalt.

The nation at peace under Solomon was a first foretaste of what was to come during the rule of the few good and great kings, which Judah had post-Solomon, such as Hezekiah and Josiah. These were prophesized ahead of time by Isaiah: "Behold, a king will reign in righteousness, And princes will rule with justice . . . My people will dwell in a peaceful habitation, In secure dwellings, and in quiet resting places . . . Blessed *are* you who sow beside all waters, Who send out freely the feet of the ox and the donkey" (Isa. 32:1, 18, 20).

The prophecies also predict the Messiah and His peaceful reign, still to occur, over the promised land. Having said that, Isaiah includes a warning, which also harks back to Solomon's imperfect peace gained through statecraft and wisdom: "Woe to those who [rely] on Egypt" (Isa. 31:1). Solomon had not defeated any of Israel's enemies; he had merely kept them at bay for a time through treaties and trade agreements, capitalizing on Egypt's weakness at the time.

Thieberger has analyzed Solomon's judicial system, and he concluded that Solomon consolidated a central supreme court and court of appeal, which could overrule the decentralized local courts. Solomon could overrule local judgments in a similar way to the enforcement administered by Samuel and then David. In effect, Solomon also secularized the civil law by banishing Abiathar, the former high priest at Nob,[44] for having supported Adonijah and his claim to the throne. By doing so, the king fulfilled God's judgment

---

43   Josephus, ibid.
44   Nob was a town near the Mount of Olives and in the vicinity of Jerusalem.

against the house of Eli.[45] As fourth in descent from Eli, he was the last of the priesthood from Eli's house. At the same time, Solomon seemed to have dispensed with the priestly casting of lots by use of the Urim and Thummim[46] located on the priest's tunic. This was despite the fact that a sole high priest, Zadok, still officiated in Jerusalem. Zadok, in tandem with the prophet Nathan, had supported Solomon's accession.

Instead, Solomon built and judged at a Hall of Judgment,[47] or Court of Justice, which stood near the palaces and temple. It was a beautiful, cedar-paneled construction projecting royal power, legal unity, rule of law, and a desire for justice. Within it, Solomon operated a very different system to what had gone before when judgments were deliberated at city gates as people came and went. Justice was administered now behind closed doors and in privacy. There was, again, an Egyptian influence: the pharaoh or his vizier made judicial decisions for petitioners in a large hall of justice. The Egyptians symbolized justice as a pair of honest scales, and the judge as a sailor who sailed on a sea of truth.[48] Neither Solomon nor the ancient Egyptians got as far as establishing a legal profession as such, but there would have been written decrees. Isaiah condemns the unfair written decrees, and presumably, they had been occurring over a very long period of time.[49]

David tasked Solomon with the building of the temple, and its dimensions all came down to him from David, who stated that he had been guided by God in all these respects:

> Then David gave his son Solomon the plans for the vestibule, its houses, its treasuries, its upper chambers, its inner chambers, and the place of the mercy seat; and the plans for all that he had by the Spirit, of the courts of the house of the LORD, of all the

---

45   1 Samuel 2:7-36
46   The possible meaning of Urim and Thummim is "lights and perfections." The presence of the Holy Spirit was required before they could be utilized.
47   1 Kings 7:7
48   N.J. Van Blerk, "The Concept of Law and Justice in Ancient Egypt, With Specific Reference to the *Tale of the Eloquent Peasant*" (M.A. Dissertation, University of South Africa, 2006).
49   In Isaiah 10:1, he is making his pronouncement about 150 years after Solomon's reign.

chambers all around, of the treasuries of the house of God, and of the treasuries for the dedicated things (1 Chron. 28:11-12).

These details are accompanied by the most precise details possible for every utensil, candlestick altar, and table to be used on temple grounds, along with the material, such as gold and silver, which David had already accumulated for them all. Solomon was given a blueprint, the internal and external furniture, and much of the raw material for that furniture. David did not say very clearly *how* he got the blueprint, only that "the LORD made me understand in writing, by *His* hand upon me, all the works of these plans" (1 Chron. 28:19). It may be, given the similarities of the plan to the one given to Moses on Mount Sinai for the sanctuary, that David had been studying that in a prayerful way.[50]

Solomon's greatest achievement is arguably the building of the temple. Like the portable sanctuary assembled in the desert, it was to be the visible manifestation on earth of a heavenly reality. The ark represented God's presence to the Israelites, but the temple would be of international significance, legitimizing Solomon's rule, as well as the spiritual dominance of Yahweh, over the nations. The king began its construction in the fourth year of his reign. He doubtlessly believed that he fulfilled the prophecies of Moses. "Then there will be the place where the LORD your God chooses to make His name abide. There you shall bring all that I command you: your burnt offerings, your sacrifices, your tithes, the heave offerings of your hand, and all your choice offerings which you vow to the LORD" (Deut. 12:11).

Construction of the temple was achieved through a levy of thirty thousand men who worked one month on with two months off. This was a way for them to pay tax to Solomon, and it allowed construction to always be done by men who were fresh—although, no doubt they had other activities such as farming and fishing when they were not working on the project. It could be argued that for the time, this relatively benign method of worker management was more enlightened than other Iron Age systems across the world through which rulers

50 Exodus 25

would require slave labor to work until they were dead. Even so, the temple's construction was extremely expensive. Hiram exacted a huge price in imported produce from Israel—vast amounts of wheat and oil delivered to Tyre each year in exchange for timber exports.[51] In the end, this was not enough, and Hiram required cities from Solomon.

The temple was built on a plateau of land that had been a threshing floor for grain and on the highest mountain summit part of Jerusalem. David, and then Solomon, had both preferred a site on a high place, which had never been used in pagan worship. It was spiritually pristine. It was also a place of deliverance where the Lord was intreated for the land (2 Sam. 24:25). David had sacrificed there, the place where the avenging angel of the Lord had paused.

It is estimated that the temple took seven years and five months to build, with much of that time spent leveling the foundation and raising up part of the ground. It was a considerable task for which the Phoenician architects and supervisors were suited. They had already worked for years to build up the city of Tyre on land reclaimed from the Mediterranean. Hiram had been working to build a temple for Melqart with his own palace nearby. Now, the Phoenicians could direct another huge construction project to create another majestic spiritual and royal space. There had to be a substantial leveling of Mount Moriah, but across a built-up section of ground supported by thick walls constructed of dressed stones about fourteen feet long. It took seven years, from 967 to 960 B.C., to build the temple. On the downward slope toward Jerusalem, Solomon would then build his palace. That project took thirteen years.

Something else was happening as well. The peaceful conditions which Solomon created, as well as the temple itself, enabled the Israelite scribes to start writing in earnest. They were able to write down the Jewish chronicles and oral histories and take them from the campfires and high place ceremonies and record them in such a way that they were preserved, eventually to become sections of our Old Testament. The royal scribes and the priests wrote all

---

this on tablets while they sat in close proximity to the temple and the palace complex. They created the national archives recounting Yahweh's dealings with them: Abraham's journeys, the clashes between Moses and Pharaoh, the crossing of the Red Sea, the wilderness years, and the capture of the land after the crossing of the river Jordan. As Henri Gaubert points out, this activity—capturing the spiritual and cultural history of a people event by event—was unique and superseded anything the Egyptians had accomplished.[52] The pharaohs had largely been concerned with propaganda, often embellishing their achievements in battle.

SOLOMON'S TERRITORIAL EXPANSION IN THE NORTH

The Bible records that Solomon fought battles in the North and expanded David's territory to the north and east (e.g. 2 Chron. 8:2-3), albeit losing Damascus. The most interesting aspect of this is that it records that he built Tadmor, or Palmyra.[53] The historian Josephus Flavius agrees that Solomon built Tadmor, although some remains may precede Solomon's development and fortification of the city. This was to control a major trade route (from Damascus to Babylon) and to protect the northern part of his empire.

Solomon also controlled Tiphsah on the Euphrates, a city due north of Tadmor and about forty miles east of Aleppo. His territory extended southwest from there to Gaza.

> And it came to pass at the end of twenty years, when Solomon had built the house of the Lord and his own house, that the cities which Hiram had given to Solomon, Solomon built them; and he settled the children of Israel there. And Solomon went to Hamath Zobah and seized it. He also built Tadmor in the wilderness (2 Chron. 8:1-4a).

"For he had dominion over all *the region* on this side of the River from Tiphsah even to Gaza, namely over all the kings on this side of the River; and he

---

52   Gaubert, ibid.
53   Palmyra is the name given to the city by Greeks.

had peace on every side all around him" (1 Kings 4:24). This meant that despite the loss of Damascus, Solomon's territory greatly expanded his father's domain. It stretched north and east of Palmyra and down through all the formerly Canaanite territory.

CHAPTER 10

A WALK THROUGH THE TEMPLE

"O Lord of hosts, God of Israel, the One who dwells between the cherubim, You are God,
You alone, of all the kingdoms of the earth. You have made heaven and earth."

—Isaiah 37:16

The functioning temple and God's presence in it were the perigee of
Solomon's success and the closest he came to God. The supernatural interface
between worship in the temple and God's felt presence would be something
talked about right across the region, to wherever the trade routes extended.
People came from far and wide to witness the extraordinary, the palpable
presence of an unseen, real Yahweh dwelling in His temple.

What was the temple like? It was exactly as Solomon had imagined it would be.
He had directed the construction, and he had imagined what its effect would be
at every viewpoint. We can consider what we would see and what we would think
of it if we could go back in time to walk in the temple grounds. The following
imaginative walk through the temple is based on the current best evidence
available.[54] We need to make certain assumptions, though, since Scripture does
not enable us to reconstruct the exact temple as one would have perceived it at
the time. For instance, in the absence of scriptural evidence, we need to assume
exactly where the twin pillars would have stood at the temple's eastern entrance.

---

54 E.g. The internal and external architectural reconstructions drawn up by Yosef Garfinkel
   and Madeleine Mumcuoglu (2016) by inputting biblical temple data into an architectural
   computer program and by considering other Jewish and pagan temple structures of the
   Bronze Age and early-to-mid Iron Age eras.

Evidence from a later southern kingdom (i.e. Judah) temple at Tel Motza,[55] just west of Jerusalem, indicates that the pillars were functional as well as decorative, holding up the entrance roof. The Tel Motza temple is not mentioned in Kings or Chronicles. So, let us go on our walk.

As we approach Solomon's Temple, we are walking uphill on just a slight incline, with the old city of Jerusalem behind us. We would then enter the sacred space of the temple through a gate in a wall almost twenty feet high. Superimposed on the stone wall is a layer of cedar beams which may have the color of light orange with a tinge of red, given the typical color of Lebanese cedar when cut and used as a building material. The interplay of colors between the dark cream or light orange wall and the superimposed cedar beams is very aesthetically pleasing.

Continuing on, visitors come to a second wall as high and impressive as the first. There are a few steps to walk up because everything enclosed inside the second wall is raised up. This is the temple court. A lot of work by Phoenician artisans has gone into leveling, raising up, and perfecting an impressive raised plane across what had been a very rocky and uneven mountainside.

We would immediately see the large, square, brass altar standing in the middle of the inner court. It is about thirty-two feet wide, thirty-two feet long, and sixteen feet high.[56] The ashes and other remains of sacrificed animals fall through its grating and onto the ground to be swept up. The sacrificial animals symbolized the future death of the sin-bearing Lamb of God, "for *it is* not possible that the blood of bulls and goats could take away our sins,"[57] even though the Jewish law requires their sacrifice. The fire on top of the altar is always ablaze, day and night.

The Bible does not indicate if there were horns at each corner of the altar, but there probably are since God had already said to Moses that He wanted them (Exod.

27:2).[58] The priest would splash the horns with the animal's blood to symbolize the blood poured out and meeting its end in death. Around the altar stand ten mobile, brass washbasins about seven feet across and about five feet high. The basins, which are six-and-a-half-feet deep, are placed on the stands, and they can be moved around on their bronze wheels as purification rituals demand. They are decorated on their outside surfaces with bulls, palm trees, and cherubs. Smaller versions of these objects have been discovered at a number of Iron Age pagan temple sites, such as Larnaca and Enkomi,[59] both Phoenician sites in Cyprus.

Near to the altar and closer to the temple stands another massive creation in brass, the largest object in the temple court. It is known as the molten sea, and it is about eighteen feet wide and nine feet deep. This large purification basin is for the priests to wash their hands and feet, and it sits on top of twelve brass oxen, three of them facing each of the four main compass points. The molten sea rests easily on their backs, despite being incredibly heavy.[60] The oxen symbolize the twelve tribes of Israel—and more besides.

The bronze basin is for sacrificial washing, a serious and absolute requirement:

> "You shall also make a laver of bronze, with its base also of bronze, for washing. You shall put it between the tabernacle of meeting and the altar. And you shall put water in it, for Aaron and his sons shall wash their hands and their feet in water from it. When they go into the tabernacle of meeting, or when they come near the altar to minister, to burn an offering made by fire to the LORD, they shall wash with water, lest they die. So they shall wash their hands and their feet, lest they die. And it shall be a statute forever to them—to him and his descendants throughout their generations" (Exod. 30:18-21).

The basin we see before us, however, has been magnified by Solomon: he allowed the Phoenicians to play with the idea. The bronze basin would not look out of place in a pagan temple forecourt! It is, of course, bigger and better than any

---

58   See also the details of the wonderful temple given in a vision to Ezekiel in Ezekiel 43:20.
59   August H. Konkel, *1 and 2 Kings (The NIV Application Commentary)*, (Grand Rapids: Zondervan, 2010).
60   The wall of the molten sea is about a foot wide, and its weight is about thirty tons.

similar pagan object—for instance, the Vase of Amathonte, a six-foot-high basin created by the Phoenicians at about the same time as the basin they constructed for Solomon and now located in the Louvre, Paris. The bulls on its handles indicated that the pagan goddess being worshipped was Aphrodite (i.e. Venus), the goddess of fertility. As Israel apostatized, post-Solomon, the object we look at now easily became a pagan vessel.

It is important to spend a little more time in the temple court to consider the sea from a Christian point of view. The sea prefigures the sea of glass in Heaven on which the redeemed of Christ stand after they have washed their robes in the Lamb's blood (Rev. 7:14, 15:2). And given Solomon's genius, it also represents an act of Creation. God conquered all the chaotic waters and gathered all the sea together into one place (Gen. 1:9). The sea is ruled over by God and is fruitful. The twelve oxen symbolize this, and the sea is usually peaceful. The watery peace is symbolized by Solomon's lily fretwork around the rim. We remember that many hundreds of years later, Christ played on Solomon's imagery: "Consider the lilies, how they grow: they neither toil nor spin; and yet I say to you, even Solomon in all his glory was not arrayed like one of these" (Luke 12:27).

If we were the Jewish high priest, we would be able to ascend eleven further steps and enter the temple building. An enigmatic bronze column about thirty-eight feet high stands on each side of the entrance, supporting its roof. On top of them are capitals about eight feet high: bronze or copper fruit baskets with rows of lilies and one hundred pomegranates. On the right-hand side is the column Solomon named Jachin, and on the left is Boaz. Like many of the other details around and within the temple, they deviate from the design of Moses' tabernacle, which had nothing like them.

These columns were a common feature in temples constructed during and after the Iron Age (e.g. in Egypt, Syria, Tyre, and Carthage), but their names were unique to Solomon. It has been said that their names are riddles, whose meanings are lost, even if they were ever known by anyone other than Solomon. But this writer believes they are probably just casual references by the king to the first words which appear on inscriptions chiseled onto the pillars. Any such inscriptions were, in fact, ceremonial and prophetic and had to do with worship; this was the case even in pagan temples with twin frontage pillars. It seems very likely that Solomon got the idea of twin pillars from Egypt, and to be consistent, he would probably have had them inscribed. The building, after all, was the temple of Yahweh.

What were the inscriptions? The Old Testament scholar R.B.Y. Scott of McGill University has speculated that "Jachin" could relate to a longer inscription of which it was the first word. For example, "Yākîn (Yahweh) kissē Dāwîd, ûmamlaktô l'zar'ô ʻad ʻōlām," which means "He (Yahweh) will establish the throne of David and his kingdom to his seed forever."[61] This could also, therefore, be a reference to Solomon himself. Likewise, the "Boaz" inscription could have been something like, "B'ōz Yahweh yismah melek," which means, "In the strength of Yahweh shall the king rejoice."[62] The expression coming from David's psalm could allude to the fact that this pillar represented Solomon's father, David.[63]

However, Solomon was fond of riddles, and if the pillars were riddles, there could be more to it. They could be parts of a rebus riddle and perhaps not complete in themselves. Solomon innovated when he carried out the temple's construction, and the Phoenicians he brought in were involved in the casting of the pillars, the molten sea, and the many smaller brass temple objects. Perhaps the riddle spans the three biggest objects, essentially pagan in their origins but used by Solomon to say something about Yahweh.[64] [65] The riddle consists of an invoking of a truth about Yahweh across the three biggest brass objects we see as we approach the temple. The riddle is spoken by three pagan-derived but reimagined temple objects, the pillars, and the molten sea. Constructed by pagan

---

61   Also see Psalm 89:4.
62   Also see King David's Psalm 21:1a.
63   R.B.Y. Scott, "The Pillars Jachin and Boaz," in *Journal of Biblical Literature*, Vol. 58, No. 2 (June, 1939), 143-149, doi:10.2307/3259857.
64   Like the twin frontage pillars, the molten sea seems to have been a construction inspired by pagan temple worship in countries surrounding King Solomon's territory. Similar Assyrian, Hittite, and Aramean basin and bull objects and reliefs have been found by a number of archaeologists.
65   See *The Conflict Myth and the Biblical Tradition* by Debra Scoggins Ballentine (2015) for a discussion of these in light of Solomon's reimagining of such objects.

artisans under instruction from Solomon, they were reconfigured and set out on display in homage to his God, Yahweh. If we stand at the entrance to the temple and read from right to left (north pillar, south pillar, molten sea), the riddle says: "He (Yahweh) founds (Jachin) with strength (Boaz) the sea," as in Psalm 93:1-4. The psalm even ends with reference to the temple: "Your testimonies are very sure; Holiness adorns Your house, O LORD, forever" (Psalm 93:5).

As we look at the pillars and their garden imagery and consider all the other imagery of flowers and pomegranates, we think of the Garden of Eden. Are these pillars representations of the tree of life and the tree of the knowledge of good and evil? The temple complex is like a microcosm of Heaven and Earth, as God intended it to be. Here we are on Earth, and we think back to its earliest days after its creation. Palm trees, the garden. We are walking toward Heaven, the Holy of Holies, where God dwells amidst His cherubim. The temple is, in fact, a new and perfected creation. It is also the universe.

If this approaches the reality of Solomon's mindset as he built the temple, it is actually part of a more general motivation or driving force within the king. Throughout the temple, he brought in foreign influences from Phoenicia, Egypt, Assyria, the neo-Hittites, and other sources round about without actually relying overly on any one of them. Solomon was synthesizing and refining what he was aware of in homage to his God, constructing something unique out of it all, which he perceived to be aesthetically pleasing to himself and presumably to Yahweh also. The general impression, though, is of a temple somewhat similar to certain types of Iron Age Phoenician temples. Like King Solomon's temple, these were built on an east-west axis facing the all-important Mediterranean Sea (rather than being oriented east according to the solar cycle); they were modest in size; they had sacred pillars representing deity; there was a raised-up, sacred space within, and so on.[66]

Solomon also accepted a common division of internal temple areas into three rooms built along a longitudinal axis, east to west, and ending in a

---

66   Meir Edrey, "Towards a Definition of the Phoenician Temple," in *Palestine Exploration Journal,* Vol. 150, No. 3, 184-205 (2018), doi: https://doi.org/10.1080/00310328.2018.1471652.

shrine room, very similar to the Iron Age post-Hittite temples at Ain Dara and Emar, which were dedicated to Baal, Astarte, and Ishtar. Unfortunately, this meant that the temple was also constructed in such a way that it could facilitate pagan worship when Judah rebelled against Yahweh. For instance, the temple was already positioned on an east-west axis and so facilitated the worship of Astarte, according to the southern setting position (in an eight-year cycle) of the planet Venus.[67] [68]

In a front wall almost sixty feet wide and forty-five feet high, the stonework gleaming white in the sunshine, the temple building entrance is twenty-one feet wide and has two enormous doors made of cypress wood inlaid with gold leaf to accentuate the carvings of cherubim, palm trees, and flowers. We see the beautiful carvings glitter in the sunlight. The temple entrance is facing east. The temple's front wall stands serene in beautiful and unornamented simplicity.

The temple is about one hundred and sixty feet long, and there is an outbuilding for storage and lodging three stories high, whose lower roof adjoins the temple walls right and left. Most of the temple's windows are set high up along its sides. Above the entrance and elsewhere around the building are the protruding roof beam ends arranged in groups of three (triglyphs). These support the roof. The beam triglyphs are just over six feet apart from each other, high up on the front, back, and side walls of the temple.

Entering through the doorway, surrounded by three recessed doorframes built to signify the holiness of the place we are entering,[69] we walk westwards into the Ulam, or entrance hall, which is one story high, about thirty-six feet wide and about eighteen feet long.[70] It is empty, designed to help one prepare for the holy place within. In front of us stand another set of doors made of cypress wood and decorated with gold-overlaid carvings of palms, flowers, and cherubim. This

67   César Esteban and Daniel Iborra Pellín, "Temples of Astarte Across the Mediterranean," *Mediterranean Archaeology and Archaeometry*, Vol. 16, No. 4, 161–166.
68   Astarte's star symbol was Venus.
69   Megan Sauter, "The Doorways of Solomon's Temple," Bible History Daily online, October 27, 2020, https://www.biblicalarchaeology.org/daily/biblical-artifacts/artifacts-and-the-bible/the-doorways-of-solomons-temple.
70   The details in this description can be found in 1 Kings 6.

time, we have four recessed doorframes surrounding doors, rather than three, to indicate the increasing holiness of the space beyond.

Through these doors is the Hechal, or sanctuary, which is completely paneled in cedar wood. Again, everything is gold-overlaid with many more palm trees, flowers, and cherubim. Nature and the living creatures are all praising God. We walk in silently and cross the gold-striped, cypress wood floor. The sanctuary is just over fifty-two feet high and is the largest of the temple's rooms. The roof is made of cedar beams, and recessed windows high up on the walls let in a subtle light which causes the golden carvings to gleam and glimmer. The precious stone decorations on the Hechal walls glitter like diamonds.[71] As the theologian Margaret Barker points out, all this symbolizes the Garden of Eden.[72]

As we walk across the Hechal, we get the feeling that we are in a stylized garden and have also left the Earth behind. We are in a mystical space, which represents paradise on Earth and paradise in Heaven. Solomon is saying that here the two locations are both present. God's kingdom has come in this form on the summit of His holy mountain, and we are walking through it, His garden temple. The temple priests composed songs about and for this place. In future times, the righteous will be like the palm trees we see glittering all around us. "The righteous shall flourish like a palm tree, He shall grow like a cedar in Lebanon. Those who are planted in the house of the Lord Shall flourish in the courts of our God" (Psalm 92:12-13).

Straight ahead, almost sixty feet away and just in front of yet another door, is the incense altar. It is about five feet high and three feet long, and it has horns at each corner like those on the altar for burnt offerings outside.[73] Pure gold candelabras stand on either side of the incense altar, and each contains five candlesticks, which shine out day and night. Beside these is a gold-covered table for the shewbread: twelve loaves of unleavened bread to set before Yahweh's face and which represent the twelve tribes. They were set in two equal piles, and

---

71   2 Chronicles 3:6
72   Margaret Barker, *The Gate of Heaven: The History and Symbolism of the Temple in Jerusalem* (Sheffield: Sheffield Phoenix Press, 2008).
73   We can infer the horns from Ezekiel 41:22.

a system of golden rods was used between the loaves to allow air to circulate between them and prevent them from crushing each other. Incense rose up beside or above the loaves, symbolizing praises to God. After a week, they were eaten by the priests in the sanctuary and were replaced by twelve more. Day and night, the lampstands on each side of the altar beam out a diffuse light. All around is a wonderful sense of peace.

The inside of the temple and its decorations are lavishly plated in gold, and this will be superseded by the Debir, where everything from floor to ceiling is gold. Solomon acted as pagan kings, cladding as much as possible in gold. It was the metal of royalty and of the gods, everywhere from Ancient Egypt and its temples through Solomon's time and into the Assyrian empire, where both Esarhaddon and his son Ashurbanipal, self-styled king of the world, plated their temple interiors with gold.[74] [75]

Behind all the golden objects of worship are five steps leading up to another carved wooden door, this time of pine wood, overlaid with gold and just over ten feet wide. It has a pentagonal doorframe. Again, Solomon borrowed this concept from pagan temples: these people groups symbolized the sacredness of an inner temple space by creating a number of recessed doorframes at its portal. Solomon developed this into an increasingly complex set of doorframe structures. We already walked through a three-framed and then a four-framed recessed doorway. Now we have Solomon's pentagonal-recessed doorframe construction. It signifies that the space behind the doorway is extremely holy and absolutely off-limits to almost everyone. The wall this door is set within is not made of stone. It is a cypress wood partition.

We are far into the temple, and the door opens into a Debir, or Holy of Holies, space shrouded from us by a drawn blue, crimson, and purple linen curtain, the veil of the screen, fastened by gold chains and decorated with cherubim.[76]

---

74   Alan Millard, "King Solomon in his Ancient Context," *Bible and Spade*, Vol. 15, No. 3 (Summer, 2002), 67.

75   Often silver was used as well, but Solomon only used gold. Even the door hinge sockets were gold.

76   Numbers 4:5—the screen's construction is according to the instructions given by God to Moses in Exodus 26:31-33.

Drawing it back, we find a room designed as a cube, about thirty-two feet high, wide and deep—like the perfect cube Holy of Holies in Moses' tabernacle but a lot larger. The room is completely overlaid with gold, including the floor and ceiling. Six hundred talents of gold have been used (2 Chron. 3:8). The weight of gold used is twenty-two tons, and its value at the time of writing is $1.4 billion. The room has no windows, and it is in complete darkness unless light streams through the drawn back curtain behind us.

We are now in the heavenly realm, having walked up and into it from the earthly Garden of Eden. The spiritual journey from earthly to heavenly is symbolized by the drawing back of the curtain, the created realm and its substance. Only those who can mediate between Heaven and Earth are to be here—those who can bring penitence on behalf of the people and who can offer God's blessing back to them. Only the officiating priests were allowed into the sanctuary, but only one man, the high priest, was allowed to enter the Holy of Holies and only once a year in the seventh month of Tishri on the day of expiation or atonement, the extinguishing of guilt through suffering or a penalty. We in future times can enter the space the Debir symbolizes through the blood of Jesus, our great High Priest.[77]

The outspread wings of two carved cherubim meet in the middle of the room while their other wings touch opposite walls. Their combined wingspan is thirty-two feet. Made of olive wood, they are overlaid in gold and are about eighteen feet high. Underneath their wings stands the ark of the covenant and within it the tablets on which the Ten Commandments are inscribed. They are divine beings linked to God's presence. They do not represent God but merely His servants:

> And the cherubim lifted their wings and mounted up from the earth in my sight. When they went out, the wheels *were* beside them; and they stood at the door of the east gate of the LORD's house, and the glory of the God of Israel *was* above them. This *is* the living creature I saw under the God of Israel by the River Chebar, and I knew they *were* cherubim" (Ezek. 10:19-20).

---

77 Hebrews 10:19-20

Solomon wanted to convey the truth that God is served and worshipped, not just by humanity but by His celestial beings. Was the concept, though, borrowed from pagan temples, which often had guard figures set inside to protect the deity bring worshipped? Commentators have sometimes said that this is a contravention of the third commandment: no graven images or likenesses are to be permitted.[78] However, Solomon was actually obeying a specific commandment to Moses, although he substantially increased the size of the covering cherubs which Moses had created at Sinai.

> And you shall make two cherubim of gold; of hammered work you shall make them at the two ends of the mercy seat. Make one cherub at one end, and the other cherub at the other end; you shall make the cherubim at the two ends of it *of one piece* with the mercy seat. And the cherubim shall stretch out *their* wings above, covering the mercy seat with their wings, and they shall face one another; the faces of the cherubim *shall be* toward the mercy seat (Exod. 25:18-20).

The Israelites understood that Yahweh was all-powerful. He did not need any help from guardian creatures. They are there, though, to provide Him with a chariot throne as He is enthroned above the cherubim in Heaven. Solomon built what David wanted, and it symbolized heavenly reality and the meeting place of Heaven and Earth on Mount Zion's summit.[79] It is here where God dwells. By having the cherubim wings meet in the middle, Solomon created God's throne. Yahweh sits above the wings, and the ark is His footstool. But He is aniconic: He is there, but any representation of Him is absent.[80] The intent is to show that Yahweh ruled over Solomon's empire from its center, the temple, and He bestowed or delegated the empire to Solomon, who reigned from his palace nearby. Sitting invisibly on His huge cherubim throne before us, Yahweh turns the temple into the palace of Yahweh. Jeremiah, who witnessed the temple and its destruction by Babylonia,

78   Exodus 20:4-6; Deuteronomy 5:8-10
79   1 Chronicles 28:18; Isaiah 37:16
80   T. N. D. Mettinger (1982) for an analysis of the meaning and significance of the cherubim throne.

harks back to this reality: "A glorious high throne from the beginning *is* the place of our sanctuary" (Jer. 17:12).

The overwhelming impression we get as we start our return journey to leave the temple is one of flawless perfection. God is enthroned in Heaven and Earth in His temple. Everything else is peaceful and ordered, created to worship Him. The ark, once enclosed in a tabernacle two hundred years prior, is now protected in a completely dark silence within the Debir, and the Debir is protected by the rest of the temple. As Steven Weitzman says in his commentary on Solomon, the temple has a "transcendent quality."[81] It is both humankind's realm and God's realm. It became this as soon as the ark was placed within it.

We have also walked westward within the temple with our backs to the sun, which has risen in the east. The temple has a Phoenician pagan orientation, facing the Mediterranean, but not a pagan solar one. Nevertheless, the temple could be used for sun worship if the curtain was drawn back, allowing the sun's rays to stream through the Hechal and into the Debir. Any worship such as this would precipitate judgment from God's throne.

THE ARK OF THE COVENANT

If the entire temple was created to protect the ark, what is the ark's significance? It is quite a small object, after all, about four feet, six inches long and two feet, two inches wide with the same dimension in height. It is made of acacia wood and overlaid with gold leaf outside and inside; superimposed outside is a more ornate gold molding. Its top surface is a lid of solid gold: the mercy seat. The Israelites referred to this lid as the *kaporet,* which is derived from *kaper,* which means "to atone for sins." On either end of this surface stands or kneels a cherubim, with its wings outstretched over the mercy seat. We cannot say from the written accounts what their exact postures were.

Unlike anything else in antiquity, its contents are hugely significant but so, too, is its surface. Both are associated with Yahweh's presence. Inside the box are the Law Codes, or Ten Commandments, given to Moses at Mount Sinai. These were

---

81   Weitzman, ibid.

inscribed by Moses on two rectangular tablets of stone. It is likely that these were blue in color, created from sapphire stone or lapis lazuli. Jewish tradition has it that they were about a foot-and-a-half long and wide and about nine inches thick with five commandments inscribed on each. They served as God's contract and alliance with Israel. Obedience to the Law guaranteed the protection of Yahweh. The ark also contained other manifestations and assurances from Yahweh; Aaron's rod, which demonstrated miraculous powers in Egypt and during the exodus journey; and a gold pot of manna.

The mercy seat served at certain times as Yahweh's throne. Its purpose and function are described very well by the Bible scholar Henri Gaubert: "It was here that Yahweh came when He wanted to speak to Moses, and later with Joshua, and, in circumstances of exceptional gravity, with some of the high priests."[82] This was exactly as God had said, as recorded in Exodus. This was where He said He would come. And it was Yahweh Who was worshipped. The ark and its throne for Him were greatly revered. God's throne is in Heaven, but it is also here in the temple. And taking no form, He speaks from a place between the cherubim and above the mercy seat.[83] King David wrote, The LORD *is* in His holy temple, The LORD's throne *is* in heaven (Psalm 11:4a).

Two gold-plated rods were permanently in position, fixed across the longest sides of the ark through rings. These had been in position for transport when Israel, in their long journey from Egypt, was nomadic. The biblical account describes the ark's history before it is placed by Solomon in the temple. It is no inert object. It is, in fact, repeatedly connected to accounts of miraculous provision as well as miraculous destruction. It has to be handled with absolute care. When the Philistines captured it during the battle at Eben-Ezer, it caused them so much trouble that they became absolutely desperate to get rid of it. Eleven books in the Old Testament and New Testament refer to the ark.

---

82   Gaubert, ibid.
83   Exodus 25:22

CHAPTER II

THE ROYAL COMPLEX OF PALACES

"But Solomon took thirteen years to build his own house;
so he finished all his house. He also built the House of the Forest of Lebanon."

—1 Kings 7:1-2a

We retrace our footsteps until we are outside the temple. We walk across the temple court, pass through a south-facing doorway in the temple court wall, and walk down a flight of stairs. At the foot of the stairs, we enter a smaller courtyard, and on our right stands the magnificent royal palace, its walls constructed from polished stone. Its roof is constructed from cedar wood. Further to the right is a smaller palace wing in which the Egyptian queen resided. Surrounding the palace with its royal apartments are a number of adjoining buildings for the greater household—other wives and concubines permitted to live there as well as the king's personal guard stationed in a number of guardrooms. This complex served entirely as living quarters. The palace has a front courtyard and also a more private back courtyard next to the living quarters.[84] We can see that, overall, the entire palace complex is about ten times the size of the temple above us.[85]

Still walking south, we soon step into another complex, this time military and judicial. We walk straight into the Hall of Pillars, a magnificent waiting

---

84 This assumption about palace courtyards is the best which can be made currently. See the archaeological summary provided by Garfinkel and Mumcuoglu (2016).
85 Ibid.

room where various legal matters were probably settled by court officials. The Hall is about eighty-eight feet long and fifty-two feet wide, and its pillars all support a cedar beam canopy. If we are standing there, the House of the Forest of Lebanon is on our right, and the Throne Hall paneled inside with cedar where Solomon gave his judgments is on our left. It is in this hall where Solomon judged between the two women claiming the one child as their own.

The Throne Hall also served as a public reception hall: Solomon probably received the Queen of Sheba here. We do not know its measurements. We do know that the king's wood, ivory, and gold throne within it is reached by walking up six steps, each flanked by lions, and on each side of the throne, a lion stands beside the armrest.[86] The six steps are derived from a pagan model for thrones positioned on elevated platforms. Solomon sat on the seventh heaven, where God resides. Egyptian and Phoenician thrones in that time also had a number of steps up to them, and they believed in the existence of seven heavens. These corresponded to the seven classical, observable planets known to the Sumerians and Akkadians: the moon, the sun, Mars, Venus, Mercury, Jupiter, and Saturn. Was Solomon saying that he was God's representative on Earth? According to the Midrash, the six steps also symbolize the six days of Creation and the six types of land defined in the Torah, which Solomon said he ruled over.

In the House of the Forest of Lebanon, we can admire Solomon's armory upstairs and the three hundred beaten golden shields used by Solomon's bodyguard when they escorted him on royal visits. Alongside these are another three hundred smaller gold shields. The House is two stories high and contains the armory and the state treasury. It is about 180 feet long and about ninety feet wide, and its ground floor contains sixty massive cedar trunks, almost thirty feet high, separated from each other by gaps of about nine feet. Four rows of trunks each contain fifteen pillars. It is as if we are in a manmade forest with rows of trees stretching out before us. Looking up, we see that the treetops are blocks of cedar carved with leaves and that ribs protruding on either side from each pillar touch the ribs of the next trunks. It is like a roof of intertwined forest branches, but on all that rests the actual roof of cedar.[87] Three rows of square windows set high up in the two side walls let in the light, and the impression is of looking at gleams of light streaming through the branches of a forest. The House of the Forest of Lebanon is the most impressive of all the palace buildings to which we are allowed access. It alone is more than three times the size of the temple in terms of the area it takes up.

Walking south from the Hall of Pillars and its connecting buildings on either side, we step through the main wall of the complex and continue down to the city. Looking back at the House of the Forest of Lebanon, we can see that it is built to last. It was still there, in fact, 250 years after Solomon in Isaiah's time when other palace buildings were gone.[88] On the outsides of a number of the palace buildings, we see sculpted trees and all sorts of plants carved high up on the stone walls like a white stone version of the hanging gardens of Babylon. As the sun's rays shine on the palace, the meticulous intricacy of the carvings of each and every leaf gives the viewer the impression that the plants and trees are moving in the breeze.[89]

---

87   This reconstruction follows Thieberger's portrayal, which relies on the meanings of certain Hebrew terms, such as *zela*, meaning rib.
88   Isaiah 22:8
89   Josephus, ibid.

CHAPTER 12

THE KING ON THE BRAZEN SCAFFOLD

"Then Solomon stood before the altar of the Lord in the presence of all the assembly of Israel, and spread out his hands (for Solomon had made a bronze platform five cubits long, five cubits wide, and three cubits high, and had set it in the midst of the court."

—2 Chronicles 6:12-13a

When the temple consecration ceremony occurred in the harvest month of *Tishri*, Solomon processed in the opposite direction from the journey we just made, beginning at the old sanctuary in Jerusalem. With the Levites carrying the ark and the holy vessels, the king ascended up toward the temple. Musicians and singers were with them, and as they approached the Boaz and Jachin pillars, they were probably singing new dedicatory psalms created for the ceremony rather than anything from the recent or ancient past. The first of these quotations is from Solomon's Song of Ascents: "Unless the LORD builds the house, They labor in vain who build it; Unless the Lord guards the city, The watchman stays awake in vain" (Psalm 127:1). "Lift up your heads, O you gates! Lift up, you everlasting doors! And the King of glory shall come in. Who is this King of glory? The LORD of hosts, He *is* the King of glory" (Psalm 24:9-10).

There were also many other people present—tribal leaders and heads of families—and everyone involved themselves in a huge animal sacrifice of sheep and cattle before the ark. But the assembly divided at the pillars, and everyone

101

but the king and the priests remained outside at the sacrificial site in the temple forecourt. The king and priests stepped through the doorway into the sanctuary and then through the curtain into the Holy of Holies. There the priests set the ark underneath the golden cherubim wings, and Solomon offered up incense in the sanctuary.

There was a great musical noise of cymbals, harps, and lyres in the Hekal. One hundred and twenty priests blew their trumpets, and suddenly the singing and all the instruments blended into one cry of praise: *"For He is* good, For His mercy *endures* forever."[90]

As soon as the priests exited the Holy of Holies, the cloud of God's presence filled the temple, and the priests were unable to continue with their duties. The Presence was so powerful that everyone fled outside to the twin pillars and beyond. Solomon responded by latching on to a psalm which has now been lost to us. His quotation from it is all that remains. The situation warranted immediate improvisation, and the king thought of the most appropriate possible response. He tried to take command of the situation again and said to God, "'The LORD said he would dwell in the dark cloud. I have surely built You an exalted house, And a place for you to dwell in forever.'"[91]

Solomon exited the temple and then ascended a brazen scaffold (a platform made of bronze) that he had commanded to be made and to be placed in the middle of the temple forecourt. It was seven-and-a-half feet wide and the same dimension broad. It was four-and-a-half feet high.

Solomon then knelt and launched into a blessing and dedication speech in which he proclaimed that his father told him that it was God's stated will that Solomon build the temple. He also acknowledged that no earthly temple could contain God, and he immediately asked for God's mercy. Remarkably, he prophesied in his speech many of the future events for his people, including possible defeats in battle followed by their exile and later return to the land, events which were hundreds of years into the future. The king then stood up

---

90   2 Chronicles 5:12-13
91   1 Kings 8:12-13

on the scaffold and blessed all those present, ending his speech with these magnificent words:

> "And may these words of mine, with which I have made supplication before the LORD, be near the LORD our God day and night, that He may maintain the cause of His servant and the cause of His people Israel, as each day may require, that all the peoples of the earth may know that the LORD *is* God; *there is* no other. Let your heart therefore be loyal to the LORD our God, to walk in His statutes and keep His commandments, as at this day" (1 Kings 8:59-61).

Solomon's speech, as recorded in Scripture, is arguably the best and most lucid speech in all of Old Testament Scripture.[92] He was well capable of honoring God and His temple with a speech which was all-encompassing, including details of his people's past, present, and future journey of faith with both its trials and its victories. But there was nothing apocalyptic about it and nothing of a future Messiah. A religious observer of the king on his scaffold would be led to conclude that the millennium and the rule of the Messiah had arrived. The Messiah was sitting on the throne of Israel, and he possessed a kingdom which, in due time, would fill the Earth. Solomon declared that God will dwell in Solomon's temple forever, and he informed those present that God's eternal reign had just started on Earth. Solomon made it possible: "'I have surely built You an exalted house, And a place for You to dwell in forever'" (1 Kings 8:13).

The king then walked to the altar located in the forecourt, knelt down again before God, raised his hands skyward in a prayerful way, and sought to renew the covenant between God and Israel. Solomon described a number of situations where Israel must fulfill the requirements of this covenant and when God would forgive their sin against Him, executing fair judgment on the innocent and the guilty. God could be supplicated at the temple. He could be sought after through repentance, and He would meet the needs of the people concerning justice,

---

92   Having said that, there is evidence from archaeological remains of Mesopotamian pagan temple dedication ceremonies that Solomon borrowed some of the speech elements from them. These similarities are described in the *Olam Hatanakh,* a biblical encyclopedia approved by the Israeli Ministry of Education.

protection, and defense from enemies. Israel can also seek Him as the God over all nature to address their needs in times of drought, famine, and plague. Solomon also aligned himself with something communicated later through the prophet Isaiah: God would hear and answer foreigners' prayers at the temple.[93] And in general, Solomon emphasized the effectiveness of prayer. God heard and responded to worshipers' prayers.

Solomon then rose to his feet again and turned directly to the assembly to bless them. "Israel," he said in a loud voice, "has arrived, and they are now at rest." God is a Keeper of all His promises to Israel, and they were fulfilled that day. His words would have sounded majestic, confident, and perfect for the ceremonial occasion. It is actually "a praying out of the Pentateuch," as Dale Ralph Davis has observed.[94] Solomon took hold of texts within Leviticus 26 and Deuteronomy 30 and prayed them out to Yahweh, juxtaposing Yahweh's attributes of severity and mercy while holding them together. Daniel and Nehemiah would offer similar prayers in later times. It was a seemingly authentic prayer and oration, and it ended with the following simple but profound words:

> "He may incline our hearts to Himself, to walk in all His ways, and to keep His commandments and His statutes and His judgments, which He commanded our fathers. And may these words of mine, with which I have made supplication before the LORD, be near the LORD our God day and night, that He may maintain the cause of His servant and the cause of His people Israel, as each day may require, that all the peoples of the earth may know that the LORD *is* God; *there is* no other. Let your heart therefore be loyal to the LORD our God, to walk in His statutes and keep His commandments, as at this day" (1 Kings 8:58-61).

The book of 2 Chronicles records that as soon as Solomon had finished, fire came down from heaven and consumed the burnt offering and sacrifices. This is the same experience as the one recorded in Leviticus when the fire consumed

---

93   Isaiah 56:7
94   Davis, ibid, 89.

the burnt offering on the altar.[95] The fire was God's signal to Israel that His sacrificial conditions had been met: the people had turned away from sacrificing to idols and instead had followed His commands as to acceptable sacrifice to Him. The fire showed the people they could fellowship with a holy God because the sacrificial blood atoned for their souls. It was a signal to them that they should continue in the ways He had set out to them (as in Leviticus). He would then continue to abide with them.

God's glory also appeared in the temple as a cloud—again, very similar to the glory appearing to the people in the series of events to do with the tabernacle and recorded in Leviticus. The cloud displayed God's presence but at the same time hid Him from view. God's will was clear enough: it was inscribed on the tablets within the temple's ark. God Himself remained obscure. It had to be like that. Because of God's holiness, no one could see God's face and live (Exod. 33:22-23).

The temple was then dedicated with burnt offerings. There were so many that Solomon consecrated much of the courtyard for the activity because the altar could not contain it all. The festivities lasted for fourteen days.

God's presence in a dark, smoky cloud within the temple required the priests to urgently vacate the premises, and we are left with the possibility that the Presence was unbearable. It seemed something akin, almost parallel, to an event in Heaven, still in the future and located in the heavenly realm, which aspects of the temple represented. In Revelation, celestial beings are required to vacate God's temple because of the smoke coming from God's glory. This time, the smoke is a sign of God's wrath and the prelude to the last plagues being poured on the Earth. It would make an observer of these unpredictable events at Solomon's temple wonder if they had suddenly been blessed by God's supernatural presence but were also in great danger of slipping into judgment. Are there aspects to this temple which provoked God toward rage? "Then one of the four living creatures gave to the seven angels seven golden bowls full of the wrath of God who lives

---

forever and ever. The temple was filled with smoke from the glory of God and from His power, and no one was able to enter the temple till the seven plagues of the seven angels were completed" (Rev. 15:7-8).

CHAPTER 13

THE POWER OF THE TEMPLE

"Then the word of the Lord came to Solomon, saying:
'Concerning this temple which you are building . . . '"

—1 Kings 6:11-12a

God's only clear will was that an altar be built in that place.[96] God neither confirmed to the king that Solomon should now build a temple or forbid him to build it. He knew ahead of time that Solomon would want to build a temple.[97] Since God knows everything, He also knew that Solomon's good motives would be compromised and that his polluted temple would be destroyed. At the same time, though, He read the king's noble motives and told him that if he walked always according to God's commandments, then He would live amongst His people. The tone of Scripture in 1 Kings suggests that although it is not Yahweh's clear will that Solomon build the temple, it was blessed by God's gracious favor. God recognized Solomon's good motives and was able to bless the endeavor.

It is very difficult to evoke the atmosphere which the temple had within it, but it would certainly have been more potent than anything we have ever experienced in a sacred building. The sudden arrival of God's overpowering presence made the place unbearable for the priests and everyone else for a time. At all times after that, there was the ever-present necessity to preserve the peaceful and predictable order of things through prayer and ritual; and

---

96   1 Chronicles 21:18
97   2 Samuel 7:13

sometimes, especially post-Solomon, the people confused the two and offered up ritual when only prayer would have done. One wrong move in such a place could spell personal or even national disaster. This was the place, after all, where King David had seen the destroying angel of death and the drawn sword which had killed seventy thousand. This was where he had built his altar. The frisson of potential further judgment may still have hung in the air.

The temple was a place of pilgrimage, a place which took away from the scattering of pagan high places set on other peaks. It was also a centralizing focus for Israel as a nation, a numinous jewel set within the structure of Solomon's statecraft, built to glorify Yahweh. It was also a source of national life, and it was able to prolong the timeline of the southern kingdom of Judah after the nation split apart under Rehoboam. It played a key role in the national re-awakenings, times when the royal dynasty turned back to God—for example, under Jehoshaphat and Hezekiah.

There is great power in the temple's music. One of Solomon's innovations is that he took the level of music which Egypt used in their temples and reinvented its use for his own temple. The professional temple musicians in Egypt were the most esteemed and valued musicians in the land. Taking that on board, Solomon professionalized Israelite temple musicianship; for instance, he exempted the singers and musicians from doing anything else at all.[98]

The temple housed the presence of Yahweh and something of His glory, but much of the ceremony surrounding it displayed the power and glory of Solomon. We know that Solomon fashioned two hundred targets (large shields) and three hundred smaller shields of beaten gold. He stored these in his armory, the Palace of the Forest of Lebanon. These were for ceremonial purposes and also served as an impressive show in public of some tokens of his wealth. Carried by soldiers and commanders of the palace guard, they surrounded the king as he walked in procession to the temple and its altar. There, he offered up the customary sacrifices. We can infer this because when his son had to replace them with

98   1 Chronicles 9:33

less valuable shields made of bronze, this is what he continued to do. But when Solomon was in procession toward the temple, the sight was dazzling, literally. The sun overhead shone off a very large amount of polished gold. Having to shield their eyes, the people were ecstatic concerning the glory of Yahweh, Who lived now with His people and with the king's own gold-reflected glory.

What was going on, though, in Solomon's mind? The details we have of him in relation to the temple do not capture any religious or even emotional zeal after its inauguration. This is in contrast with his father David and his deep, heartfelt loyalty to Yahweh. We remember how he danced and sang before the ark as it was in procession. Surrounded by the golden orb of reflected sunlight on his beaten, golden shields, Solomon was completely calm. The external appearance of glory and majesty satisfied his heart. Wealth, more than anything else, motivated him now.

The temple stood above Jerusalem for about 350 years until the Babylonians destroyed it in 586 B.C. A second temple was built in its place with construction beginning about 520 B.C. As Israel Drazin comments, the first temple "was the apex of Solomon's reign."[99] It was a sign of redemption for Israel, but at the very same time, it was a national high point manifested in gold and light at the start of a precipitous descent toward the darkness of exile and the desperate plight of the Jews forced to live out their precarious existence in Gentile lands.

---

99   Israel Drazin, *The Authentic King Solomon* (Jerusalem: Gefen Publishing House, 2018).

CHAPTER 14

SOLOMON'S WISDOM IN OLD TESTAMENT SCRIPTURE

"Behold, I have done according to your words; see, I have given you a wise and understanding heart, so that there has not been anyone like you before you, nor shall any like you arise after you."

—1 Kings 3:12

Three complete books in the Bible are, in some way or other, explicitly linked to Solomon's authorship. Proverbs is recorded as his work in its first verse: "The proverbs of Solomon the son of David, king of Israel" (Prov. 1:1). The Song of Songs, or the Song of Solomon, is also explicitly referenced: "The song of songs, which *is* Solomon's" (Song of Sol. 1:1). Solomon is referred to several times in the third person, sometimes favorably and sometimes otherwise. Ecclesiastes is less explicit, but the biblical narrative implies twice that its author is Solomon. At the start, the author is described as "the Preacher, the son of David, king in Jerusalem," while slightly later, the author reminisces again: "I, the Preacher, was king over Israel in Jerusalem" (Eccles. 1:1, 12).

THE SONG OF SOLOMON

We can see the author and his passions clearly in the Song of Solomon, which is a unique love poem that defies analysis. Within Scripture, it is a *hapax legomenon* in itself in what it includes (e.g. *"selahim"* possibly means "branches") and what it omits. For instance, there is no reference in it at all to God, Israel, or sin. Although it is considered as composed of 117 verses, there is no definitive structure and no easy way to separate out different sections. We believe that it contains two dream sequences within it. The Song explores human sexuality as it can affect and consume lovers when awake and when asleep. It comes with all the longing, agonized hope, fulfillment, and restlessness of love. It can be difficult to tell which lover is speaking sometimes as everyone involved—the watchmen, girls, and shepherds—are carried along.

Some commentators have read secondary, allegorical, and spiritual meanings into much of the lyrical poetry, going beyond sexual love between a male and a female lover (e.g. that the song signifies the relationship between God and Israel or between God and His Christian bride, the Church). A problem with this is that the Song is about two lovers very much on the same plane of existence, and both are more or less equally desirous of the other. In Christian theology, the love relationship between God and His Church is characterized as imbalanced. God loves us far more than we love God, and it is His love for us that enables us to have any love at all for Him. At the same time, though, the central theme of love, as well as a number of the Song's motifs, do have a transcendent significance.

The Song of Solomon is also a very physical and sensual poem, one that is full of nature—trees, animals, valleys, mountains, springtime, vineyards, and gardens. It has no plot as such but reveals and describes two lovers united in their desires for each other but always restless and on the move, searching for the other and for fulfillment—the promises of love. There is no conclusion or climax. But suddenly, the poem leaps upwards, and love takes us toward eternity and then shifts downward again and into Solomon's vineyard. The song is a unique and spectacular literary work:

> Set me as a seal upon your heart, As a seal upon your arm; For love *is as* strong as death, Jealousy *as* cruel as the grave; Its flames *are* flames of fire, A most vehement flame. Many waters cannot quench love, Nor can the floods drown it. If a man would give for love all the wealth of his house, It would be utterly despised. Solomon

had a vineyard at Baal Hamon; He leased the vineyard to keepers; Everyone was to bring for its fruit A thousand silver *coins*. My own vineyard *is* before me. You, O Solomon, *may have* a thousand, And those who tend its fruit two hundred" (Song of Solomon 8:6-7, 11-12).

Evidence within the song reveals that it dates from a time when Israel was united with its capital in Jerusalem. For instance, "O my love, you *are as* beautiful as Tirzah, Lovely as Jerusalem" (6:4a). Tirzah became the capital of the Northern kingdom of Israel (until Omri moved it to Samaria), and its ruins are found in the northern West Bank, northeast of Nablus. No later author from Judah would have commended a woman as having the beauty of Tirzah, and likewise, no Northern author would have held up Jerusalem as the viewpoint from which other territories were surveyed—as the Song does. Egypt and its Iron Age linguistic and poetic styles and motifs were also influential.

The Song, for instance, frequently alludes to the female lover as the male lover's sister (Song of Sol. 4:9-12, 5:1, 8:8). This description comes from ancient Egyptian love songs from Solomon's era and from before it and from a time when physical signs of emotional closeness were taboo unless two people were closely related (e.g. siblings).[100] There is the additional meaning of permanence— only your siblings are with you throughout your life. We know from the song that Egypt was an influence, anyway: "I have compared you, my love, To my filly among Pharaoh's chariots" (1:9). This verse references the Egyptian horses Solomon was acquiring in trade. But the influence also extends to less obvious lyrical motifs. All this confirms Solomon as the poet.

The Song of Songs is considered the greatest of the songs known to the Jews because Solomon, in his wisdom, lyricizes about themes and ideas which connect to God and His perspective on the human story. In the first part of Solomon's reign, the vineyards were in good condition, a pleasure to visit: "Let us get up early to the vineyards; Let us see if the vine has budded, *Whether* the grape blossoms are open, *And* the pomegranates are in bloom. There I will give you my love" (7:12). But by Isaiah's time, the vineyard had been bad for some

---

100 Adolf Erman, *Life in Ancient Egypt* (New York: Dover Publications, 1971), 154.

time: "Now let me sing to my Well-beloved A song of my Beloved regarding His vineyard . . . So he expected *it* to bring forth *good* grapes, But it brought forth wild grapes" (Isa. 5:1, 2b). Later still, Jesus continued the vineyard narrative through a number of different parables in which His Father is the Lord of the vineyard. Through redemption, the saved will render to their Lord the fruit in season, but first, the evil workmen will kill the owner's son. The prophets are continuing with the song's human love, tragedy, pain, and separation motifs, but they take on a transcendent meaning.

PROVERBS

In this book, Solomon records his monotheistic faith as central to wisdom. To emphasize it, he repeats the starting point for acquiring wisdom in Proverbs 1:7 and Proverbs 9:10. "The fear of the LORD *is* the beginning of wisdom, And the knowledge of the Holy One *is* understanding" (Prov. 9:10). Human wisdom relates to faith in God and to understanding through this of the differences between right and wrong. If one applies this knowledge, life can be as happy and fruitful as possible, and many traps and pitfalls are avoided. It is important to walk in the right way (walking toward God), and Solomon's proverbs define that way.

Proverbs is both transnational and universal, and it surpasses the wisdom of other wise men (as recorded in 1 Kings 5) and who would have been present at Solomon's court. Unlike more worldly wisdom, Solomon's proverbs are applicable to wherever and whenever we find ourselves. For instance: "Where *there is* no revelation, the people cast off restraint; But happy *is* he who keeps the law" (Prov. 29:18).

In one short sentence, Solomon predicted that if a tribe or nation had no great vision or ideal to unify and guide them, they would throw off moral restraint, and they and their civilization would decay and collapse. He added that vision is insufficient in itself. The people must also all obey the moral law. Solomon connected vision with God's revelation of the law and linked them to happiness, the experience of joy, and the absence of anxiety.

Like the Song of Solomon, though, the king's proverbs also occasionally borrowed from Egyptian literature—this time, from its wisdom literature. If Egyptian viziers and wise men had alighted on the truth, Solomon was pleased to republish or extend their aphorisms and their meanings. There were strands of Egyptian wisdom originating far back in time, from the fifth dynasty, and the Egyptians of Solomon's time knew them as the Maxims of Ptahhotep, an elderly vizier to the pharaoh who wrote his wisdom down for the benefit of the author's son, who would soon take over the role at court. They make for wonderful reading, and here are a few examples:[101]

- "The human race never accomplishes anything. It's what God commands that gets done."
- "Great is the Law."
- "To listen is better than anything, thus is born perfect love."
- "Do not blame those who are childless, do not criticise them for not having any, and do not boast about having them yourself."
- "Do not repeat a slanderous rumour, do not listen to it."
- "He who has a great heart has a gift from God. He who obeys his stomach obeys the enemy."

Solomon was also influenced by more recent Egyptian wisdom literature, particularly that of the scribe Amenemope, who lived around 1100 B.C., during Egypt's twenty-first dynasty. Again, the writings are instructions to his son as to how one can live a kind, wise, self-controlled, and moral life while avoiding pride and self-advancement, which lead inexorably to a fall. Although Solomon includes some of it seemingly more or less verbatim in his proverbs, he also sometimes retains the subject matter while altering the treatment of it. In both cases, he likes the wisdom greatly, since it fuses reasoning with poetry. A couple of very close parallel texts follow, and it is agreed by Egyptologists and historians that Solomon's proverbs post-date Amenemope's writings and not the other way around.[102] Here are some proverbs to compare:

---

101   Christian Jacq, *The Living Wisdom of Ancient Egypt* (New York: Pocket Books, 1999).
102   S. R. K. Glanville, *The Legacy of Egypt* (Oxford: Oxford University Press, 1942).

- "Do not overwork to be rich; Because of your own understanding, cease! Will you set your eyes on that which is not? For *riches* certainly make themselves wings; They fly away like an eagle toward heaven" (Prov. 23:4–5).
- "Toil not after riches; If stolen goods are brought to thee, they remain not over night with thee. They have made themselves wings like geese. And have flown into the heavens" (Amenemope, ch. 7).
- "Do not rob the poor because he *is* poor, Nor oppress the afflicted at the gate" (Prov. 22:22).
- "Beware of robbing the poor, and oppressing the afflicted" (Amenemope, ch. 2).

It is likely that Solomon put his proverbs to use in his kingdom in the same way the Egyptians had done for almost two thousand years by the time Solomon reigned. The Egyptians used them for instruction and training—the education of scribes and other public servants as well as in a more general education for school students in reading, writing, and morals. Some of Solomon's proverbs were used to educate and train children in writing, reading, and reasoning, while some were used in group or individual discussions between tutors and young adults (e.g. the warnings given in Proverbs 7).

We can view this borrowing and reapplication of Egyptian proverbs much as the various initially pagan temple structures which Solomon borrowed from all around. Reapplied into a monotheistic faith, they all grew in stature and, as Thieberger observes, "take on a new aspect."[103] They became innovations divorced from their pagan origins and from the capriciousness and disinterest of pagan gods.

It seems clear from the archaeological evidence that Solomon took some of his wisdom material from Egypt, but this does not detract from it coming from the pen of Solomon. Solomon made it his own. It served his purposes, wherever it came from. We know that Solomon's wisdom far exceeded that of Egypt.[104]

---

103 Thieberger, ibid, 243.
104 1 Kings 4:30

ECCLESIASTES

Rabbinic tradition says that Solomon wrote this book later in life. Its original title is *Koheleth*, which means "the convener of, and preacher to assemblies,"[105] or a meeting of wise men. We can assume that the man referred to as the Koheleth is Solomon as he addressed his assembly of sages. This assembly was not equivalent to a metaphysical school of philosophy. In a structure which had no modern equivalent, it would have been interfacing with diplomats, civil servants, and educators. The assembly worked to formulate and agree on final revisions of works stemming from their activity (i.e. Proverbs and Ecclesiastes).

There seems to be a number of writers from the assembly who inputted into the work, but they were all responding to Solomon's questions, also recorded, such as: "'Vanity of vanities,' says the Preacher; 'Vanity of vanities, all *is* vanity.' What profit has a man from all his labor in which he toils under the sun?" (Eccl. 1:2-3).

We were created to be eternal but instead are required to build and enjoy things which are transient. This causes the wise to lament—they see that everything and everyone turns to dust no matter what our efforts are. Solomon's lament was not peculiar to him alone. He did not fear death. But he sought the value of life, given the inevitability of death. The reassurances within the text that life has meaning are unconvincing, so he repeats the question: what does man gain?

Ecclesiastes is Solomon's lament. It reflects on his tendency to dive into work—almost to the point of disappearance—his unbridled enjoyment of women, and his acquisition of almost unlimited wealth. He was materially successful across the board, but because he has broken the law in all these things, there was an unexpected and dreadful emptiness in his soul. He was saying: appreciate this. The emptiness is part of life. These are truths for everyone whose ambitions take them down the roads which he has trodden. Without God, one ends one's life in futility. Nothing has been gained when we are standing at the shores of eternity.

---

105 *The Complete Jewish Bible, s.v.* "Kohelet – Ecclesiastes – Chapter 1," accessed April 30, 2021, https://www.chabad.org/library/bible_cdo/aid/16462/jewish/Chapter-1.htm.

Even if we are standing on the rocks which represent our greatest achievements, the view across the sea before us is a bleak one because the achievements have no eternal significance. It was all "grasping for the wind" (Eccl. 1:14).

Like Song of Songs, Ecclesiastes defies attempts to define its structure. Some attempts have met with a limited degree of acceptance among scholars. There is an investigation of life and then a series of conclusions, both sandwiched between two poems. It is not possible to say that Solomon wrote this book, but it *is* possible to say that the book is about him. It accurately details his later musings, his frame of mind, and his conclusions about life in the form of an autobiography—a fictional one in the sense that it is written only as *if* Solomon wrote it, but also a biographically accurate one with the exception of the allegory about old age. Solomon died in his sixtieth year. Perhaps, though, he had become like an old man.

PART 2
A TIME TO SPEAK

BY: MARGARET P. ROY

IN "PART 2: A TIME to Speak," I examine, in some detail, various portions of Solomon's writings from the three books we believe that he wrote: Proverbs, Ecclesiastes, and the Song of Solomon. My aim is not to provide a verse-by-verse Bible study of the three books nor a detailed commentary, but instead to select and highlight certain parts of these books which have meant something to me over the course of my Christian life. In addition, I believe that the subjects covered within Solomon's writings are still relevant to our lives today. Solomon has much wisdom and useful advice for us in the present day on various issues, such as maintaining a healthy marriage, committing to sexual purity, handling the aging process, caring for elderly people, stating a position on euthanasia, and battling the dangers of too much wealth and the "prosperity gospel." In other words, Solomon still speaks to mankind today.

The Song of Solomon is a book which has always intrigued me, and I have heard various opinions on what this book is about. I have also listened to sermons where one or two verses are plucked from the Song of Solomon and woven into a sermon, usually on the subject of Christ's love for His Church. Not being entirely satisfied with these explanations, I decided to make a study of it for myself by seeking any Christian books which contained insight and understanding of what the book is really about. These findings are presented in my chapter about the Song of Solomon. This wonderfully poetic book provides a plethora of descriptive language on courtship (which does not always go smoothly), the passionate love between a man and a woman, the marriage covenant, and sexual love within marriage. I look at the cultural background of the period in which it was written in order to try to clarify what the story is about and to explain the various metaphors and analogies within it. I do not believe that the Song of Solomon is simply an allegory which describes the love of God the Father for His Church or of Christ for His Bride. In my view, it is an account of a love relationship between a youthful Solomon and a young girl, the Shulammite, whom he eventually marries.

For the Book of Ecclesiastes, I focus on a number of portions in various chapters. A time for every purpose under Heaven (Chapter 3) reminds us that there is a right time and a wrong time for many activities which we undertake in life. "Two are better than one" (Chapter 4:9-12) teaches us the value of helpful interactions with others, including within marriage. Solomon's writings on prosperity and the dangers of too much wealth (Chapters 2 and 5) provide a cautionary tale for our present day and for our churches. Finally, Chapter 12 paints a rather sad picture of old age but starts with an unction to young people to remember their Creator in the days of their youth. I have outlined a number of ways in which young folk can remember their Creator and what this really means. Subsequent verses outline the physical and mental problems which accompany aging and frailty, followed by a metaphoric description of death which is certain to come to every person born.

Interspersed throughout my reflections, I have quoted different verses written by Solomon in the Book of Proverbs—for example his warnings about adultery, excessive riches, alcohol abuse, and foolish and perverse speech. In Chapter 20, I focus specifically on Proverbs 8:22-36, which is a wonderful portion of Scripture in which Solomon describes Jesus Christ, our eternal Savior, being present with His Father even before the Earth was formed and then witnessing His Father God's creation of the Earth! What amazes me is Solomon's divine inspiration about Christ because he lived over nine hundred years before Christ came to Earth.

For more in-depth Bible study of Solomon's writings, I can recommend the books from which I have quoted and acquired information. For a study of Solomon's three books, Henry M. Morris's book, *The Remarkable Wisdom of Solomon*, is excellent. For the book of Ecclesiastes, *The Message of Ecclesiastes* by Derek Kidner will help you understand as you read. And *God's Pursuing Love* by Ray Bentley and *A Song for Lovers* by S. Craig Glickman are recommended for studying the Song of Solomon.

CHAPTER 15

A TIME FOR EVERY PURPOSE UNDER HEAVEN

"To everything there is a season,
A time for every purpose under heaven."

—Ecclesiastes 3:1

There are times and seasons in all of our lives and also in our Christian walk with God. There are also different times and seasons in the life of a church or ministry. Solomon tells us in Ecclesiastes 3:1-8 that there is a time for certain things or actions to occur, and then that time passes. Not everything happens all the time without ceasing or without being interrupted. He has written here about twenty-eight forms of activity set out in fourteen pairs of opposites. In each pair of opposites, it is right at one time in life to do the one and, at another time, to do the other. It is not about whether the activity is right or wrong but about the time or season when the activity is carried out. There is a right time and a wrong time to carry out each activity. According to Derek Prince, if a church is being guided by the Holy Spirit and if Christ is allowed to be Lord in that congregation, then the church body will do the right thing at the right time. He wrote, "This is the source of all true liberty, harmony and unity" as opposed to "bondage, discord and disunity."[106]

Let's look at the verses in detail.

---

106 Derek Prince, *Foundations for Righteous Living* (Preston: Derek Prince Ministries UK, 1998).

A TIME TO BE BORN AND A TIME TO DIE (3:2A)

Each person alive in the world started off their life by being born, and each person finishes their life when they die physically. Nothing can alter that reality; it is by God's design that we are born, and it is because all living things are in a fallen state on earth that we die. No scientist or medical professional can change the facts that every human is born of a woman and one day every human body will die. Ephesians 1:11 says that God "works all things according to the counsel of His will."

Not one of us chooses the time or year when we are born into this world. Neither do we choose who our parents are or whether they are rich or poor. Think about that: none of us can decide on or pick the day of our own conception or of our birth. We have no control over it whatsoever. An obstetrician may intervene and plan a birth for a certain day by medical induction or caesarean section, but the baby itself is unaware.

The same applies to our death. We have a number of years allotted to us on this earth by God, which I believe cannot be altered, and our life will come to an end at the point when God permits it. However, life can be shortened unnaturally by suicide, murder, or drug and alcohol abuse, which I do not believe are ever in the will of God for a life. It is the evil in mankind which causes someone to murder either a child or an adult, and surely, that could not be God's plan for the victim's life. However, I believe that any person in these categories will not be rejected by God and can still find eternal life if they have trusted Christ as the Savior of their soul. Many former drug addicts or alcoholics who have become Christians have their lives shortened due to the effects of addiction on their physical organs, but they will still inherit eternal life in Heaven with the Lord.

A TIME TO PLANT AND A TIME TO
PLUCK WHAT IS PLANTED (3:2B)

For many years before, during, and after Solomon's time, agriculture was the main activity for earning a living. This part of the verse speaks of sowing a crop and then later harvesting it—the practice of sowing and reaping. Jesus told a number of parables, including the parable of the sower, which described planting a crop and later harvesting it (Matt. 13:1-9, 18-23). A common theme was the tending of a vineyard and then the subsequent grape harvest, which He compared to the harvest of souls who would accept Him as Savior (Matt. 20:1-16; Matt. 21:28-43; Mark 12:1-11; Luke 13:6-8; Luke 20:9-17).

Planting and plucking up could also refer to starting a business or a ministry or moving into a new home when these activities are in line with God's will for us at the time. It is also important to finish these if and when God indicates. A business or ministry may be the right thing to do for a certain period of time, but that does not mean that it will always be God's will to continue with it throughout life.

A TIME TO KILL AND A TIME TO HEAL (3:3A)

When would there be a time to kill? The killing of germs or diseases is in order and also the killing of venomous snakes, spiders, or insects in order to protect and preserve human life. In war and conflict, the consequences are often the killing of enemy soldiers and sometimes, sadly, civilians also.

The opposite of killing, according to the verse, is a time to bring healing. After destruction, there must be a mending and a restoration. If we go through a painful time in our life when bad habits, oppression, or inner bondages are broken by the power of God's Holy Spirit, it can feel that there has been a rending deep inside. After that, we need to allow God's healing balm to penetrate our inner being and restore the torn parts to health and strength.

A TIME TO BREAK DOWN AND A TIME TO BUILD UP (3:3B)

There is a correct time to destroy old buildings or equipment when they can be of no further use. In my home city of Glasgow, Scotland, there was a huge demolition program in the 1970s to get rid of many of the old three-story tenement flats which had become rundown, unsafe in stormy weather, and unsuitable living conditions for families. In their place were built new flats, houses, and shops. A number of completely new towns were created with modern shopping centers. This happened in many cities throughout the U.K. in the 1970s and 1980s.

Breaking down could also refer to the destruction of prejudices, racist attitudes, discrimination, false doctrines, and pride. Building up comes from the restoration of harmony, love for one another, equal rights for all, and the end of discrimination on the grounds of sex, disability, or race. Once false doctrines are exposed, good, solid Bible teaching will nurture people spiritually and cause them to grow in the knowledge of God and His truth.

A TIME TO WEEP AND A TIME TO LAUGH; A TIME TO MOURN AND A TIME TO DANCE (3:4)

There are times of weeping and mourning throughout our lives. This could be weeping over our sin and its effects, sadness over the death of a loved one, anguish for a child who has gone astray, depression or discouragement, or the emotional pain associated with suffering of various kinds. Weeping can also occur when a person is deeply touched by the Holy Spirit, Who can penetrate deeply into the emotional being, causing tears to flow, which are not necessarily tears of sadness.

Weeping should not be prevented either in oneself or in others because it can bring inner healing and restoration of stability. The Bible tells us that God knows about every fallen tear. King David begged God to "put my tears into Your bottle" (Psalm 56:8). God promises in Psalm 30:5, "Weeping may endure for a night, But joy *comes* in the morning." And Isaiah 25:8 assures us that one day when Christ returns to the earth, "The Lord God will wipe away tears from all faces." Ultimately, when we reach the Heavenly City, we have God's promise that there will be no weeping there ever again as "God will wipe away every tear" (Rev. 7:17). In ancient Israel—and even in some Eastern cultures today— mourning for a dead relative was a very noisy and ostentatious occasion, with much wailing and loud crying.

There are happy, joyful times in life also: a wedding, the birth of a child, success in employment or study, recovery from illness or trauma, or simply a quiet sense of all being well. Solomon tells us that there is also a time to dance. Dancing normally denotes celebration and happiness when the physical body is free to express the joy rising within one's being. Derek Prince cautions against church groups getting into various degrees of bondage by repeating certain patterns of behavior week after week, such as hand-clapping, dancing, shouting, or speaking in tongues. Christians can assume that because God blessed the group along certain lines once that He will always bless the group if they manifest the same behaviors. However, the Holy Spirit cannot be worked up and made to comply with man's wishes. In a church group, there is a time for joy and praise and a time to dance, but there is also a time to weep and mourn, perhaps in deep intercession.[107]

A TIME TO CAST AWAY STONES AND A TIME TO GATHER STONES (3:5A)

Stones are removed and cast away from a field to prepare it for planting a crop. Large stones in fields can block drainage canals and have to be dug out and cast away. God gave the people of Israel instructions to "ruin every good piece of land [of your enemy] with stones" (2 Kings 3:19). Isaiah the prophet compares Israel to the Lord's vineyard and writes that God dug the earth and "cleared out its stones, And planted it with the choicest vine" (Isa. 5:2). Metaphorically speaking, we can have stones or even boulders lying within our being, which block the flow of the Holy Spirit through us. These could be pride, gossip, slander, bitterness, jealousy, or lust—to name a few. Isaiah 62:10 instructs the people to "build up the highway! Take out the stones." Thus, a smooth road could be created for everyone to pass through, just as the Holy Spirit needs a clear channel through which to flow in us.

In the Old Testament, gathering stones was essential to building a structure, constructing a marker or memorial stone, or building a heap to cover a burial— as Joshua did on two occasions (Josh. 7:26, 8:29) and Joab did to cover Absalom's grave (2 Sam. 18:17). In Genesis 31:45-49, Jacob told his brethren to gather stones and make a heap which was to stand as a witness between him and Laban, signifying that one would do no harm to the other. The heap of stones was

---

107   Derek Prince, *Foundations for Righteous Living* (Preston: Derek Prince Ministries UK, 1998).

named Galeed, or Mizpah, which means, "May the LORD watch between you and me when we are absent one from another" (Gen. 31:49). Joshua was instructed by God to take twelve stones out of the River Jordan; the stones were to serve as a memorial to future generations that the waters of the Jordan were stopped to allow the Israelites and the priests who bore the ark of the covenant to travel across the river on dry ground (Josh. 4:3-9).

Elijah took twelve stones, according to the number of the tribes of the sons of Jacob, to build a new altar in the name of the Lord on which he placed a sacrifice. He then prayed that the people would know that the Lord God is the God of Israel and that Baal was a false god. The fire of the Lord fell and consumed the burnt sacrifice, plus the wood and the twelve stones (1 Kings 18:31-38). As a result, the people fell on their faces and knew without a doubt that the Lord of Israel is, indeed, the true God.

A TIME TO EMBRACE AND A TIME TO REFRAIN FROM EMBRACING (3:5B)

In marriage, there is a time for close contact and for sexual activity, and this should not be neglected. Paul wrote that couples should not deprive one another except when they agree by mutual consent to commit themselves to a time of prayer and fasting, but this should only be temporary (1 Cor. 7:5).

But there are also times for many other activities which couples can share in a meaningful way. These activities can also build up and strengthen the bond between husband and wife. Spending time simply talking to each other is highly important in the nurturing of a marriage, as well as sharing fellowship with other believers, praying together, and serving the Lord together in a public capacity.

Sometimes, public displays of affection are not appropriate (e.g. in some cultures, especially in the Middle East). Or public embracing may cause upset to someone struggling to recover from sexual abuse or an abusive relationship. It is good to be sensitive to how others around you might feel about public displays of affection.

A TIME TO GAIN AND A TIME TO LOSE (3:6A)

There will be prosperous times and lean times in our lives—times when money is plentiful and times when it may be short. Like Paul, we can learn to be content in whichever state we find ourselves (Phil. 4:11).

A TIME TO KEEP AND A TIME TO THROW AWAY (3:6B)

Henry M. Morris writes that we should keep good habits and attitudes and throw away the bad ones.[108] Other things we should throw away are items from our pre-conversion days which may affect our spiritual life adversely: occult objects and books, masonic regalia, music downloads if they are dark or Satanic, types of clothing, and even toxic relationships where someone has a seriously negative effect on our emotions or spirit.

A TIME TO TEAR AND A TIME TO SEW (3:7A)

When does deliberate tearing occur? In the sphere of medicine, there is tearing in some types of surgery, during childbirth or tooth extraction, and in the lancing of an infected wound. In all of these cases, a time of sewing up the wounds would follow. In Bible times, people sometimes tore their skin out of extreme anguish or grief (Jer. 16:6). In the Book of Job, Job accuses one of his "comforters," saying, "He tears *me* in His wrath, and hates me" (16:9). Meanwhile, Bildad addresses Job as, "You who tear yourself in anger" (Job 18:4). In Hosea 6:1, we read that it is the Lord who has torn, but that He will also heal: "He has stricken, but He will bind us up."

Garments which are torn can be mended again, as can broken relationships, where it may feel as if a tearing has occurred within one's spirit. Healing of severed friendships can take place when the time is right, and this is usually after forgiveness has been put into action.

---

108   Henry M. Morris, *The Remarkable Wisdom of Solomon* (Green Forest: Master Books Inc., 2001).

A TIME TO KEEP SILENCE AND A TIME TO SPEAK (3:7B)

This is a very important portion. Many people talk continuously, which can lead to them saying hurtful or meaningless things or being insensitive to another person's needs. We should try to be aware of the person to whom we are speaking and allow them to say something, too. Psalm 19:14 says, "Let the words of my mouth . . . Be acceptable in Your sight, O LORD." There is often a time to be silent and wait, either on God or on others to have their say. Prayer is not merely talking to God: there is also a time for waiting quietly before Him in His presence with our heart open to what He wants to say to us.

Solomon cautioned in Ecclesiastes 5:2, "Do not be rash with your mouth, And let not your heart utter anything hastily before God. For God *is* in heaven, and you on earth; Therefore let your words be few." Proverbs 4:24-26 instructs, "Put away from you a deceitful mouth, And put perverse lips far from you." And in Proverbs 10:19, he writes, "In the multitude of words sin is not lacking, But he who restrains his lips *is* wise." It is not of any benefit for Christians to get into heated arguments either face to face or on social media.

Proverbs 15 outlines a number of contrasts between words of perversity and wholesome speech. Verse one says, "A soft answer turns away wrath, But a harsh word stirs up anger." The words that we speak can either dissipate anger or arouse it.

Verses two, seven, and twenty-eight make a comparison between the tongue of the wise and the mouth of fools:

- "The tongue of the wise uses knowledge rightly, But the mouth of fools pours forth foolishness" (v. 2).
- "The lips of the wise disperse knowledge, But the heart of the fool does not do so" (v. 7).
- "The heart of the righteous studies how to answer, But the mouth of the wicked pours forth evil" (v. 28).

Furthermore, in verse four, Solomon wrote, "A wholesome tongue is a tree of life, But perverseness in it breaks the spirit." Perverseness means deviating from what is right and good, therefore perverse words lead to distress, depression, and defeat.

Finally, verse twenty-three says, "A word spoken in due season, how good it is." The right word spoken at the correct time can encourage and strengthen another believer and bring joy to both speaker and hearer.

There is, of course, a time when we should speak but may be afraid to do so due to fear or shyness. There are occasions when Christians should speak up boldly about issues they should take a stand on (e.g. abortion or sex education for very young children). We may be scared of the consequences of speaking up for what is right, but God promises to sustain us. Jesus promised in Luke 21:15, "For I will give you a mouth and wisdom which all your adversaries will not be able to contradict or resist." With God speaking through us, we have nothing to fear.

A TIME TO LOVE AND A TIME TO HATE (3:8A)

A time to love is obvious, and we are commanded to love the Lord God with all our heart and to love our neighbor as we love ourselves (Lev. 19:18; Matt. 19:19). But when would it ever be right to hate? We are instructed to hate every false way (Psalm 119:128) and to hate doublemindedness (Psalm 119:113). David expressed hatred for the enemies of God (Psalm 139:21-22). We are also to hate sin both in ourselves and in others but to love the person who sins. In addition, we must hate the devil and all his works and emissaries: they have been defeated at the cross when Christ gave His life for mankind, and they will one day be bound and cast into outer darkness. We must have no communion with these forces of darkness. Victory over their effects comes only through the blood of Jesus and never by our own human efforts.

A TIME OF WAR AND A TIME OF PEACE (3:8B)

Throughout history, there have been many wars and conflicts and then a time of peace. Sadly, there are still wars being fought today (e.g. in Syria since 2011, in Yemen and various parts of Africa). There have been two world wars, the Korean War, the Vietnam War, two Gulf wars, war in Afghanistan, and wars against ISIS. Jesus told us what our attitude should be when He said, "You will hear of wars and rumors of wars. See that you are not troubled; for all *these things* must come to pass, but the end is not yet" (Matt. 24:6). So, we are not to be disheartened but are to watch and pray as we await the second coming of the Lord Jesus (Luke 21:36).

GOD HAS MADE EVERYTHING BEAUTIFUL IN ITS TIME (3:11A)

God made His original creation beautiful and said that it was all very good (Gen. 1:31). God did not make it evil or bad. The emphasis is not on human decision but on God's decree, and everything happens at the time when God wills it. God's timing is perfect.

GOD HAS PUT ETERNITY IN THEIR HEARTS (3:11B)

Each person has an innate awareness that God does exist and does have a purpose, albeit one which is, at times, mysterious and incomprehensible by our human mind. Every human being has a longing for eternal life, even though this longing may be suppressed at times.

The rest of verse eleven says, "No one can find out the work that God does from beginning to end" (3:11). Neither science, nor research, nor philosophical reasoning, nor historical studies can find this out. The future is unknown to us, but God knows everything that will happen, and only He knows the exact time when Christ will return (Matt. 24:36).

CHAPTER 16

TWO ARE BETTER THAN ONE

"Two are *better than one,*

Because they have a good reward for their labor.

For if they fall, one will lift up his companion.

But woe to him who is alone when he falls,

For he has no one to help him up.

Again, if two lie down together, they will keep warm;

But how can one be warm alone?

Though one may be overpowered by another, two can withstand him.

And a threefold cord is not quickly broken."

—Ecclesiastes 4:9-12

TWO ARE BETTER THAN ONE (4:9)

"Two are better than one" is certainly true in the marriage relationship. Genesis 2:18 tells us, "The LORD God said, 'It is not good that the man should be alone; I will make him a helper comparable to him.'" The King James Version uses the word "helpmeet"; "meet" is an adjective, meaning "suitable." Other Bible versions translate "a help meet" as "a helper suitable for him" (NIV) or "a helper fit for him" (RSV, ESV). Got Questions Ministries explains it this way: "She is compatible with her husband . . . well-suited to him, one who completes him in every way and who brings harmony . . . to the relationship."[109]

However, the verses beginning with "Two are better than one" do not refer only to a marriage relationship. There can be close friendships in which each person is a support to the other emotionally, socially, and prayerfully. The apostle Paul usually had a fellow-traveler and missionary when he undertook his journeys to visit church groups or to spread the Gospel of Christ. Barnabas, Silas, Timothy, Philemon, Trophimus, Tychicus, and Mark are all mentioned in this context in the Book of Acts. Sopater of Berea accompanied Paul to Asia (Acts 20:4). Paul wrote in 2 Timothy 4:11, "Luke is with me. Get Mark and bring him with you, for he is useful to me for ministry." Even when he was imprisoned for preaching the Gospel, Paul had fellow bondservants, such as Aristarchus (Col. 4:10) and Epaphras (Col. 4:12; Philem. 1:23).

The apostles Peter and John ministered together in Jerusalem (Acts 3:1-11) and traveled together to Samaria (Acts 8:14), while Silas and Timothy took the Gospel to Macedonia (Acts 18:5). Ecclesiastes 4:9 says, "They have a good reward for their labor." Two people serving God in unity can achieve far more than one person working alone. Even today, many single missionaries often work in pairs linked with missionary families. God gives different spiritual gifts to each of us, and it is important to discover just what your giftings are. Often, God calls two people to serve Him in ministry together, and each has very different gifts and talents that complement one another. Ephesians 4:12 and 16 tells us that the spiritual gifts are for the work of the ministry and the edifying of the body of Christ, where each part of the body does its share and is joined to work in unity.

ONE WILL LIFT UP HIS COMPANION (4:10)

"For if they fall, one will lift up his companion." Support from a fellow believer is invaluable if a person is struggling with their faith, depressed, discouraged, or suffering illness or injury. It is always much more difficult to bear sorrow or

---

109 "What does it mean that a wife is supposed to be a helpmeet / help meet?," GotQuestions. org, https://www.gotquestions.org/wife-helpmeet.html (accessed December 1, 2020).

cope with trouble on your own, and the devil has more opportunity to attack and weaken one's faith and cause hopelessness. The rest of verse ten says, "But woe to him *who is* alone when he falls. For *he has* no one to help him up." We need one another. In addition, Jesus promised that "where two or three are gathered together in My name, I am there in the midst of them" (Matt. 18:20). Not only do we need one another, but we also need Jesus with us as well.

THEY WILL KEEP WARM (4:11)

"If two lie down together, they will keep warm." This seems like a strange expression. According to Derek Kidner, people traveling on long journeys during Solomon's time would sleep outdoors by night and would lie next to one another, or even next to their donkey, for heat.[110] So, the expression refers to mutual help, closeness, and unity between two people, including, but not limited to, marriage.

A THREE-FOLD CORD IS NOT QUICKLY BROKEN (4:12)

When trials and spiritual attacks try to overpower us, one person on their own "may be overpowered by another, two can withstand him, And a three-fold cord is not quickly broken." A three-fold cord means that all three people are of one mind and one spirit; the three strands of a cord or rope are entwined together as one and are thus stronger than each individual strand alone.

The three-fold cord also describes a godly marriage (i.e. husband, wife, and the Lord God). Derek Prince explains in *The Marriage Covenant* how the cord of three strands illustrates marriage as it was designed by God at Creation: the binding together of three—the man, the woman, and God. The relationship between the man and woman is on the horizontal plane; but when God is added to the relationship, there is a new dimension, and God is an integral part of the marriage. The three-fold cord forms an inseparable link bound by the covenant of marriage. Derek gained further insight after conversing with a rope-maker, who told him that a rope made of two strands is quite weak, and one made of four strands is not stronger than one made of three strands. The optimum strength is

---

110   Derek Kidner, *The Message of Ecclesiastes* (Downers Grove:Inter-Varsity Press, 1976).

where all the strands touch one another, and this only happens with a rope made of three strands! One or even two of the strands can be under pressure, but if the third strand (God) holds, the rope will not break.[111]

Similarly, Joni Eareckson Tada writes in her book about her marriage to Ken:

> If the man and woman twine their lives around each other in marriage, that is good and they'll be stronger for it. But if both of them twine themselves around the living God, that's best of all. It's a union that will hold through anything that life—or even hell—might throw at them. Because nowhere else—and with no-one else—will you have quite the chance to experience union with Christ than through a hard-fought-for, hard-won union with your spouse. It's trials that really press you into the breast of your Savior. The cord of three strands.[112]

111   Derek Prince, *The Marriage Covenant: The Biblical Secret for a Love That Lasts* (New Kensington: Whitaker House, 2006).
112   Ken and Joni Eareckson Tada, *Joni & Ken, An Untold Love Story* (Grand Rapids: Zondervan, 2013).

CHAPTER 17

SOLOMON'S EXHORTATION TO YOUTH

"Remember now your Creator in the days of your youth."

—Ecclesiastes 12:1

What does it mean to "remember now your Creator in the days of your youth" (Eccl. 12:1)? Does this merely mean that you must not forget about God? No, there is a lot more to it than simply not forgetting. In his book *The Message of Ecclesiastes*, Derek Kidner puts it this way: "To remember God is no perfunctory or purely mental act: it is to drop our pretence of self-sufficiency and commit ourselves to Him. Remembrance can be a matter of passionate fidelity."[113] Therefore, when God exhorts us, through the words of Solomon, to remember our Creator when we are young, He means that we should commit our whole life to God while we are in our youth and, during that period of life, learn to be faithful to His commandments and teaching.

If you commit your whole life to God whilst in the days of your youth, at the time when you have full physical and mental fortitude, then you will lay down patterns for living which will sustain you in your walk of faith as you go through life and when you reach old age. A person can come to faith in Christ at any age; the way of salvation is open to all, and not everyone becomes a

---

113   Derek Kidner, *The Message of Ecclesiastes (Bible Speaks Today)* (Downers Grove: InterVarsity Press, 1976).

Christian during their youth. But Solomon is urging his readers to "remember God" in their youth, so this must have importance in God's plan for believers.

I came to know Christ as my Savior when I was a young person at the age of twenty-one, after being caught up for just under a year in a cult called the Children of God (see Chapter 42 for an overview of this cult's teachings and lifestyle). My commitment to Him and my decision to follow Him wholeheartedly has sustained me through the decades that have followed. I can look back and see how God has guided my life, how He has been with me through trials and troubles, such as chronic illness and the resultant employment difficulties. He has always provided for my needs and protected me from times of possible danger. He has also changed and transformed my nature and taken away many fears which plagued my life as a child and teenager.

Youth is the time when people aim to find their place in the world—a time for starting work or for study at college or university. For the Christian young person, it can also be the time for going on short-term missions, helping with children's work, engaging in musical activities, and finding out what your calling is and where your giftings lie in a church setting, so that you know in which spheres God wants you to serve Him.

TEMPTATIONS AND DANGERS

But youth is also the time when the sex drive—which has been placed in us by God—is at its strongest, and it is a time of great temptation to explore sexual activity. In today's Western culture, it has become almost the norm for teenagers to start becoming sexually active at a young age without any thought for the consequences, which include teenage pregnancy and sexually transmitted infections. In a healing prayer conference held in 2018 in North Carolina, Clay McLean described it this way: "Sex has become a toy, a plaything." He described Christian couples who decide to live together as carrying on a relationship where God is shut out; whereas, we should include God in our relationships. Not only teenagers but also many adults seem to think nothing of engaging in sexual activity with whomever they may be dating. Television dramas and movies feed these behaviors to the masses and propagate the idea that sex with multiple partners is normal and commonplace.

In recent years, advances in medical science have given us the contraceptive pill, the morning-after pill, and a vaccine to protect against high-risk types of Human Papilloma virus, transmission of which is linked to having multiple sexual partners and which can cause cervical cancer in women. This vaccine is now being given in the U.K. to all girls and boys aged twelve to thirteen. These advances have reduced risk and caused many people to dismiss the dangers associated with fornication and with having several different sexual partners.

I also have to mention the tragedy of readily available abortion, including the recent provision of "Do it yourself" home abortions using medication. In 2018, 23.7 percent of pregnancies in England and Wales were terminated, with ninety-eight percent of these carried out for contraceptive or social reasons. And in 2019 in Scotland, the number of abortions was over thirteen thousand, the second highest number ever recorded for this country.[114]

ONE FLESH

Physical consequences are not the only issues which result from extramarital sexual activity. Whenever a man and a woman engage in sexual intercourse, the Bible describes them as "becom[ing] one flesh" (Gen. 2:24). Jesus Himself quoted the Genesis Scripture when answering the Pharisees' questions about divorce: "'For this reason a man shall leave father and mother and be joined to his wife, and the two shall become one flesh'" (Matt. 19:5). Why is the expression "one flesh" used? "Flesh" is a figure of speech called *synecdoche*, which means that a part of a thing is used to represent the whole. Therefore, God is not only referring to the physical flesh, but also to the whole person as an individual with all their component parts.

"One flesh" means much more than physical, sexual union. It means two people become one; it is a personal union of a man and a woman at all levels of

---

114 "Scotland abortion numbers second highest ever on record," Right to Life News.com, August 28, 2020, https://righttolife.org.uk/news/scotland-abortion-numbers-second-highest-ever-on-record.

their lives. The apostle Paul carried this further by warning that sexual activity with a prostitute means that a man makes himself one body with her (1 Cor. 6:16-17). Paul is decrying physical oneness with a prostitute because the other kinds of oneness which every sexual act should mirror are absent and because every sex act is supposed to be a uniting act. C. S. Lewis likened sex without marriage to tasting food without swallowing and digesting it.

WAITING UNTIL MARRIAGE

Here is another way in which young people can "remember their Creator." As they commit their lives fully to God, they can fully commit the sexual part of their being to Him. According to God's command and instruction in His Word, this means abstaining from all sexual activity until marriage. Why is it so important to wait and to keep sexual activity for only within marriage? Why has God ordained this to be the way? Does He just want to deprive young people of enjoyment and make them miserable? No, because it was God Himself Who designed the sexual act and Who intricately created the sexual organs. The key to the mystery is covenant.

Derek Prince explains, "The difference is that the marriage union is preceded by a mutual covenant which means a total commitment to one another, in front of witnesses. Sexual activity which occurs before such a covenant is made between the man and woman constitutes immorality."[115] When two bodies become one flesh physically, they also become one spiritually, bonding them forever in a covenant relationship. When sexual union expresses love within the covenant of Christian marriage, God is glorified; but if sexual union expresses lust or selfishness, Satan is glorified. Christopher and Rachel McCluskey put it this way: "The spirit of making love in Christian marriage, bonding spirit to spirit, soul to soul, and body to body in three-dimensional union, is entirely different from simply having sex."[116]

---

115   Prince, *Marriage Covenant*, ibid.
116   Christopher and Rachel McCluskey, *When Two Become One: Enhancing Sexual Intimacy in Marriage* (Grand Rapids: Fleming H. Revell, 2004).

The Bible clearly shows God's attitude towards the marital union and to the high regard in which marriage must be held. "Marriage *is* honorable among all, and the bed undefiled; but fornicators and adulterers God will judge" (Heb. 13:4). Putting all of this together shows us the reasons for waiting until marriage before engaging in sexual activity. However, we must also remind ourselves that God can and does forgive all forms of sexual sin if a person comes to Him in repentance and asks for His forgiveness and cleansing. Christ died for every sin, including sexual sins. We have only to think of the New Testament accounts of Jesus encountering the woman caught in adultery or the Samaritan woman at the well. He loved these women and most likely understood the reasons for their carnal lifestyles, and He offered them forgiveness and cleansing from their sins of the body. He did not condemn them as the religious leaders had done. It is the same for both men and women today; if they become Christians, God forgives and removes the stain of sin and makes their lives pure. In addition, there can be inner healing for any prior emotional trauma.

CHAPTER 18

SOLOMON AND PROSPERITY

"The rich and the poor have this in common, The Lord is the maker of them all."

—Proverbs 22:2

Solomon became a very wealthy man, and the Bible tells us that it was God Who gave Solomon his riches and prosperity (1 Kings 3:12-13). Furthermore, God gave him riches and honor, which he had not asked for (v. 13). Solomon wrote that he acquired whatever he wanted (Eccl. 2:10). In 1 Kings 10:14-28, we read about the vast quantities of gold, silver, and ivory which he procured and used to make various implements and furnishings for his palaces. He also possessed huge numbers of horses, chariots, and horsemen. Solomon had greater possession of herds and flocks, more than any before him in Jerusalem; he also acquired many male and female servants and singers (Eccl. 2:7). He owned houses, vineyards, gardens, orchards, and water pools (Eccl. 2: 4-6). But he despondently concludes his account of all that he had acquired by saying that "all *was* vanity and grasping for the wind. *There was* no profit under the sun" (Eccl. 2:11).

In Ecclesiastes 5:19, he considered that wealth is pointless if a person cannot use it and enjoy it: "As for every man to whom God has given riches and wealth, and given him power to eat of it, to receive his heritage and rejoice in his labor— this *is* the gift of God." The word used here for "riches" in Old Testament Hebrew is *neh'kes*, meaning riches or treasure, from a root meaning "to accumulate."[117]

---

117 *Bible Study Tools, s.v.* "Nekec," accessed March 9, 2021, https://www.biblestudytools.com/lexicons/hebrew/kjv/nekec.html.

Solomon warns, "He who loves silver will not be satisfied with silver; Nor he who loves abundance, with increase. This also *is* vanity" (Eccl. 5:10). But he says, "A *good* name is to be chosen rather than great riches, Loving favor rather than silver and gold" (Prov. 22:1). Solomon also praises the acquisition of wisdom over that of gold in Proverbs 16:16: "How much better to get wisdom than gold! And to get understanding is to be chosen rather than silver." But again, he admonishes, "He who trusts in his riches will fall" (Prov. 11:28).

Timothy writes in the New Testament, "Those who desire to be rich fall into temptation and a snare, and *into* many foolish and harmful lusts which drown men in destruction and perdition" (1 Tim. 6:9). He also writes that "the love of money is a root of all *kinds* of evil," warning that greed had caused some to stray "from the faith . . . and pierced themselves through with many sorrows" (1 Tim. 6:10).

In Matthew 6:19-20, Jesus tells his followers to "'not lay up for yourselves treasures on earth, where moth and rust destroy and where thieves break in and steal; but lay up for yourselves treasures in heaven, where neither moth nor rust destroys and where thieves do not break in and steal."

In Proverbs 22:2, Solomon writes, "The rich and the poor have this in common, The Lord *is* the maker of them all." Rich or poor, we all belong to the same God, and it is He Who created each one of us. Being rich does not automatically bring happiness or contentment, as we can see from looking at the tragic lives of some wealthy celebrities and musicians. Solomon writes of "one who makes himself rich, yet has nothing; *And* one who makes himself poor, yet *has* great riches" (Prov. 13:7). Proverbs 10:22 gives us a wonderful promise: "The blessing of the Lord makes *one* rich, And He adds no sorrow with it." If the blessing comes from God, then there is no toil, anxiety, or affliction that comes with it and nothing we can strive at to make it happen.

IS IT WRONG FOR CHRISTIANS TO BE WEALTHY?

So, is it wrong for a Christian to be wealthy and to acquire many possessions and property? Sometimes, God blesses Christians with riches, and if they are following Christ with a humble and unselfish spirit, they can use their financial resources to support and build up churches and Christian ministries. First John 3:17 says, "But whoever has this world's goods, and sees his brother in need, and shuts up his heart from him, how does the love of God abide in him?" Loving our brothers and sisters includes helping those who are in financial need.

Kenneth Frampton was a wealthy property developer in London and a Christian. He gave large amounts of his money to Christian causes, and in 1965, he set up the Deo Gloria Trust, which is still in operation; the Trust's purpose is to support numerous evangelistic projects, including providing information on cults and on the dangers to young people of getting involved in the occult and false teaching, and the Contact for Christ service.[118] He honored God by using his wealth to help and support others, and he was a humble, kind man.

Joni Eareckson Tada has given much of the money which she has made over the years from her books, art, and media events to set up the "Joni and Friends" charity, which reaches out to and supports people affected by disabilities throughout the world.[119] Projects run by the charity include the Wheels for the World project, which provides wheelchairs for disabled children in poorer countries, international family retreats, and global internships for training in disability ministry.

These wealthy people have taken what God has given them and have contributed to spreading His love around the world. They have allowed God to use them to support His ministry.

THE PROSPERITY GOSPEL

The prosperity gospel is a movement operating in several nations of the world. This movement teaches that financial blessing and physical health are always the will of God for every believer and that if you have faith in God, He will always deliver health, security, and prosperity to you. By means of positive confession,

118   www.deo-gloria.co.uk
119   www.joniandfriends.org

visualization, faith, and even by giving financial donations to teachers of this gospel, the believer will in return receive physical healing and financial blessing. The atonement is interpreted to include the alleviation of sickness and poverty, which are both viewed as curses or lack of faith. In my view, the dangers inherent in prosperity teaching are financial fraud, exploitation of the poor, idolatry of man, and sometimes a refusal to seek medical help. Donations are requested in live gatherings or from televangelists on various television programs. These donations, according to the "seed faith" teaching of the prosperity doctrine, will grow in value and multiply; and this increase will return to the donor in due course. A *Time* magazine poll in 2006 reported that seventeen percent of Christians in the United States identified with the prosperity movement.[120]

My main concerns regarding this teaching are that it just does not work in practice, and it is not biblical, as we can see from the verses about wealth and poverty from Solomon's writings. Solomon did not request riches nor demand prosperity (though he may have desired them), nor did he "claim" it from God based on promises He thought God had made. He knew that there are days of prosperity and days of adversity for every person: "In the day of prosperity be joyful, But in the day of adversity consider: Surely God has appointed the one as well as the other, So that man can find out nothing *that will come* after him" (Eccl. 7:14). Solomon mentions the poor in many of his proverbs. For example, Proverbs 29:7 says, "The righteous considers the cause of the poor." And in Proverbs 14:21, "He who has mercy on the poor, happy *is* he." Also, "He who oppresses the poor reproaches his Maker, But he who honors Him has mercy on the needy" (Prov. 14:31).

Financial prosperity is not promised to every believer nor, in fact, to every person in the world. I know many Christians who live continuously on a low income, but their faith is strong; they serve their church diligently; and they share Christ with others. The apostle Paul knew times of blessing but also times of hardship and had learned to accept both states. He writes, "Not that I speak in

120 David Van Biema and Jeff Chu, "Does God Want You to Be Rich?," Time.com, September 10, 2006, http://content.time.com/time/magazine/article/0,9171,1533448,00.html.

regard to need, for I have learned in whatever state I am, to be content: I know how to be abased, and I know how to abound. Everywhere and in all things I have learned both to be full and to be hungry, both to abound and to suffer need. I can do all things through Christ who strengthens me" (Phil. 4:11-13).

The Christian life will include times of suffering, but that does not mean that God has forsaken us or has turned His back on us. These are the times for testing of faith and growth in both perseverance and endurance, which are a sign to those around us that we have faith in God no matter what comes our way. Many dedicated Christians suffer greatly with illnesses and disabilities from which God does not heal them, even when they have faith for healing. I believe that God can and does heal our physical bodies, but only God alone can instigate this.

We do not know the reasons why all Christians are not made well by God's power, either instantly or gradually. But putting pressure on people to give donations of money so that they can be healed in return is totally wrong and is certainly unbiblical. It leads to feelings of guilt, confusion, and worthlessness in individuals who get caught up in this teaching. Striving for healing and personal wealth takes away from the peace which Christ promised that we would walk in, as we trust Him with our whole life in every area. Only God can give us these things, just as it was God Who gave Solomon his riches and possessions. One day, when we pass into eternity and dwell in Heaven with Jesus our King, all sickness and disability will be gone, and there will be no lack of anything.

COSTI HINN CAME OUT OF PROSPERITY TEACHING

Costi Hinn, an American pastor and teacher and nephew of Benny Hinn, grew up in the midst of prosperity teaching and knew no other way of Christian living. He believed in the doctrine implicitly until he began to have serious doubts during a time when he met the young woman who would later become his wife. She did not have a background in the prosperity gospel.

Costi also started to experience guilt regarding his wealthy lifestyle and his high expenditure on luxury hotels, the most expensive cars, and top designer clothing. He realized that he and his family were acquiring riches from receiving the donations given by attendees at healing meetings all over the USA and Canada. People were flocking to these meetings because they were seeking physical healing and were told that the more they gave, the more God would honor them with healing.

Costi eventually had to leave the prosperity gospel behind because of his newly found convictions. He has no hatred and bitterness for those still involved in it, but he feels that he must speak out to warn people and to show them how false the doctrine is. You can read his enlightening and honest story in his book, *God, Greed, and the (Prosperity) Gospel.*[121]

THE PERSECUTED CHURCH

In many countries in the world, Christians are experiencing great suffering and often living in poverty. What do we say to them with regard to the prosperity gospel? The answer which is often given is that persecuted Christians are in the minority and are a special case. But according to Paul, "And if one member suffers, all the members suffer with *it*" (1 Cor. 12:26). Persecuted Christians are members of the Body of Christ just as we are; in addition, persecution and harassment of Christians is actually increasing across the globe, as Jesus predicted in Matthew 24 would happen at the end of the age.

Persecuted Christians are not in a minority. In his review on Christian persecution commissioned by the U.K. Foreign Secretary, Jeremy Hunt, at the end of 2019, the Bishop of Truro found that both the geographic spread of persecution and the severity of it are increasing year after year. Christians are the most persecuted religious group in the world. According to the Pew Report, in 2016, Christians were suffering harassment in 144 countries of the world, up from 128 countries in 2015.[122]

---

121   Costi Hinn, *God, Greed, and the (Prosperity) Gospel: How Truth Overwhelms a Life Built on Lies* (Grand Rapids: Zondervan, 2019).

122   "Global Uptick in Government Restrictions on Religion in 2016," Pew Research Center, June 21, 2018, https://www.pewforum.org/2018/06/21/global-uptick-in-government-restrictions-on-religion-in-2016.

Richard Wurmbrand, who was tortured and imprisoned for preaching the Gospel in Romania in the 1960s, challenged believers in free nations to be aware of and support their brothers and sisters who are persecuted and martyred for their Christian faith. He writes, "Free Christians are part of the same Body of Christ that is now beaten in prisons in restricted nations, that even now gives martyrs for Christ."[123]

---

123 Richard Wurmbrand, *Tortured for Christ (30th Anniversary Edition)* (Living Sacrifice Book Company, 1998).

CHAPTER 19

OLD AGE AND DEATH

*"Before the difficult days come, And the years draw near when you say,
'I have no pleasure in them.'"*

—Ecclesiastes 12:1

THE AGING PROCESS (ECCL. 12:1-5A)

In the second part of Ecclesiastes 12:1, Solomon begins to write about old age and a time of life when nothing seems to give pleasure any more. In the course of my secular employment, I have encountered elderly people whose days indeed have no pleasure in them. They may be confined to bed, have to be given food and liquids through a straw, suffer from incontinence, are no longer able to hold a conversation, or have been overtaken by dementia. Others, perhaps not in as extreme a condition, are confined to their home; mobility is impaired; and the pleasures of holidays, driving a car, shopping, reading, or other hobbies are a thing of the past.

Many commentators assume that Solomon himself was an elderly man when he wrote this passage, but there is no evidence that he lived to a great age. However, in common with most people, he would have observed the effects of aging in family members and friends and was thus able to describe the signs of old age so clearly and, with his writing gifts, so poetically. We know that Solomon saw his father David at the end of his life, bedridden and continuously

151

feeling cold so that Abishag, a young virgin, was instructed to lie with him simply to keep him warm.

Unless cancer or another serious illness or accident takes us earlier in life, it is a sure and certain fact that we will reach old age and will live through the years when our physical and mental health gradually decline. I am glad that Solomon penned these lines in Ecclesiastes 12, describing the results of the aging process and the reality of its limitations in the lives of people who were previously active. The actual moment of death is also described. The passage shows us that God knows all about this stage of life, and therefore, we can be reassured that He is still with us, still loves us, and still wants us to trust Him as we age. In Isaiah 46:4a, we have God's promise: "Even to *your* old age, I *am* He, and *even* to gray hairs I will carry *you*." Before then, we can be aware of the needs of our elderly relatives and friends.

Ecclesiastes 12:1-6 is abundant with highly descriptive metaphors, yet it paints a very sad picture. There have been various explanations given in analyzing each metaphor, as outlined here. In chapter twenty-nine, "Solomon on the Couch: The King's Personality," there is a further view of Ecclesiastes 12.

Ecclesiastes 12:2—"While the sun and the light, The moon and the stars, Are not darkened, And the clouds do not return after the rain."

This points to a sense of depression and hopelessness. There is no longer the resiliency of youth, when trials and illness were, in most cases, transient and there was hope of recovery. Now with old age, the body is in decline; there will be no recovery of strength; and life is nearing its end.

Ecclesiastes 12:3—"In the day when the keepers of the house tremble, And the strong men bow down; When the grinders cease because they are few, And those that look through the windows grow dim."

"The keepers of the house tremble" could refer to the arms and hands, which become weak and shaky. "The strong men bow down" could refer to the legs, which support the body but are now failing; bone and muscle function deteriorate with age. "The grinders cease because they are few" may refer to the molar teeth, most of which are no longer present. Fortunately, today, dentures and dental implants can remedy this. "Those that look through the windows grow dim" could refer to diminished eyesight or total blindness, which can come with old age. It could also be a picture of a person suffering from dementia: they look but cannot make sense of what they see due to the mental confusion resulting from damaged brain cells, which locks them into another world.

Ecclesiastes 12:4—"When the doors are shut in the streets, And the sound of grinding is low; When one rises up at the sound of the bird, And all the daughters of music are brought low."

This passage points to difficulties interacting with the outside world because of frailty. In other words, many elderly people become housebound or isolated due to mobility problems, dementia, blindness, and other limiting afflictions. "The sound of grinding is low" points to deafness and inability to distinguish sounds. "When one rises up at the sound of the bird" may refer to the time that an elderly person awakes. Many elderly people suffer from insomnia during the night, or they awaken too early, at the time the birds start to sing.

"The daughters of music are brought low" could refer to a lack of desire for the joys found in entertainment or the joys and celebrations of youth. However, music and singing can be very enjoyable and therapeutic for elderly people, including those suffering from dementia. Singing and music touch a part of the being which is not affected by physical illness. An American organization called Music and Memory was set up to provide personalized music programs on iPods for people with dementia living in nursing homes and assisted living facilities. Results show that residents are calmer, happier, and more sociable while listening. In the U.K., broadcaster Sally Magnusson set up a similar charity called Playlist for Life, after observing how her mother, who suffered from dementia, responded so positively to songs and music with which she was familiar when nothing else seemed to help.

Ecclesiastes 12:5—"Also they are afraid of height, And of terrors in the way; When the almond tree blossoms, The grasshopper is a burden, And desire fails. For man goes to his eternal home, And the mourners go about the streets."

They have a fear of height due to feeling unsteady, having a loss of balance and a consequent fear of falling.

"Terrors in the way" refers to the elderly becoming more anxious and fearful. A decline in mental capacity makes it more difficult to cope with the issues of everyday living.

"The almond tree blossoms" could refer to the white hair of the aged, like a flourishing almond tree produces white blossoms.

"The grasshopper is a burden" could mean that even tiny things produce irritation and agitation, or it could be a picture of a grasshopper crawling slowly and laboriously, due to injury or cold, instead of hopping.

"Desire fails" could refer to general enjoyment of life or specifically sexual desire, which wanes in old age. Some versions of the Bible include the Hebrew expression, "when the caperberry fails." Caperberries were used as a stimulant for appetite and had aphrodisiac properties. See chapter twenty-nine for further exploration of this imagery.

DEATH (ECCL. 12:5B-7)

Ecclesiastes 12:5b—"For man goes to his eternal home, And the mourners go about the streets."

The end of every person's life is physical death, and every person's soul goes into eternity. Solomon lived a long time before Christ was born, so he did not know about salvation through His sacrificial death on the cross; but he obviously believed in eternal life at a time when people believed in Sheol as the place of the dead.

"And the mourners go about the streets" refers to when someone dies. The funeral procession will pass through the streets so that relatives and friends can mourn for the deceased. This still happens today in most nations of the world: a funeral is a public occasion, and the mourners will walk or travel with the coffin to the burial place or crematorium.

Ecclesiastes 12:6—"*Remember your Creator* before the silver cord is loosed, Or the golden bowl is broken, Or the pitcher shattered at the fountain, Or the wheel broken at the well."

The actual moment of physical death is portrayed so poetically in verse six. Let's look at the metaphoric language and its possible meanings.

"The silver cord is loosed" speaks of a chain made of silver which suddenly snaps and is irreparably broken. The connection between the physical body, and the spirit is severed in an instant.

"The golden bowl is broken" could represent a gold oil lamp, which had been suspended on the silver chain, which then breaks, causing the golden bowl to fall and break in an instant.

"The pitcher shattered at the fountain" describes a water pitcher which has broken, and therefore, its usefulness is over.

"The wheel broken at the well" paints a similar picture. When the wheel breaks, its functionality is gone, and the system for drawing water from the well (perhaps using the water pitcher) is interrupted and ended. Some commentaries say that the metaphoric language describes the heart and circulatory system.

Derek Kidner explains the verse this way: "A picture of our familiar selves; the transience of the simplest, most basic things we do. There will be a last time for every familiar journey, every routine job."[124] No matter whether a person dies in infirmity or old age, or suddenly in an accident, the process is the same: the familiar actions of daily life cease in an instant and stop forever.

Ecclesiastes 12:7—"Then the dust will return to the earth as it was, And the spirit will return to God who gave it."

Scientists have discovered that all of the fifty-nine elements found in the human body are present in the Earth's crust. The remains of the physical body, in whichever way it is disposed of, will eventually return to the dust of the earth, as do the physical remains of animals and birds. Genesis 2:7 and 3:19 also tell us that our bodies are made from the dust of the ground. Solomon writes in Ecclesiastes 3:19-20 that both man and animals come from the dust and will return to the dust after death.

---

124 Derek Kidner, *The Message of Ecclesiastes* (Downers Grove: Inter-Varsity Press, 1976).

"And the spirit will return to God who gave it" refers to the spirit within each of us, which cannot die and will live on into eternity. Even Solomon acknowledged this, despite not knowing about the salvation wrought by the sacrificial death of Christ on the cross.

THE QUESTION OF EUTHANASIA

There are moves by various lobby groups to make assisted suicide legal in the U.K. and in more states in the USA. Is it right for a person to choose to be helped to die by a physician because of severe and incurable suffering? Or if we trust Him totally with our whole life, should we wait for our natural lifespan to be completed in the time allotted to us by God?

I believe that assisted suicide is wrong before God and wrong for society as a whole. Mainly, it is wrong before God because we are made in God's image (Gen. 1:27) and are thus different from the animal kingdom. That is why it is perfectly allowable to have your pet dog or cat euthanized by a veterinary surgeon if it is suffering incurable physical distress. Animals are not made in the image of God, but human beings are. The teaching of the theory of evolution muddies the waters by causing people to think that we have evolved from animals similar to modern-day chimpanzees, and therefore, we are simply a higher form of animal life. Following on from that belief, some think that it gives justification to euthanize people in the same way as is done with an animal. But God says that we are made in His image. Also, our body is described as being "the temple of the Holy Spirit . . . you are not your own . . . [but] were bought at a price" (1 Cor. 6:19-20). We have great worth and value in God's sight.

In Canada, where assisted suicide has been legal since 2016, the government has consulted on expanding the procedure to include the mentally ill, "mature minors," and people whose deaths are not imminent. Canadian hospices are coming under pressure to provide assisted death or risk losing their funding. Assisted dying is also legal in some states in the USA and in the state of Victoria in Australia. In the U.K., the British Medical Association, which has opposed assisted dying since 2006, launched a poll in February 2020, asking its members for their views on supporting or opposing assisted suicide. Results showed that forty percent of British doctors voiced their opposition to legalizing assisted suicide, stating that they have a duty of care to patients and have concerns about the risk to ill and vulnerable patients.[125] In a similar survey by the Royal College of Physicians in early 2019, 43.4 percent of respondents said that the RCP should be opposed to a change in the current law on assisted dying.[126] In June 2021, a new bill to legalize assisted dying was lodged at the Scottish Parliament with a consultation about changing current legislation to take place later in the year.

Joni Eareckson Tada, a committed Christian who has been quadriplegic since the age of seventeen following a diving accident, has written an excellent book called, *When Is It Right to Die?* She does not advocate legalizing euthanasia, despite having struggled with her paralysis, coping with depression and suicidal thoughts in her youth, and being confined to a wheelchair for about fifty years. She writes realistically about her own struggles and those of several families who have wrestled with end-of-life questions and gives encouragement, comfort, and biblical advice. She believes that every person has worth.[127]

Joni also wrote in an article in *Decision Magazine* that she believes the push to legalize assisted suicide originates from a fear of suffering and an attitude of entitlement, which includes the right to arrange the timing of one's own death. She advocates instead for more research into dealing with pain and other distressing symptoms, plus the provision of spiritual input to allay people's fears and help them understand the reality of eternity.[128]

There is also the effect of a decision to end one's life on a whole network of relationships. Any suicide has a devastating and long-term effect on family, friends, and acquaintances. Joni wrote in *Christianity Today* that a person's

---

125 "Physician-assisted Dying Survey," British Medical Association.org, January 20, 2021, https://www.bma.org.uk/advice-and-support/ethics/end-of-life/physician-assisted-dying-survey.

126 "The RCP clarifies its position on assisted dying," Royal College of Physicians online, Accessed March 10, 2021, https://www.rcplondon.ac.uk/news/rcp-clarifies-its-position-assisted-dying.

127 Joni Eareckson Tada, *When Is It Right to Die?: Suicide, Euthanasia, Suffering, Mercy* (Grand Rapids: Zondervan, 1992).

128 Joni Eareckson Tada, "When Is It Right to Die?," Decision Magazine.com, June 1, 2019, https://decisionmagazine.com/when-is-it-right-to-die.

decision not to end their own life in the face of suffering matters to society and positively affects the cultural drift and moral resolve of a society.[129] Conversely, the acceptance of assisted suicide weakens the moral resolve. Paul wrote in Romans 14:7, "For none of us lives to himself, and no one dies to himself." When a person dies, a lot of people are affected.

One group that advocates against assisted suicide is Affirm the Dignity of Life (www.adfinternational.org), a faith-based, legal advocacy organization which protects fundamental freedoms, promotes the dignity of all people, and speaks out against euthanasia.

Another group is Care not Killing (www.carenotkilling.org.uk), an alliance of several organizations which are opposed to the legalization of assisted suicide in the U.K. and aims to promote more and better palliative care. Yet another one is Not Dead Yet (www.notdeadyet.org), a disability rights group, active in the USA and the U.K., which opposes assisted suicide and euthanasia for people with disabilities.

FURTHER CONSIDERATIONS

Please go to Appendix A and B sections for further considerations of interactions with the elderly and concerning Solomon's contemplations of death.

---

129 "Why suicide is everybody's business," Christianity Today.com, March 14, 2018 https://www.christianitytoday.com/ct/2018/march-web-only/joni-eareckson-tada-suicide-everybodys-business-euthanasia.html.

CHAPTER 20

PROVERBS, GOD'S CREATION, AND OUR ETERNAL SAVIOR

"Rejoicing in His inhabited world, And my delight was *with the sons of men."*

—Proverbs 8:31

Solomon obviously received special inspiration from God to write in Proverbs 8:22-36 about the creation of the world in a similar way to that which is described in Genesis 1-2. But not only does he write about the creation of the world but he also writes about Jesus Christ being with the Father in Heaven before even the physical world came into being and, furthermore, about Christ being present to witness God creating the world. Solomon must have received special revelation of these wonders; and in one part of the passage, it is as though Christ is narrating the story about Himself instead of Solomon telling it.

Let's look at the words from verses twenty-two to thirty-one, which are obviously spoken by Jesus in the first-person singular:

"The Lord possessed me at the beginning of His way,
Before His works of old;
I have been established from everlasting,
From the beginning, before there was ever an earth.
When *there were* no depths I was brought forth,
When *there were* no fountains abounding with water.
Before the mountains were settled,

Before the hills, I was brought forth;

While as yet He had not made the earth or the fields,

Or the primal dust of the world.

When He prepared the heavens, I *was* there,

When He drew a circle on the face of the deep,

When He established the clouds above,

When He strengthened the fountains of the deep,

When He assigned to the sea its limit,

So that the waters would not transgress His command,

When He marked out the foundations of the earth.

Then I was beside Him *as* a master craftsman;

And I was daily *His* delight,

Rejoicing always before Him,

Rejoicing in His inhabited world,

And my delight *was* with the sons of men."

This portion of Proverbs 8 shows that God had provided the means of our eternal salvation through Christ, even before He had created the world. Before the depths, the fountains, the mountains, the hills, the Earth, or the fields ever came into existence, Christ was present with the Father from everlasting, from the beginning. It would be the same Jesus Christ, Son of God, Who would pay the price for us by His sacrificial death on the cross after His short life on the Earth. This ties in with John 1:1: "In the beginning was the Word, and the Word was with God, and the Word was God."

In John 17:5, we can read Christ's prayer to His Father, in which He speaks of the glory He had before the world was. And later, He says to the Father, "You loved me before the foundation of the world" (17:24). First Peter 1:19-20 also says that Christ was "foreordained before the foundation of the world." Micah 5:2 speaks of Christ as "the One to be Ruler in Israel, Whose goings forth *are* from of old, From everlasting." It is remarkable that Solomon wrote this passage in Proverbs 8, hundreds of years before Micah, John, or Peter.

In the passage in Proverbs 8, Christ says twice, "I was brought forth" (v. 24-25). Although He was not created in a physical sense, He was indeed brought forth from His Father to become a man, to be born from the womb of Mary, and to live on Earth and die to save us from sin's penalty.

Looking at the description of the creation of the world here, it speaks of the very foundations, the ultimate beginning of the Earth, before there were plants or living creatures. The mountains and hills, the heavens, the clouds, the fountains of the deep, the sea and its tidal limits were all marked out by God as He spoke them into existence from the beginning when the Spirit of God "hover[ed] over the face of the waters" (Gen. 1:2). Jesus describes in Proverbs 8:24 the "depths" and "fountains" of the deep, which aligns with the second day of Creation, when the firmament was created to divide the waters above it from the waters below it (Gen. 1:6-7). He "drew a circle on the face of the deep" (8:27) and "marked out the foundations of the earth" (8:29). Compare this with the passage in Genesis 1:9-10, that says, "Then God said, 'Let the waters under the heavens be gathered into one place, and let the dry *land* appear; and it was so. And God called the dry *land* Earth, and the gathering together of the waters He called Seas." The "primal dust" referred to in 8:26 could refer to the smallest of particles of which the Earth was made or even the chemical elements and atoms. Genesis 2:7 tells us that man was formed *"of* the dust of the ground."

The passage also tells us that Jesus Christ rejoiced at what the Father had created (8:31), and He said, "My delight *was* with the sons of men," which refers to the human beings whom God had created. What a thought—that Christ delights in us; we bring Him great joy! Christ says that He was daily the delight of His Father and was beside Him as a Master Craftsman: Christ is also Creator!

CREATION AND SALVATION THROUGH CHRIST CANNOT BE SEPARATED

This is why it is important that Christians believe in a literal Creation, as outlined in Genesis 1 and 2. Many believers say they believe most of what is written in the Bible, but they cannot legitimately accept the Genesis account of Creation.

As a result, they find other ways to explain how the natural world came about, like theistic evolution or even the entire theory of evolution itself. Or they accept that God created the world but that it happened over a long period of millions of years. When we consider the Proverbs passage above, where it is obviously Christ speaking and Solomon writing the words, we can conclude that the Creation is not only described in the Book of Genesis but also here in Proverbs and in other parts of Scripture, too (Rom. 1; Col. 1:16). So, if we deny the Genesis account, we are denying part of the truth concerning Christ and His coming to the world to save us. He took part in Creation; He was with the Father in Heaven; and the plan that He would become our Savior was made before the foundation of the world. The Genesis account of Creation is part of the whole story of salvation and must be believed, rather than being sectioned off as a part of the Bible that we cannot grasp with our mind and find difficulty understanding.

WHAT ABOUT SCIENTIFIC KNOWLEDGE?

I studied and gained an honors degree in biological sciences, but I have no difficulty in believing the account of a literal, six-day Creation. During my studies, I found it very difficult to believe in the theory of evolution—which was universally taught as truth at school and university—even before I was a Christian. All I could see again and again was evidence for a Designer, a Creator. I marvel at the intricate functioning and complex anatomy of a mammalian kidney, for example. Or the human eye! Have you ever looked at the diagram of the eye, which has so many different layers and types of cells? Then try to explain how the various parts of that organ work together to allow us to be able to see! The reproductive system in animals and humans is unbelievably intricate, and much of it still cannot be explained by scientists; yet new life is produced again and again. And how do muscles work? The lecturers always struggled to try to explain how the muscle fibers worked together at different times to produce movement, and there was a theory to help with understanding this.

But despite the advances in scientific knowledge and the increasing detail within animal and plant structure, which can now be viewed through the electron microscope, MRI scanning, or internal photographic probes, many people still refuse to believe that the natural world has been designed and put together by a Creator Who is the God of the universe. However, the more I studied these things, the more I saw the hand of God revealed, and I continually rejoice and praise Him for His wonderful and fascinating, created world.

CHAPTER 21

THE SONG OF SOLOMON

"My beloved is *mine, and I* am *his."*

—Song of Solomon 2:16

The book in the Bible entitled the Song of Solomon is sometimes called the Song of Songs, indicating that it is the prime song amongst many that Solomon wrote; it has also been called *Canticles,* which means "a number of songs." Martin Luther named it *Das Hohelied,* meaning "the noblest song."[130] First Kings 4:32 tells us that Solomon wrote 1,005 songs, but we only have this one song in the Bible.

The Song of Solomon, which was written around 945 B.C., depicts a courtship leading to marriage between Solomon and a young woman, whom the daughters of Jerusalem call "The Shulamite." There is some debate and uncertainty about her title. Some commentators believe she came from a place named Shulam, whereas others say that Shulamite is derived from the Hebrew word for peace—"shalom"—and is the feminine equivalent of the name Solomon. Her first name is not given anywhere in the song.

Throughout most of my Christian life, I had always been taught that the Song of Solomon was simply an allegorical story which told of Christ's love for His Bride, which is the Church, and of the Christian's love for Christ. While that may be one of the meanings which can be taken from this book, I believe that there is more for us to see and learn.

---

130 M. G. Easton, *Illustrated Bible Dictionary* (London: T. Nelson and Sons, 1893).

It was not until recent years, while I was attending a Bible teaching course at a local church, that I was introduced to David Pawson's explanation of the meaning of the Song of Solomon. Pawson encourages us to read it at face-value as a love story and explains the meaning of much of the text. He sheds light on many of the parts of the book which do not seem to make sense as an allegorical account and are difficult to process spiritually.[131] Song of Solomon is full of metaphoric language; and the story is written somewhat like the pieces of a jigsaw, and the parts do not appear in chronological order. This may seem strange, yet many modern films follow this pattern where the scenes flit back and forward in time. Once we put all the pieces of the jigsaw together, we see far more clearly what the poetically written story is telling us.

THE STORY TOLD IN THE SONG OF SOLOMON

Solomon had a country estate in Baal Hamon, where he had planted an extensive vineyard, had many orchards, and even kept livestock. He had appointed tenant farmers on his estate who carried out the horticultural work and farming tasks, while selling their produce to make a living. There was one family there who were engaged in this agricultural work; it is thought that the father had died leaving sons and a younger daughter. The sons, or perhaps stepsons, put pressure on their young sister to go out and work in the fields and vineyards every day. Working outdoors in the strong sunshine caused the girl's skin to become darker, unlike the women in the cities who tried to preserve their skin and remain as pale as possible.

One day, Solomon, the son of King David, traveled out to visit his country estate and caught sight of a young girl at work in the fields. He was captivated with how beautiful she was and could not take his eyes from her. Unable to deny his feelings, he approached her, and they struck up a conversation. She had no idea that he was the future King Solomon, but she was attracted to him and was taken aback that a handsome man from the city should be interested in a poor, country

131 David Pawson, "Song of Solomon – Unlocking the Bible" accessed June 3, 2020 https:// www.davidpawson.co.uk/resources/unlocking-the-bible.

girl like herself. She was the Shulamite of the Song of Solomon. Nevertheless, they fell in love and began a passionate courtship until eventually, he told her that he wanted her to become his wife. She was thrilled at this prospect and did not want to let him go back to the city, in case she never saw him again. But in line with Jewish custom regarding courtship and marriage, he told her that he must go away and prepare a place for her but that he would definitely come back for her and take her as his bride. He left and returned to the city.

Let us return to the Shulamite. She had to wait patiently for her lover to return, and she had no idea when this would occur. She did not find the waiting easy and could not stop thinking about him. Even when she was asleep, she dreamed about him; in the dream, she went into the city and searched everywhere for him, asking the city watchmen if they had seen him. The watchmen were unkind to her. Perhaps they looked condescendingly on her, knowing that she was a country girl who worked in agriculture and was not refined like the women of the city and should not be seeking her lover there. The only way she could try to contact him was by sending a message via the daughters of Jerusalem.

"Daughters" in the Bible is often used for any female inhabitant of a place or city, so these daughters appear to be young women who lived in Jerusalem. The Shulamite begged them to tell her beloved, if they happened to see him, that she was sick with love for him. She also gave the young women some advice and told them, on more than one occasion, that they should not awaken love or artificially stir up love until the time was right. This suggests that they were unmarried girls; and if they were at all able to contact Solomon, it could be that they were maidservants in one of his palaces.

One day, the young girl was outdoors with others when all of a sudden, they saw clouds of dust on the horizon and then caught sight of a large and very ornate chariot, pulled by several horses, approaching the estate where they dwelled. She asked who this could be, and someone told her that it was the wedding party of Solomon. As the dazzling chariot drew near, she looked up and saw that it was her beloved, the man who had courted her, asked her to be his wife, and promised to return for her and take her to the place he had prepared for her. He was King David's son, Solomon, from the city of Jerusalem, and he was thoroughly captivated by her beauty and had come to claim her as his bride. It is a Cinderella love story: a poor, country girl, her skin darkened by the sun from laboring outdoors, married to one of the greatest and wealthiest kings ever known.

Some Bible expositors say that the story told in the Song of Solomon also includes a young shepherd, and it was he with whom the Shulamite fell in love and courted. It is unclear from the passages whether this is part of the story. Many commentators believe that the "shepherd with his flocks" is Solomon himself. Solomon writes in Ecclesiastes 2:7 that he "had greater possessions of herds and flocks than all who were in Jerusalem before me." We know that his father, King David, had worked as a shepherd in his youth and owned great flocks. Perhaps Solomon periodically went to look over his flocks of sheep when he visited his country estate, in a similar way to the queen of the United Kingdom going to view her many horses, which are stabled and looked after at her country estates. We can also think of Christ, Who called Himself the Good Shepherd and Who cares diligently for His flock; the sheep get to know His voice (John 10:3-5). The Shulamite herself had a flock of goats to care for: after asking where her lover pastured his flocks, the Shulamite is instructed to feed her kids (goats) beside the shepherds' tents (1:8). She may have wondered who Solomon was and, having met him, wanted to find him again.

A CELEBRATION OF MARRIAGE

The Song of Solomon is a celebration of romantic love, courtship, and marriage between a man and a woman. The language which is used speaks of a deep and meaningful relationship and of intimacy and sexual union. The Song of Solomon contains many beautiful images of erotic love.[132] It contains several passages which describe the couple praising each other's bodies and delighting in their sexual union.[133] That this love song is in the Bible shows us how important the bond of love between a man and a woman and its development into the

---

132   Douglas E. Rosenau, *A Celebration of Sex* (Nashville: Thomas Nelson, 2002).
133   Christopher and Rachel McCluskey, *When Two Become One: Enhancing Sexual Intimacy in Marriage* (Grand Rapids: Fleming H. Revell, 2004).

commitment of marriage is to God. Henry Morris writes, "The marvellous phenomenon of sexual love and reproduction, with the amazing complex of mechanisms involved, could never have originated by some random evolutionary process. God created it all and He has reminded us of its grandeur by including this beautiful Song of Solomon in his divinely inspired scriptures."

Solomon most likely wrote this Song when he was a young man. In his book *The Remarkable Wisdom of Solomon*, Henry Morris outlines his belief that the Shulamite was Solomon's first wife, and perhaps his first love, and that they were married and had a son, Rehoboam, before Solomon was crowned king.[134] Since Solomon became king at the age of twenty and reigned for forty years, after which Rehoboam became king at age forty-one, this would give credence to Morris' belief. Morris continues by saying that this love relationship was ordained by their Creator. God had called Solomon to be king of His chosen nation: the future establishment of His everlasting Kingdom as promised to his father, David, must include a properly prepared wife for Solomon. At that time in the Middle East, people married at a young age, often before the age of twenty.

WEDDINGS IN ANCIENT ISRAEL

To help us understand the story which is being told in the Song of Solomon, it is useful to know what a wedding would be like in the time of Solomon and in the days when Christ lived on Earth. Weddings in the West in modern times bear no real resemblance to weddings in ancient Israel. However, Jewish weddings in modern times still follow some of the practices which were the norm in ancient Israel.

The wedding in ancient times comprised three definite stages:

1. The contract
2. The consummation
3. The wedding celebrations

---

134 Henry Morris, *The Remarkable Wisdom of Solomon* (Green Forest: Master Books, 2001).

Having chosen the man who was to be her husband, the bride's father would draw up and sign a *ketubah*, or legal contract, between him and the prospective husband. From this point, the boy and girl were legally married; this was the betrothal, but it was not the same as our engagement event of today. The betrothal marked the first stage of marriage; but the union was not yet consummated, and there was a time gap before this would take place. During the time gap, which could last up to seven years, the bridegroom was usually required to make a payment to the bride's father and to provide wedding jewelry for his bride. Sometimes, the jewelry included a headband made of coins, and there is speculation that it may have been one of ten headband coins which was lost by the woman in the parable of the lost coin (Luke 15:8).[135]

The second stage of the wedding was the *chuppah*, or sexual consummation, and this generally took place in a room in the bride's or bridegroom's house. In the culture of the day, the bride was expected to be a virgin, and because most girls married in their teenage years, virginity was the norm. The parable of the ten virgins who were bridesmaids, which Jesus tells in Matthew 25, describes this part of a wedding in New Testament times. The bride waited with her bridesmaids for the bridegroom and his companions to arrive. This event usually took place at night, which explains why it was so important for the bridesmaids to have their oil lamps ready with enough spare oil in case the bridegroom was greatly delayed. In the parable, the bridegroom is, indeed, greatly delayed—so much so that the ten bridesmaids fall asleep. They were supposed to wait for the call that the bridegroom was on his way to take his bride. They had to be ready and prepared, or they would miss the moment, and it would be too late to assist the bride to dress and be ready for her beloved. Once the companions of the bridegroom noisily announced his arrival, the bridesmaids must get up and get the bride ready to be claimed by the bridegroom. She would be veiled and wearing as much jewellery as her family could afford. He came to take his bride,

---

135   Pat Alexander, ed., *Lion Encyclopedia of the Bible* (Colorado Springs: Chariot Victor Pub, 1986).

and they entered the specially prepared *chuppah* room, where they consummated their marriage.

The custom was for the bridegroom's companions to wait nearby as witnesses and celebrate what was happening. An allusion to this event is used by John the Baptist when he said in John 3:29, "He who has the bride is the bridegroom; but the friend of the bridegroom, who stands and hears him, rejoices greatly because of the bridegroom's voice. Therefore this joy of mine is fulfilled." John the Baptist is comparing himself to a groomsman, and Christ is the Bridegroom Who takes His Bride, the Church, to Himself when He returns in power and glory at the end of the age. John is rejoicing because of the Bridegroom's victory in claiming His pure and spotless Bride. We can see this further in 2 Corinthians 11:2, where Paul writes figuratively, "For I have betrothed you to one husband, that I may present *you as* a chaste virgin to Christ."

Jesus was also alluding to the marriage customs of His culture when He told His disciples that He was going away to prepare a place for them in His Father's house and that He would return and take them to be with Him (John 14:2-3). Jesus is the true Bridegroom, and every person who trusts in Him as their Savior is a part of the Bride of Christ (Eph. 5:32). One day, we will all be united with Christ, and there will be a great wedding feast, the Marriage Supper of the Lamb (Rev. 19:7). But for now, we must wait for the time appointed, just like the ten virgins did, because no one knows the day or hour of Christ's return (Matt. 24:36).

After the *chuppah*, a wedding procession, comprised of the bridal couple with their relatives and friends, made its way with much joy and singing to the bridegroom's house, usually by the light of torches and oil lamps. There, the wedding feast began, and this could last for up to seven days. The parable which Jesus told about the wedding feast, where those who were invited went in and then the door was shut, describes this stage in a wedding. Also, in the parable of the ten virgins, the five foolish ones, who did not have enough oil for their lamps and had to go away to buy some oil, returned for the wedding feast but were too late: the door was shut; the feasting had begun, and they could not enter. The parable is a warning to us to always be ready and to be diligent in maintaining our Christian faith with the help of the Holy Spirit (the oil) because we do not know the hour of our Bridegroom Jesus' return, and there may be a delay. After all the celebratory feasting had ended, the bridegroom and bride had fully completed the ritual of marriage and could start their married life together in the place which the bridegroom had prepared for them to live.

The marital union is used in the New Testament to represent the love between Christ and His Bride, which comprises the company of all true believers. Having given practical instruction to husbands and wives to live in harmony in Ephesians 5:32, Paul states that marriage is a profound mystery, but that he is ultimately talking about Christ and the Church. In Revelation 21:2, we see the Church "as a bride adorned for her husband." And then the wedding supper of the Lamb takes place as described in Revelation 19:7-9. It is, indeed, a mystery, and we will not be able to understand it fully until we ourselves attend the wedding of the Lamb of God.

MARY AND JOSEPH

The story of Mary and Joseph, which is well known in all Western countries, makes sense when we consider the three stages of marriage which took place at that time in Israel. Mary and Joseph had undergone the first stage and had signed the *ketubah*, and therefore, they were one hundred percent legally married but had not had sexual relations (Stage Two). When Mary became pregnant by the Holy Spirit, Joseph thought about divorcing her privately until the angel spoke clearly to him about the conception within Mary by the power of the Holy Spirit and the forthcoming birth of Christ (Matt. 1:18-21). To divorce her privately meant that his reputation, not Mary's, would be harmed, and he would most likely pay a dowry back to Mary.

The Bible says that Joseph was a righteous and upright man, and this option would mean that he was not going to openly and publicly accuse Mary of having sexual relations with another man. Matthew 1:25 tells us that Joseph obeyed the angel and took Mary as his wife but that they had no sexual union until after she had given birth to her firstborn son, Jesus.[136]

PSALM 45: A ROYAL WEDDING

Psalm 45 depicts a description of a secular royal wedding, but it is also a messianic psalm wherein it speaks of Jesus Christ. Verse 2 says, "You are fairer than the sons of men." This is obviously referring to Christ, and this portion is also quoted in Hebrews 1:8-9.

Verses fourteen and fifteen describe the bride being brought to the bridegroom: "She shall be brought to the King in robes of many colors; The virgins, her companions who follow her, shall be brought to You. With gladness and rejoicing they shall be brought; They shall enter the King's palace."

THE LANGUAGE OF THE SONG OF SOLOMON

Following on from the viewpoint that the Song of Solomon is a love story between Solomon and his beloved Shulamite, let us look at and examine some of the descriptive texts and metaphorical language which appear in this book. My aim is not to provide a commentary nor to go through this book verse by verse. I do not claim to have all the answers, nor do I have a complete understanding of the meaning of everything which Solomon has written. The Song of Solomon is a rather mysterious book, and at times, we are not even sure who is speaking in the various dialogues. My purpose in writing is instead to highlight and examine some of the verses and words which I have found enlightening and which have caught my interest and deepened my understanding of the character of Solomon and of his beloved Shulamite.

TREES AND PLANTS

First Kings 4:33-34, which speak of Solomon's great wisdom, says that he "spoke of trees, from the cedar of Lebanon even to the hyssop that springs out

---

136 Steve Rudd, "Marriage in the Bible and Ancient and Jewish Wedding Customs: The Three Stage Ritual of Bible Marriages," Bible.ca, https://www.bible.ca/marriage/ancient-jewish-three-stage-weddings-and-marriage-customs-ceremony-in-the-bible.htm (accessed December 6, 2020).

of the wall." He had great knowledge of plant life and trees, many of which are mentioned in the Song of Solomon.

1. "A bundle of myrrh *is* my beloved to me" (Song of Sol. 1:13).

The bundle of myrrh which the Shulamite says is like her beloved would have been a scent bag full of crushed myrrh, which would have been hung around her neck or used to perfume clothing. Myrrh trees produce a resin, which is distilled to extract the essential oil, which also has healing and antiseptic properties. Myrrh is mentioned in the book of Esther (2:12) as being one of the perfumed oils used over a six-month period to prepare Esther and the other girls for their meeting with the king. The Shulamite would most likely have prepared herself in a similar way for her wedding. Myrrh was one of the three special gifts brought to Christ at His birth by the wise men (Matt. 2). But the significance of the myrrh in this case most likely refers to its use in the preparation of a body for burials, as we read regarding Christ's body after His death (Luke 23:56-24:1; John 19:39).

2. "My beloved *is* to me a cluster of henna **blooms**" (Song of Sol. 1:14).

The Shulamite girl compares her beloved to "a cluster of henna *blooms* In the vineyards of En-Gedi." Henna is a small, thorny shrub which has fragrant white flowers in spring. The leaves are used to make dye. S. Craig Glickman puts it this way: "En-Gedi was an oasis in a desert wilderness: it was green, bright and fresh. The king was like an oasis of life in a desert of monotony where she found refreshment from being with him. Since the henna blossoms are the loveliest flowers in that oasis, he was indeed very special to her."[137]

3. "I *am* the rose of Sharon" (Song of Sol. 2:1).

The rose of Sharon is actually a crocus-like flower or tulip, which grows prolifically around the plain of Sharon, which lies between the mountains of central Israel and the Mediterranean Sea. The Hebrew word *habasalet* in Song of

---

137   S. Craig Glickman, *A Song for Lovers* (Downers Grove: InterVarsity Press, 1976).

Solomon 2:1 has been translated as "rose," but the plant is not a rose as we know it in the West. Rose of Sharon flowers grow easily and cover the dry, barer areas of the plain, giving it a pinkish hue, almost like heather. When the Shulamite says she is a rose of Sharon, she is meaning that she is just a lowly, common wildflower and not anything special.

It is the Bride, the Shulamite, who calls herself the rose of Sharon. Some Bible expositors say that Jesus is the Rose of Sharon. Jesus never described Himself in that way. He said of Himself, "I am the door" (John 10:9); "I am the good shepherd" (John 10:11); "I am the bread of life" (John 6:35); "I am the vine" (John 15:5); "I am the way, the truth and the life" (John 14:6). But He never said, "I am the Rose of Sharon."

4. And "the lily of the valleys" (Song of Sol. 2:1).

Similarly, when the Shulamite describes herself as a "lily of the valleys," she is also referring to a wildflower which is common in Israel. The lily of the valley here is probably a deep-blue hyacinth type of plant. Again, Christ is never described as a lily of the valley, nor is the Body of Christ, as some Christian teaching would suggest.

5. "Like an apple tree among the trees of the woods, So *is* my beloved" (Song of Sol. 2:3).

Apple trees, as we know them, do not grow in the Middle East. Therefore, the apples mentioned in several places in the Song of Solomon (2:5; 7:8, 8:5) probably refer to the apricot tree, which also produces beautiful blossoms in spring, or the quince, which produces fragrant fruit. The Hebrew word used in Song of Solomon for apple is *tappuah*, which means fragrance and was a familiar symbol for romance in the culture of that time.

6. "Spikenard and saffron, calamus and cinnamon" (Song of Sol. 4:14).

In chapter four of the Song of Solomon, he outlines various fragrant plants: "Fragrant henna with spikenard, Spikenard and saffron, Calamus and Cinnamon

. . . frankincense, Myrrh and aloes" (4:13-14). Spikenard, or nard, is a fragrant essential oil, which was very costly, and is derived from the plant *Nardostachys jatamansi*; in Mark 14:3-9, we read about the woman who poured a flask of expensive spikenard over Jesus' head. Saffron, a type of Crocus, is native to the Middle East, and the dried flower parts are used for seasoning and yellow coloring of food. Cinnamon, which is derived from the bark of Cinnamomum trees, which are members of the laurel family, was used in perfumes as well as for flavoring.[138] *Calamus*, which is the Latin word for "cane," was another aromatic ingredient in expensive perfumes. *Calamus*, cinnamon, and spikenard did not grow in the Middle East but only in India and Sri Lanka. The mention of these plants by Solomon points to early and extensive trade links between Israel and South Asia.

Frankincense is an aromatic gum resin containing fragrant oil which was used for perfume and incense; it is mentioned in the Pentateuch regarding the incense used in the sanctuary (Exod. 30:34-36) and was one of the three gifts brought by the Magi to the infant Jesus (Matt. 2:11).

Aloes, which are succulent plants of many varieties, are mentioned in combination with myrrh in other verses in the Bible. Myrrh and aloes were used for perfuming (Psalm 45:8) and for embalming the dead (John 19:39).

THE DAUGHTERS OF JERUSALEM

Who are these daughters of Jerusalem whose words and questions are interspersed amongst the communications of the Shulamite and her beloved? In the Bible, "daughters" can refer to any woman, to female inhabitants of a place or city, or to women who professed to follow the religion of a particular city. In the Song of Solomon, these daughters appear to be inhabitants of Jerusalem who are mostly young, unmarried women. Or they could be female servants who worked within Solomon's palaces and houses. In Ecclesiastes 2:7-8, he writes that he had many servants and many singers, both male and female. It is likely that when the

---

138 *Britannica*, s.v. "Plants," accessed March 10, 2021, https://www.britannica.com/browse/Plants.

Shulamite married King Solomon, she would have had her own female servants who attended her in much the same way as members of the royal family have ladies-in-waiting. These maidservants would grow close to Solomon's bride, and they would share many conversations, as women often do.

In Song of Solomon 1:3, the Shulamite says that because of Solomon's attractive character, which she depicts as being like "ointment poured forth," the daughters of Jerusalem loved him: "Therefore the virgins love you" (1:3b). In a marriage, other people should be able to see what an honorable person the wife has for a husband and vice versa: others who look on should see a healthy relationship and be themselves enriched by this marital union. Children and young people should, in this way, be able to form a good opinion of the married state, or they will become disillusioned and think that marriage is not worthwhile. Consequently, they may not seek to form deep relationships with the opposite sex.

THE LANGUAGE OF ROMANTIC LOVE

We can now examine some of the language which the lovers in the Song of Solomon use in order to express their deep love for one another:

"I *am* dark, but lovely (1:5-6)."

The Shulamite tells the daughters of Jerusalem not to stare at her because of her darkened skin. She says she is "dark, but lovely" and explains to them how her brothers forced her to work outdoors in the vineyards; and this is how the sun had deeply tanned her skin. She compares her dark skin to "the tents of Kedar," which were made of black cloth and inhabited by nomadic tribes, and also to the dark "curtains of Solomon" (1:5). The daughters of Jerusalem would have maintained a pale skin in order to look refined and because paler skin was seen as a prerequisite for gaining a husband.

"I have compared you, my love, To my filly among Pharaoh's chariots"(1:9).

This seems a strange compliment to pay to the young woman whom he adores! But the meaning of it is this: Pharaoh's chariot was pulled by several pairs of horses, but a prize mare was chosen to lead the chariot all alone at the front. That mare was uniquely noble and the most beautiful of all the horses. This is how special his beloved was to him—a chosen prize who surpassed all other women.

"His banner over me *was* love" (2:4).

The Shulamite sees Solomon's love as a banner covering her and protecting her. This should be the experience of every woman when she is in the company of her husband. He should be present to protect and comfort his wife when necessary. S. Craig Glickman views the banner which she refers to here as the high, wide banner which was used in battle to show the soldiers which way to go.[139] A banner is seen by other people, and therefore, those around the couple would be well aware of the husband's love for his wife; this causes a wife to feel secure in her husband's love.

"'O, my dove . . . Let me see your face, Let me hear your voice" (2:14).

Doves in Israel would often hide in the rocky gaps in the mountains, and nobody would see or hear them. Solomon is comparing his lover to one of these doves, and he wants to hear her speak to him more and thus get to know her better. He doesn't want her to be hidden any more like she was while laboring in her vineyards, but he desires to see her beautiful face and hear the sound of her voice. How important verbal communication is, especially between two people in a courtship and in marriage. In today's society, with the preponderance of social media usage, where it is all too easy to post things which can lead to misunderstandings and strife, how different and more fulfilling it is to talk face to face. This is the best way to get to know someone, and it's the pathway to forming deep friendships. Young people in particular need to practice and work at talking to one another without the constant distraction of messages and updates on their mobile phones.

---

139 Glickman, ibid.

"My beloved *is* mine, and I *am* his" (2:16).

The Shulamite is longing to have and hold her beloved fully in matrimonial union. In the next verse, she urges him to return hastily "like a gazelle Or a young stag Upon the mountains" which separate them. It could be that Solomon has returned to Jerusalem after visiting her, and she is missing him.

"Do not stir up nor awaken love Until it pleases."

This warning appears three times in the Song of Solomon:
1. The Shulamite tells the daughters of Jerusalem this in Song of Solomon 2:7.
2. Solomon gives this warning to the daughters of Jerusalem in Song of Solomon 3:5.
3. The Shulamite again quotes his warning to the daughters of Jerusalem in Song of Solomon 8:4.

Since this exhortation appears three times, I believe that God is saying that it has an important message for us in the present time. It is warning us not to stimulate love artificially, not to try to manufacture love to suit our own purposes, and not to push too hard if a budding relationship is obviously not in the will of God. It is telling us to wait for God's time and to know that in His perfect plan for our lives, He will bring the person across our path whom He wants us to marry. God is to be trusted, and we must believe that He has our best interests at heart in this most serious of matters—that of finding our marriage partner. It is not wise to rush into a marriage if we are not certain that it is the will of God for our lives.

Sometimes, God calls us to wait; and while we wait, we can live a totally fulfilled life as a single person if we look to God and trust Him totally to make provision for us. In addition, it is not wise for single women in churches to chase after a particular man whom they believe would make a good husband for them, especially if he has shown no interest in having a relationship with them. Men are quite capable of noticing a woman and approaching her to ask her out if they want. The above verse warns us not to manipulate or pursue love until the time is right and God gives us the partner of His choosing. The last word—"pleases" or "please"—can also mean "is proper." So, the warning could include a reminder not to let passions be stirred too strongly such that sexual activity takes place before marriage. An excellent book for those waiting on God for a marriage partner is *God is a Matchmaker* by Derek Prince and Ruth Prince.

At the same time, God may often *not* choose a partner for us. God's will can be broad in these matters, yet He asks us to choose a partner within His will. In other words, there are many potential life partners within God's will for us, as long as they are equally yoked in faith to Jesus and they likewise choose us. The author Jerry Sittser has written extensively about this.[140]

"Catch us the little foxes that spoil the vines" (Song of Sol. 2:15).

Because she had vineyards to look after, the Shulamite would have had experience with wild foxes—most likely the Syrian fox—and their cubs causing damage to her tender grapes, and she would need to control these animals. What she is saying to her beloved Solomon is that she does not want anything, however small, to interfere with the tender, new love which they have for each other.

In his book *A Song for Lovers,* S. Craig Glickman puts it this way: "The foxes represent as many obstacles or temptations as have plagued lovers throughout the centuries: guilt, mistrust, jealousy, selfishness, pride, unforgiveness, unacknowledged faults."[141] He also notes that because the verse says, "Catch us"—meaning "let *us* catch" rather than "let *me* catch,"—it shows that both of them must resolve to protect and preserve their love. It is a joint effort.

"And see King Solomon with the crown With which his mother has crowned him on the day of his wedding" (Song of Sol. 3:6-11).

Solomon's wedding procession, as described in these verses, was a truly magnificent sight as it came gliding out of the wilderness (v. 6). Solomon was

---

140   Jerry Sittser, *The Will of God as a Way of Life* (Grand Rapids: Zondervan, 2004).
141   Glickman, ibid.

seated in his palanquin, which had been specially made out of cedarwood from Lebanon with posts of silver, a back of gold, the seat of purple cloth, and the interior lovingly and intricately wrought in needlework by the daughters of Jerusalem. The palanquin was surrounded by "sixty valiant men" of Israel (v. 7), each with a sword upon his thigh. It was like a full-dress military wedding where only the best would do. In ancient Israel, the bridegroom wore a crown on his head. Verse eleven tells us that King Solomon is wearing "the crown With which his mother crowned him On the day of his wedding." This does not refer to a king's regal crowning.

The closest we can get to picturing the scene would be to see on television a royal wedding procession travel through the streets of London, England, with the ornate carriages surrounded and protected by the household cavalry in military uniform, with each rider bearing a sword by his side. In keeping with Jewish wedding customs, it is likely that the event described here is Solomon's return to take his chosen bride to be his wife.

S. Craig Glickman writes, "A wedding should have great significance because it marks the entrance into a whole new way of life where two people become one. Living together before marriage minimizes the significance and newness of this special binding together as one."[142] At a wedding in modern times, the man and woman make their vows in front of witnesses, and this should not be taken lightly. Most weddings include a time of feasting and sharing with relatives and friends. In the time of Solomon, there could be many days of feasting for the guests after the legally binding betrothal and usually after the consummation of the marriage.

"Behold, you *are* fair, my love! You have dove's eyes behind your veil" (Song of Sol. 4:1).

The Shulamite bride is prepared and dressed for her wedding. Brides were veiled in ancient Israel. This is what allowed Laban to trick Jacob into marrying Leah instead of Rachel, whom he loved. He had sexual relations with Leah,

---

142 Ibid.

thinking she was Rachel, and only discovered the trick the next morning, once her veil was removed.

"Your hair *is* like a flock of goats" (Song of Sol. 4:1).

This seems a strange compliment to pay to his beloved! However, in the culture of that time where the economy was based on agriculture, a flock of goats denoted great wealth and abundance. Similarly, Solomon compares her teeth to a flock of shorn sheep (4:2) and her temples to the halves of a pomegranate (4:3). These similes have highly positive connotations.

"A garden enclosed *Is* my sister. . . A fountain sealed" (Song of Sol. 4:12).

Solomon describes the Shulamite as, "A garden enclosed . . . A spring shut up . . . A fountain sealed." In the Middle East, where water is often in short supply, if a spring of pure water was discovered, then the landowner would build a wall around it, seal the fountain, and protect it by locking it with a key, so that no one could steal the water or misuse it. Solomon saw his beloved in this way, like a life-giving fountain which he jealously wanted to protect and cherish.[143] It also refers to her premarital chastity: she had kept herself sealed until she met the man she was to marry. After their wedding, Solomon can enter the garden, as described in chapter four, and unseal the precious fountain so that it becomes a well of living waters.

In the New Testament, Paul describes believers as being marked with a seal by the Holy Spirit, Who guarantees our inheritance in Christ (Eph. 1:13, 4:30). This means that we belong completely to Christ and that He protects our salvation and eternal inheritance from any interference by Satan.

"I have come to my garden . . . Eat, O friends! Drink, yes, drink deeply, O beloved ones" (Song of Sol. 5:1).

Solomon uses metaphors pertaining to food and wine to describe the sexual enjoyment of their union. There are sensations of "sight, smell and taste"

---

143 Ray Bentley, *God's Pursuing Love* (Calvary Chapel Publishing, 2003).

described in these verses.[144] The word "garden" in Greek is *paradeiso* and denotes a place where everything between the couple is perfect.

The Shulamite, who sees herself as a garden, has asked him to "blow upon my garden, *That* its spices may flow out. Let my beloved come to his garden And eat its pleasant fruits" (4:16). This shows the bride as she invites her bridegroom to consummate their union. Solomon then says, "I have come into my garden" (5:1): her garden is also his garden as they unite in the consummation.

Many believe that the second part of the verse is an instruction to the couple by God Himself to eat and drink deeply of sexual love within marriage. It confirms to us that God is present with a Christian couple during their lovemaking and that He is pleased with their enjoyment. He is glorified in it, and therefore, there should be no feelings of guilt or shame.

"My sister, *my* spouse" (Song of Sol. 4:9-10, 12; 5:1-2).

The use of the term "sister" along with "spouse" denotes complete purity in the woman as though she is a female friend to Solomon; yet, she is now his wife as well. He speaks amidst the ardent passion experienced by the newly married couple.

The Two Dreams

Two dreams which the Shulamite experienced are recorded in the Song of Solomon. The first one is described in 3:1-5. Since the account begins with the words, "By night on my bed," it seems accurate to say that she was asleep and dreaming, although some commentators believe otherwise.

In her dream, her beloved has gone away, and she is looking for him but does not know where to find him. She goes outside and wanders around the city looking for him; then, at last, she finds him and will not let him go. I think she may have had this dream during the interval when Solomon had left his country estate where she lived and worked and had returned to Jerusalem to make preparations

---

144 Ariel Rudolph, "The Bible and Agriculture," Israel Today online, November 10, 2019, https://www.israeltoday.co.il/read/the-bible-and-agriculture.

to marry her. In line with Jewish marriage tradition, he would return and claim her as his bride when the time was right. She must have been feeling anxious and was worried that he may not return for her, especially since she felt somewhat unworthy of his love. But in the dream, she finds reassurance and comfort because she found him and held onto him.

The second dream appears in 5:1-7. Again, some commentators do not think this passage is about a dream but rather about a real event. However, looking at the account as a dream, her beloved knocks at her door and "put[s] his hand By the latch" (5:4). However, she does not feel like getting up for him as she is already in bed. He leaves the dwelling; and then she regrets not answering the door to him, so she gets up, dresses, and unlocks the door. Her beloved has left some myrrh perfume for her on the door latch: her "hands dripped *with* myrrh" (5:5).

She then goes out to look for her beloved. She asks the city watchmen if they have seen him, but they are unkind to her and pull off her veil. She encounters the daughters of Jerusalem, but on this occasion, they, too, are unkind and mocking, asking her what is so special about her beloved (v. 9).

Whether the dream ends here or not is unclear, but in the next passage, she tells the daughters of Jerusalem that he is the "Chief among ten thousand" (v. 10). This descriptive phrase was a common expression in Israel, meaning simply "the greatest of all." Solomon was, indeed, the greatest earthly king for a brief period of history, but Christ will be King of kings forever. Jesus said of Himself in Matthew 12:42, "a greater than Solomon *is* here."

The Shulamite then gives a long description of her beloved in glowing, complimentary terms, finishing with the phrase, "Yes, he *is* altogether lovely. This *is* my beloved, And this *is* my friend" (v. 16). She shows gratitude at having his love and even tells them, in a beautifully poetic way, how much she admires and adores his physical body (v. 10-15). The wife speaks favorably about her husband to the daughters of Jerusalem.

How much better it is for a woman to speak well of her husband when she talks to her female friends. I am always saddened when I hear a woman speaking ill of her husband, criticizing him and complaining about his behavior. Ingratitude and pride are the main roots of problems which arise in a marriage. A wife should respect her husband and not always insist on getting her own way.

"My beloved put his hand by the latch of *the door*" (Song of Sol. 5:4).

This sentence seems a strange expression in the New King James Version. Yet through his research, Fred H. Wight[145] realized that in Middle Eastern countries at that time, the door latch and lock were on the inside, and anyone entering had to put their hand through a hole in the outer door to reach the latch or key and open the door. Leaving fragrant, liquid myrrh on the door latch was a sign to her that he had come to see her, like an affectionate love note left behind.

This second dream has similarities to the first in that she is anxious that she has missed her beloved when he came looking for her, and she looks for him once more in the city where nobody wants to help her. She wakens and realizes that her beloved has not forsaken her, nor is he lost somewhere. If her dream occurred after she was married, when she would most likely have her own special bedroom in the palace, it could indicate that Solomon was perhaps away on important duties. She was missing his company and she was adjusting to being the wife of a king, which meant time spent apart from him. It is difficult to see the second dream as a real event because it would be unlikely that a woman would go out alone and walk through the city by night with her head veiled, which would tend to mark her out as a prostitute, whereas she was, in reality, the fiancée or wife of King Solomon himself. In my opinion, it is a dream.

"O my love, you *are as* . . . Awesome as *an army* with banners" (Song of Sol. 6:4).

Solomon compares the beauty of his beloved to a great, conquering army with unfurled battle flags, which would cause awe in the eyes of a beholder. He says that her eyes have overcome him: they are almost too lovely and penetrating to

---

145   Fred H. Wight, *Manners and Customs of Bible Lands* (Chicago: Moody Publishers, 1953).

gaze into.[146] Then in verse ten, a question is asked by the ladies who are mentioned in verse nine (i.e. the daughters, the queens, and concubines): "Who is she?" They compare her appearance and presence to a progression of gradually increasing light, starting with the dim light of dawn, then the silvery brightness of moonlight, and finally as the full brightness of sunshine. They finish their description by quoting Solomon's words that she is "awesome as an army with banners." The picture of a great conquering army is also a type of the Church of Christ, who with Christ as the Head, will one day be totally victorious over the devil and his cohorts.

"I *am* my beloved's, And my beloved *is* mine" (Song of Sol. 6:3).

"He feeds *his flock* among the lilies," says the bride to the daughters of Jerusalem when they ask her where he has gone. This is a poetic expression of her knowledge of his love for her. The Shulamite can declare these words with certainty, even when they are apart and when he is elsewhere. She is secure in the knowledge that because of their commitment to one another, he loves her and will not leave her. S. Craig Glickman writes that marriage provides firm boundaries within which any problems are to be worked out together.[147]

"What would you see in the Shulamite—As it were, the dance of the two camps" (Song of Sol. 6:13).

The daughters of Jerusalem call the Shulamite to return. And in response to her question, "What would you see in the Shulamite?," they say that they would like the "dance of the two camps" (armies). The name of this dance is *Mahanaim*, which is the place where Jacob was met by the angels of God and where he divided his retinue into two camps or companies (Gen. 32:2). It is likely that a victory dance was initiated to celebrate this occasion.

Mike Shreve[148] explains that the dance of *Mahanaim* was a traditional title for an ancient Hebrew wedding dance, where the bridegroom and his companions danced before the bride in a demonstration of strength and mastery. Then the

---

146   Henry M. Morris, *The Remarkable Wisdom of Solomon* (Green Forest: Master Books, 2001).
147   Glickman, ibid.
148   www.shreveministries.org

bride performed a dance before the bridegroom to show her love and devotion for him and also to reveal her beauty. However, Morris believes that the *Mahanaim* dance is performed by the bride for her new husband when they are alone together. The *Dance of Mahanaim* is still performed as a female solo dance for entertainment in modern Israel.[149]

"I *am* my beloved's, And his desire *is* toward me" (Song of Sol. 7:10).

Full of admiration for the Shulamite's beauty (7:1-5), Solomon lovingly compliments his bride and expresses his desire for her in an obviously erotic manner; the mandrakes in 7:13 were a well-known aphrodisiac. She responds with this phrase, "I am my beloved's, And his desire *is* toward me" (v. 10). By this time, it is likely that the couple have been married for a period of time, and she is saying that she belongs totally to her husband.

"His desire" here means sexual desire, which is directed fully toward his bride. The same rare Hebrew word for *desire* is used in Genesis 3:16, where God tells Eve that her "desire *shall be* [for your] husband." Timothy Keller writes: "Sex is God's appointed way for two people to reciprocally say to one another, 'I belong completely, permanently and exclusively to you. It is the most powerful, God-created way to help you to give your entire self to another human being of the opposite sex."[150]

Making love is an intimate connection and a breaking down of walls between husband and wife.[151] This is part of being "one flesh," the other part being the physical union. God created the sexual organs and designed the act of sex for marriage. Sexual activity within marriage is pure and holy.

Marriage is the start of a new life together, and love between a husband and wife should continually grow and not diminish. In addition, love-making, which provides nourishment for the marriage bond, should grow and develop from the initial consummation throughout the years which follow. According

149 Henry M. Morris, *The Remarkable Wisdom of Solomon* (Green Forest: Master Books, 2001), 56.
150 Timothy and Kathy Keller, *The Meaning of Marriage* (New York: Riverhead Books, 2011).
151 Douglas E. Rosenau, *A Celebration of Sex* (Nashville: Thomas Nelson, 2002).

to S. C. Glickman, "Greater knowledge produces a deeper love. It is a growth in perfection from the initial love at the start of the marriage to a far deeper love as time passes; there is a growth in familiarity, a maturity of their relationship, a different mood from the delicate formality of the wedding night."

On the contrary, any type of sexual activity outside the confines of marriage is sin; this is clearly outlined in the Bible. As lovers, a husband and wife are to entrust the most private parts of the body to one another and to no other person.[152] In Proverbs 5:15-19, Solomon instructs every man to "drink water from your own cistern [of a pure marriage relationship] And running water from your own well." He goes on: "Let them be only your own, And not for strangers with you."

Solomon, who must have experienced a deep, loving relationship with his first wife, says, "Rejoice in the wife of your youth" (v. 18); he describes her as "*a loving deer and a graceful doe*" (v. 19), which speaks of gentleness and attractiveness. And he further exhorts husbands to "let her breasts satisfy you at all times; And always be enraptured with her love" (v. 19) before giving warnings about the dangers of adultery and sexual relations with an immoral woman (v. 20).

"Oh, that you were like my brother" (Song of Sol. 8:1).

In the culture of this time, it was not proper to express affection publicly except to members of one's family. If he was her real brother, "who nursed at my mother's breasts" (8:1), then it would be in order to kiss him in public, so she would not be despised for doing so.

"I would cause you to drink of spiced wine, Of the juice of my pomegranate" (Song of Sol. 8:2).

The Shulamite wants to take Solomon to her mother's house where she grew up and to offer him spiced wine made from the pomegranates which she had grown in her orchard. The same Hebrew word is used in the Bible to describe both unfermented and fermented wine. There is no mention of drunkenness in this passage; Solomon wrote very graphically about the consequences and

---

152   Rosenau, ibid.

dangers of becoming intoxicated with alcohol in Proverbs 23:29-35. "Who has woe? Who has sorrow? Who has contentions? Who has complaints? Who has wounds without cause? Those who linger long at the wine" (Prov. 23:29). He describes the temptation to drink to excess, but the resultant effects are, "It bites like a serpent, And stings like a viper. Your eyes will see strange things, And your heart will utter perverse things" (v. 32-33). An intoxicated person could get struck but not be aware they are hurt and not feel pain (v. 35), but despite all this, their only desire is to seek another drink on waking up (v. 35). Also in Proverbs 20:1, he writes, "Wine *is* a mocker, Strong drink *is* a brawler."

What Solomon has described so pictorially regarding drunkenness has been relevant through the centuries which followed and is confirmed in the present day. In the UK, current National Health Service guidance is as follows: "The short-term effects of alcohol misuse include accidents and injuries, violent behaviour or being a victim of violence, unprotected sex that could lead to an unplanned pregnancy or sexually transmitted disease, loss of personal possessions through theft or being unconscious, and alcohol poisoning resulting in seizures."[153] Long-term risks include liver disease, heart disease, stroke, and various cancers as well as social problems like homelessness, divorce, and unemployment.[154] It is, without doubt, of tremendous importance, especially for young people, to pay attention to the warnings which Solomon wrote down regarding excessive drinking of alcohol and of drunkenness.

"Set me as a seal upon your heart" (Song of Sol. 8:6a).

A seal had the signature of the owner or writer and was a jealously guarded possession. In Old Testament times, it was often an engraved ring, which was pressed into hot wax and then used to seal a letter or mark a document. Seals were still used to close and mark handwritten letters up until the early 1900s. The Shulamite responded to Solomon by saying, "Set me as a seal upon your heart, As

---

153   "Risks: Alcohol Misuse," NHS.uk, accessed March 11, 2021, https://www.nhs.uk/conditions/alcohol-misuse/risks.
154   Ibid.

a seal upon your arm." Ray Bentley explains what the Shulamite meant: "Mark me as your own, embrace me, encompass me, surround me, be with me, never leave me."[155] "Upon your heart" refers to his thoughts and affections, while "upon your arm" refers to his actions and his strength.

"Love *is as* strong as death, Jealousy *as* cruel
as the grave" (Song of Sol. 8:6b).

It appears to be the bride herself who is saying these deeply meaningful words to Solomon. Glickman writes, "She likened the strength of love to death, which is irreversible both by man and circumstance; death conquers all in its path. Love is also possessive in the sense of being intensely and jealously concerned for the one who is loved and their well-being."[156]

"Many waters cannot quench love, Nor can the
floods drown it" (Song of Sol. 8:7a).

Waters and floods can come and go in our lives, but they can never overcome true love. Isaiah 43:2 gives us the promise that when we pass through waters of adversity, God will be with us, and the rivers which we struggle through will not overwhelm us. In the same way, genuine love will persevere through any trials which come in married life—illness, problems with children, poverty, or strife in family relationships. Every marriage will experience times of adversity and difficulty, but we have God's promise that the love between husband and wife will not be quenched or overcome during these crises. I am well aware that things sometimes go wrong for various reasons—and I do not want to sound simplistic—but exploring these issues is beyond the scope of my writing here.

"If a man would give for love All the wealth of his house,
It would be utterly despised" (Song of Sol. 8:7b).

In his book, *The Remarkable Wisdom of Solomon*, Henry Morris explains this part of the verse as follows: "A man would be despised for reducing love and the

155   Bentley, ibid.
156   Glickman, ibid

woman he loved to an object with monetary value; love must be given and not bought. Love is not an object to be bought because love is priceless."[157]

"Solomon had a vineyard at Baal Hamon" (Song of Sol. 8:11).

Verse eleven tells us that Solomon's vineyard was at Baal Hamon, which means the "place of a multitude." He is thought to have had extensive vineyards in this location, which was most likely in Lebanon to the north of Israel. This is where the Shulamite's family leased vineyards from him and payment would change hands as described in 8:12.

Lebanon is mentioned a few times in the Song of Solomon. "Come with me from Lebanon" (4:8). Amana, Senir, and Hermon are mountains in Lebanon— "from the lions' dens, From the mountains of the leopards" (4:8). Wild animals are known to abound in Lebanon's mountain ranges. Solomon compared the fragrance of the Shulamite's garments to the "fragrance of Lebanon" (4:11) and compared her to "living waters, And streams flowing from Lebanon" (4:15). Also, when describing his wife's beauty, he says, "Your nose *is* like the tower of Lebanon, Which looks toward Damascus" (7:4).

"What shall we do for our sister In the day when she is spoken for" (Song of Sol. 8:8).

The bride is gathered with her family and wedding guests in her mother's cottage. Her brothers remind her of her childhood when "she has no breasts" (v. 8a) and how her brothers had cared for her until the day of her wedding— that is, "when she is spoken for" in marriage. She does not seem to bear a grudge against her brothers. It looks as though they had done their duty in protecting her from wrong advances from men who were not suitable for her. This is metaphorically described as "enclose her With boards of cedar" (v. 9). On the contrary, "If she *is* a wall, We will build upon her A battlement of silver" denotes her chaste life leading to something of value—in other words, a good marriage. They may have forced her to work in the vineyard, but they did do

157 Morris, ibid.

their part in preparing her for her marriage. She had also played a part by being careful and exercising healthy self-protection: "I *am* a wall, And my breasts like towers" (8:10). If only more young girls would be like her, instead of entering into sexual relations in their teenage years with many different boys without any thought of serious commitment.

"My own vineyard *is* before me" (Song of Sol. 8:12).

The Shulamite has metaphorically described herself as a vineyard a number of times. First, she says in Song of Solomon 1:6 that she has not taken care of her own vineyard; she has been too busy working and has not valued herself or thought much of her appearance. Now, in verse twelve, she can say that her own vineyard is hers to give. She is giving herself totally in every part to her husband, and she has developed a healthy self-esteem.

"The companions listen for your voice" (Song of Sol. 8:13).

The bride, or perhaps her brothers, say that her attendants are listening for his voice. In the very last verse (8:14) of the Song of Solomon, the Shulamite tells her beloved to come quickly. "Make haste, my beloved and come quickly, like a gazelle or a young stag upon the mountains of spices." The words indicate that she is calling him to come; therefore, the words here cannot be taken to represent Jesus calling for us. At the start of their courtship, in Song of Solomon 2:9, she had described him as being "like a gazelle or a young stag," leaping upon the mountains (v. 8) and then standing behind the wall of her house and looking through the windows and calling her to come away with him. Now, finally, she is impatiently waiting for him to come for her so that they can begin their married life together.

WHY IS THE SONG OF SOLOMON USUALLY INTERPRETED AS AN ALLEGORY?

The Song of Solomon speaks plainly of a godly marriage between a husband and wife who love each other. Some of Satan's strongest attacks on biblical viewpoints have been mounted against Christian marriage—never more so than in our present day. "Love between a husband and wife is seen as a divine imperative and as the fulfillment of the will of God. The Song of Solomon teaches us that romantic, sensual love is His gift for marriage, and that God honors and blesses this love between a man and a woman."[158]

Why are Christians afraid to read the Song of Solomon as an actual account of a blossoming romance leading to a godly marriage? Over the centuries, three types of philosophy that are contrary to God's Word have affected Christian thinking and have distorted God's viewpoint on marriage and sexual love—the Greek stoics, the Greek philosopher, Plato, and the Gnostic cults.

The Greek stoics despised human emotion and began the custom of using allegories and symbols to explain human passions and emotions. Plato taught that people should renounce the earthly and the physical side of love in order to acquire the spiritual because it was not possible for mankind to have both. This view has actually strongly influenced Christian teaching, especially in some church denominations. The Gnostic cults believed in separation of the physical from the spiritual; therefore, in the case of marriage, they taught that human sexuality should be renounced and that the ideal was to have a marriage with the Spirit. Again, this has influenced the doctrine taught in some church denominations, even today.

These influences have led to the Song of Solomon being spiritualized, whereby the courtship and marriage which are described therein are merely a symbol of mystical marriage with God. In the Middle Ages, biblical teachers saw the Song of Solomon as a spiritualized allegory without any reference at all to human love and marriage. Celibacy was regarded at the time as the greatest of virtues. In the sixteenth century, the Puritans and other Reformers began to see the Song of Solomon as a descriptive book which celebrated perfect married love and, therefore, a book which could be used to give instruction on God-given sexual love between a husband and wife within the privacy of matrimony. However, the Victorians in the

---

158   Ed Wheat and Gloria Okes Perkins, *Love Life for Every Married Couple* (Grand Rapids: Zondervan, 1980).

nineteenth century preferred allegorical interpretations of the Song of Solomon because discussion about sexual matters and bodily functions were considered embarrassing and immodest in this era, including by Queen Victoria herself.

The allegorical viewpoint has continued for many decades and been widely taught in churches with no consideration given to the view that the Song of Solomon contains definite teaching on love within marriage. In many churches, a literal interpretation of the book is never discussed, nor the fact that it contains a beautifully written description in exquisite poetic language of courtship, deep love, a marriage ceremony, and subsequent married life. But, as outlined above, the over-spiritualized viewpoints originate in non-Christian philosophies, which have permeated much of the Christian Church.

To the pagan mind, holiness and purity belonged to people who had renounced sex forever but not to a married couple engaging in sexual activity. Virginity became the symbol of spirituality. In the Roman Empire, the vestal virgins represented ideal virtue. Pagan attitudes toward love, sex, and marriage clashed head-on with the correct biblical teaching on these matters. Many teachings on love and marriage can be found in the Bible (e.g. Gen. 2; Prov. 5; Jesus' teachings in the Gospels including His references to Gen. 2:24; Paul's teachings in Eph. 5 and 1 Cor. 7), including in the Song of Solomon. Therefore, we must take heed and seek out correct teaching according to and in line with God's Word. Fortunately, in recent years, more churches are aware of the dangers of exclusively allegorical interpretations and are endeavoring to study the Bible in a more literal way and to keep its teaching in context.

HOW THE SONG OF SOLOMON CAN HELP US HAVE A BETTER MARRIAGE

We can learn many helpful things from observing how the couple interact and how they treat one another in the Song of Solomon. Right from the start, Solomon skillfully and lovingly built up the Shulamite's self-image; he praised her in the areas where she felt most insecure. He did not criticize her, even when she may have deserved it, and his words to her were always positive. He continually complimented her on her beauty, both of face and of body, and told her again and again how perfectly beautiful she was and the effect which she had on him.

In the Song of Solomon, we see a free exchange of love between husband and wife, and we see how they both appear to play an equal role in the love affair: it is neither dominated by the man nor by the woman. The Shulamite showed her love for him by her response to him when he praised her and complimented her. She thought of him, even when he was absent, and longed for him to come quickly and return to her side. He wanted to hear her voice and listen to her words.

CONCLUSION

In the Song of Solomon, we have a picture of Solomon's ardent love for his young wife, the Shulamite, during the years of his youth. What were the factors and experiences in Solomon's life which affected his integrity and led him to change his thinking regarding marriage and faithfulness to one wife? As he grew into maturity and eventually took many wives and concubines, including foreign women, what were the reasons which brought about his departure from God's ways? These questions are examined in "Part 3, A Time to Tear Down."

PART 3
A TIME TO TEAR DOWN

BY: ARCHIE W. N. ROY

THE TIMNA VALLEY IS TO be found about nineteen miles north of Eilat, an Israeli port and resort city on the Red Sea. The valley no longer has abundant reserves of copper ore, but the archaeological remains there reveal that copper was mined in and around the valley for thousands of years. Copper was an important commodity in the Iron Age and was used for jewelry, stone-cutting tools, weapon-making, and as a trade good. Archaeologists have investigated scores of copper mines and smelting camp sites at Timna and uncovered many different remains, including those of ancient worship practices and a variety of organic remains, such as textiles, preserved very well in the extremely arid conditions. These have usually been radiocarbon dated to the reign of Solomon. It seems that under Solomon, mining activity at Timna was increased dramatically.

Since the nineteenth century A.D., archaeologists working in the Middle East have uncovered evidence which authenticates the Bible's historical accounts. Their work in the Timna Valley is one of the more recent examples. This authentication has to do with verification of details in Scripture but can also add to Scripture. Although we will see in Part 3 of our book, for instance, that Scripture points to the rough area where Solomon's mines were located, it is silent on exactly where they were. Neither does Scripture focus in on the conditions which Solomon's miners had to endure, but these have also come to light now. The findings are disturbing in themselves, but they also point to something more compelling and significant— that there was a very dark and oppressive side to Solomon's time in power.

Timna is one of the hottest places on the planet, with summer temperatures often climbing as high as 125 degrees Fahrenheit. Copper smelting also requires very intense furnace heat. For instance, the slave labor alluded to in 1 Kings 9 would have been indescribably difficult in locations such as the Timna mines. Excavated mining shafts sink to more than ninety feet below the surface and down into the copper-rich sandstone. Heavy weights of ore would have to be mined, pulled through narrow tunnels, and then hauled to the surface. The conclusion many have reached is that these ancient sites reveal the reality of slave labor in Solomon's time. There is just no way that free laborers would tolerate such harsh conditions, even for good remuneration.

In Part 3, we consider the biblical account of Solomon's departure from God. We investigate the reasons for his drifting away and the effects of the drift for both Solomon and for Israel. The results for Israel are fairly well known. The united monarchy did not survive Solomon and the fractured state divided in two. Although the rulers of Israel were more flawed than the rulers of Judah, neither successor state was able to last for long because of apostasy and corruption. Yet far less attention has been paid to why Solomon departed from his pursuit of Yahweh and what the personal effects were for him. If we can understand both of these issues, there are surely lessons for us all. It is not merely an exercise in Bible Study, although any attempt to understand a character Scripture focuses so much on is worth pursuing for its own sake.

It is actually a study of personality. The key question is a psychological one. Are there reasons in terms of personality traits and characteristics which help to explain Solomon's apostasy? Are there explanatory factors for it which have to do with his relationships with his parents and/or siblings? We will attempt to understand the king's personality as far as it is possible, given the evidence. In Solomon's case, we have two types of direct evidence: facts concerning him and the books whose authorship is attributed to him. We consider both types of evidence. We will also consider the question of personality effects. As Solomon drifted further away from Yahweh, how did he change as a man and as a ruler? This is a good time to investigate these matters, given that we have already looked at the king's family of origin, his rise to power, and his early commitment to Yahweh. We have also looked at the broad religious and literary themes which he himself focused on as a writer inspired by God. What about the man himself and his character flaws? Is it possible to understand these things?

CHAPTER 22

THE TEMPLE AS A WORK OF THE FLESH

> When Solomon was about to build the Temple he applied to Pharaoh, King of Egypt, for builders and architects. Pharaoh ordered his astrologers to choose all the men who would die in the current year; and these he sent to Solomon. The latter, however, by simply looking at them, knew what their fate was to be; consequently, he provided them with coffins and shrouds and sent them back to Egypt.[159]

We now have to turn to the ways in which Solomon failed to measure up or to be more precise, the ways in which Solomon went adrift after the temple's construction. Given his wisdom and even his theophoric name, his change of direction is hard to understand. Indeed, the Jewish rabbis only made sense of it by creating teachings and lore around Solomon's alliance with demons, even during the construction of the temple.

The Talmud describes, for instance, a long series of events involving Solomon and some of his court officials where he sought and obtained help from demonic sources to find the *shamir*, a stone-eating worm which would enable him to have the temple's stones cut without the use of tools which may also be used in war.[160] Strangely, in very recent times, something akin to the

---

159 Rabbi Emil Gustav Hirsch, et al., *The 1906 Jewish Encyclopedia*, s.v. "Solomon," (JewishEncyclopedia.com, 2002).
160 Tractate Gittin 68a, Seffaria, *The William Davidson Talmud: digital edition of the Babylonian Talmud*, https://www.sefaria.org/Gittin.68a?lang=bi (accessed August 22, 2019).

shamir has been discovered.[161] Perhaps I should say *rediscovered*. This finding does not confirm that the Talmudic stories are true, but it does make them more intriguing. In any case, we start our next section of this book at the heart of Solomon's kingdom, the organization of a monotheistic faith through the construction of the temple.

It was by no means certain that the temple would be built. There had been conflict between the prophets as to whether it was right or wrong to have it constructed. These forces were antagonistic to each other, and each sought to influence King David. The temple builders won out, but their opponents worked to deny them this and then to delay the project. Commentators such as Henri Gaubert describe the situation in some depth. David's prophet, Nathan, was opposed to the temple idea. The king had shed too much blood in warfare, and besides that, Yahweh was content to dwell in a tent (i.e. where the ark had dwelt on Mount Sinai).

But another of David's powerful prophets, Gad, had a different mindset. In fact, Gad instructed David to build an initial altar on the threshing floor on Mount Moriah. David paid the owner for the land and did as instructed. Gad then allowed David to immediately lurch into a passion for building not just an altar but also an entire temple. The angel manifestation was taken as God's permission to build. David was devoted to Yahweh and devoted to the temple idea. In a spontaneous song before the Israelite assembly, he says: "For we *are* aliens and pilgrims before You, As *were* all our fathers; Our days on earth *are* as a shadow, And without hope. 'O LORD our God, all this abundance that we have prepared to build You a house for Your holy name is from Your hand, and *is* all Your own'" (1 Chron. 29:15-16).

Much of the materials used for the temple were plundered loot accumulated by King David from his raids into pagan kingdoms such as Edom, Zobah, Amalek, Ammon, and Moab. For instance, Solomon used much of the bronze taken from

---

161 Adam Eliyahu Berkowitz, Recently Discovered Rock-eating Worm Could Be Key to Building Third Temple," Israel365News.com, June 30, 2019, https://www.israel365news.com/132404/recently-discovered-rock-eating-worm-key-third-temple.

Zobah to create the bronze Sea for the temple courtyard, the twin pillars at the temple entrance, and much else besides.[162] The rest came from a trade agreement with Hiram, king of Tyre.

Although Solomon had great admiration for Egypt, his design for the Jewish temple drew on Phoenician architectural style and conventions as to orientation. Secondary pagan influences came from all around. Essentially, Solomon drew from pagan temple models to passionately and energetically create a ceremonial space which outshone all the surrounding examples of these models. He emulated pagan models but reimagined and repurposed their motifs. This work set two different sets of Israelites against the temple. On the one hand, the traditionalist prophets came to view it as something which was far adrift of Yahweh's earlier dealings with them and their predecessors—when they were poor. They saw the temple as something which was compromised more or less from the start because of the repurposing of pagan temple architectural follies. On the other hand, there were thousands of laborers and ex-laborers who would view *any* of Solomon's grand constructions as detrimental impositions, taking them away from their livelihoods. For some, the projects may have caused them to cast their minds back to their ancestors' slavery in Egypt.

Solomon also purposed the temple as a unifying ceremonial center for the entire nation, in contrast to the pagan tendency to create high places of worship all over the place for the worship of local gods. To this extent, he discarded the paganism around him. Yet in due time, he was happy to indulge his pagan wives and erect pagan altars, which later on infiltrated the temple. Its east-west orientation and ambiguous artistic trappings could be said to have facilitated that. The temple also restricted the minds and spirits of many in Israel and beyond, who would no longer reach out to an omnipresent God wherever they happened to be. Like pagans, they had to go to the temple or high place where their god resided.

God's presence manifested itself in Solomon's Temple and blessed it for centuries, but this does not necessarily entail that the building of the temple was His will. Permitting the temple may, as Shawn Nelson argues, have been a concession by God.[163] Nelson compares this possibility to the granting of permission to Israel to have a king, something which was also not God's will. The kings were all flawed—even David, whose ambitions and desires often followed after God but whose crimes of murder and adultery set in motion a generational outworking of killing while he was alive and reaching well beyond his lifespan.

Nelson refers to Solomon's Temple as David's Temple because David had the vision for it, amassed most of the raw material for it, and instructed his son to build it. David stated to Israel's leaders that the reason God gave him to not build it was that he had been a man of war and shed blood (1 Chron. 28:3). God had instructed David *not* to build it. Later on, though, David said to Solomon that among other things, God had said to him, "Behold, a son shall be born to you, who shall be a man of rest; and I will give him rest from all his enemies all around. His name shall be Solomon, for I will give peace and quietness to Israel in his days. He shall build a house for My name" (1 Chron. 22:9-10a).

Nelson's view is that David cannot be trusted on this matter—he is determined to go ahead with a plan God had rejected. If he cannot build it himself, at least his son can do it. David may be talking out of his essentially fleshly desire to build God a temple, misattributing the infatuation as God-given. That may be the case. Another reading of the text, though, is that God was simply telling David what He knew would come to pass during Solomon's reign. It was not His will that Solomon build it. It is also apparent in the text that David is countermanding God's will by appointing masons and giving an executive order to Solomon and the ruling elite to start the work.

Unlike the very detailed, God-given instructions for the traveling tabernacle, which was to emulate the heavenly tabernacle, there are no exact requirements for the temple's dimensions. David had an all-consuming desire and a plan as

---

163 Shawn Nelson, "David's Magnificent Temple Built in the Flesh," GeekyChristian.com, December, 2013, http://geekychristian.com/evidence-the-temple-was-not-gods-will.

well but seemed vague on the details.[164] Solomon was required to fill in the blanks. He did so, and one thousand years later, the New Testament martyr, Stephen, was saying to the synagogue's council that temple building is an example of Israel's rulers going their own way rather than obeying God. Does Stephen, under the anointing of the Holy Spirit, differentiate between the true spirit of David's desire (to create a permanent resting place for God's tabernacle) and Solomon's wrong implementation of it by building a magnificent and absorbing temple?

> ""You also took up the tabernacle of Moloch, And the star of your god Remphan, images which made you to worship; And I will carry you away beyond Babylon.' Our fathers had the tabernacle of witness in the wilderness, as He appointed, instructing Moses to make it according to the pattern that he had seen, which our fathers, having received it in turn, also brought with Joshua into the land possessed by the Gentiles, whom God drove out before the face of our fathers until the days of David, who found favor before God and asked to find a dwelling for the God of Jacob. But Solomon built Him a house. However, the Most High does not dwell in temples made with hands, as the prophet says: 'Heaven *is* My throne, And earth *is* My footstool. What house will you build for Me?' says the LORD, 'Or what *is* the place of My rest? Has My hand not made all these things?' You stiff-necked and uncircumcised in heart and ears! You always resist the Holy Spirit; as your fathers *did*, so *do* you" (Acts 7:43-51).

God's powerful and shimmering presence was in the temple for several hundred years until Ezekiel records His departing around 592 B.C., prior to the temple's destruction by Babylon. He left like a mighty, rushing wind. But it seems that God had never wanted the physical and limiting temple. It did not limit Him, but it limited the minds and spirits of believers. Today, God's temple is pretty much everywhere on Earth: ""Do you not know that your body is the temple of the Holy Spirit *who is* in you, whom you have from God, and you are not your own?" (1 Cor. 6:19).

David did not understand God's revelation to him.[165] He misattributed much to the son he saw before him, Solomon. However, God has an eternal view. It is Jesus Who will build His temple and Whose kingdom will last forever. David was captivated by God's promises and intuits that they concerned generations of his descendants on into the future, but he did not understand. Neither did Solomon. Yet he grasped hold of the promise given to his father by Nathan, and for a time, Solomon believed he was the seed who would build the temple and a kingdom which would last forever. His building work foreshadows the work of Christ and the revelation of His eternal kingdom. The temple *looks* solid, but it is a shadow of what is still to come. Neither Solomon nor his temple are the fulfillment. The prophesied kingdom is to be built over a very much longer time period.

The commentator Israel Drazin adds to the general criticism of Solomon by highlighting that while the temple was very much a focus for King David, Solomon did not actually begin its construction until the fourth year of his reign.[166] He had other priorities. When he did start building, the temple took just seven-and-a-half years. By contrast, his palace complex, considerably larger, took thirteen years to build. Just one of its buildings, the House of the Forest of Lebanon, was much larger than the temple. Furthermore, the temple was built beside the royal complex. Like the integrated but architecturally separated pagan temple and palace complexes in Egypt, Tyre, and other kingdoms, this was meant to convey the shared rulership of the king and his god.

It is not the case that Solomon's Temple was built according to a Divine blueprint. We have a record of David's instructions to Solomon as to dimensions and materials (1 Chron. 28:9-21). We can question whether David obtained these from God, given that God instructed the king *not* to build a temple at all. But thereafter, we find that Solomon did not even choose to adhere to these requirements. For instance, David's instructions frequently emphasized the use of silver for vessels, candlesticks, and tables. Solomon sometimes used gold and sometimes used brass for these, never silver. He actually did the same for

165   See 2 Samuel 7.
166   Israel Drazin, *The Authentic King Solomon* (Jerusalem: Gefen Publishing House, 2018).

objects which were to be of gold. Depending on the object, he either fulfilled the obligation or deviated from it and made the thing out of brass. Generally speaking, Solomon decided that everything inside the temple building would be made of gold, and everything outside in the courtyard would be made of brass.

God's temple in Jerusalem has been destroyed so completely—first by Babylon and then by Rome—that we have to ask to what extent was its existence ever God's will. Neither temple actually symbolized Heaven and earth perfectly. If Solomon's temple had done so, it would surely have been much more different in its dimensions, structure, and orientation, compared to the Phoenician temples it emulated in so many respects. These were built to honor and worship pagan deities such as Baal and Astarte. The patron Baal of Tyre, Hiram's capital and port city, was Melqart, and very little is known about the cult and how Melqart was worshipped. He was a god of the sea and also idolized later in relation to the sun. It is likely that worship included ritual sacrifice of infants by roasting them to death. Later in Israel's history, this Baal was enforced on the people by the apostate king Ahab and his Sidon-born, Phoenician wife, Jezebel.

Solomon's construction inferred that God was far superior to any pagan deities worshipped in other temples, but it is possible that its design placed these deities, in many people's eyes, in the same category as God, though inferior to Him. It was then all too easy for the Jews post-Solomon to slip into idolatry. The temple complex need not be ignored. It could become part of a false religion. Once it had done so, it could not be redeemed back. It had to go. The prophet Isaiah had foretold of the destruction of the temple over a hundred years prior (Isaiah 64:11). When the Babylonians destroyed it in 586 B.C., anything they could not destroy completely, such as the twin pillars, was broken up and transported in pieces back to Babylon.

Solomon's temple was built to honor Yahweh, but because of the way it was constructed, it all too easily became a temple for idolaters. For instance, depending on how the temple veil was treated, the Holy of Holies could be set apart for the high priest to enter in solemnly once a year, *or* the temple could be repurposed very easily for sun worship. The temple faced due east. Therefore, at the autumn equinox, if the curtain was pulled back, the rising sun would shine through the temple doorway and illuminate the Holy of Holies. The resultant golden brilliance could now be misperceived as that of the Canaanite solar goddess, Shapash, an associate and supporter of Baal. Worship had reverted to paganism, and the sun worship may have included attempted contact with the dead. This and similar practices precipitated the temple's destruction since God had instructed the Jews in plain language that these things were absolutely forbidden.[167] After the temple's destruction, Ezekiel, now with his people in exile, is at pains to point this out.

> He brought me to the door of the north gate of the LORD's house; and to my dismay, women were sitting there weeping for Tammuz. Then He said to me, "Have you seen *this*, O son of man? Turn again, you will see greater abominations than these." So He brought me into the inner court of the LORD's house; and there, at the door of the temple of the LORD, between the porch and the altar, *were* about twenty-five men with their backs toward the temple of the LORD and their faces toward the east, and they were worshiping the sun toward the east (Ezek. 8:14-16).

---

167 Deuteronomy 4:19; 17:2-5

CHAPTER 23

SOLOMON AS AN APOSTATE KING

"When Solomon married Pharaoh's daughter, Gabriel descended and stuck a reed in the sea, which gathered a sand-bank around it, on which was built the great city of Rome."

—Babylonian Talmud: Tractate Sanhedrin 21b

Apart from Solomon's marriages to pagan wives, there is another sign that Solomon was in danger of apostasy early on in his reign. God communicated with him as he was still building the temple. Therefore, the communication must have been during the first quarter or so of his reign. God communicated a conditional promise, and thereafter, we read of the meticulous attention Solomon paid to the temple's details:

> "*Concerning* this temple which you are building, if you walk in My statutes, execute My judgments, keep all My commandments, and walk in them, then I will perform My word with you, which I spoke to your father David. And I will dwell among the children of Israel, and will not forsake My people Israel." So Solomon built the temple and finished it (1 Kings 6:12-14).

The warning steadied Solomon sufficiently for him to remain on course and complete the temple while living according to most of God's precepts. God then revealed His presence in the temple. His Spirit dwelled there because at its completion, Solomon had still shown himself worthy of the task. In other words, Solomon had been in danger of going astray personally and in relation to the project. God's intervention enabled him to backtrack from using the project to merely show off his own wisdom and his artistic preferences and tendencies. He had been in danger of becoming too narcissistically involved. Here was David's temple, but it now belonged to Solomon: his victory in stone over and above his father. On the other hand, Solomon may have thought: is all this in vain? What would the building work lead to? Would God actually dwell in it? It would be better never to find out—by delaying its completion. Solomon may well have needed God's reassurance.

Solomon's second dream came at a time of completion when the king had finished building the temple, his own house, and some other projects he had in mind to do—the temple taking priority and being finished first. All this had been accomplished in the span of twenty years since he acceded to the throne, and it was at this point that God appeared to him "the second time, as He had appeared to him at Gibeon" (1 Kings 9:2b). The dream occurred when Solomon had moved out of David's older palace in the city and installed himself in the new palace just to the south of the temple.

God told him that He had heard his prayer and supplication made in the new temple and had honored the king's actions by hallowing the temple. God told him that He wanted to make His presence there forever. Then He immediately warned the king, and the dream became ominous.

> "Now if you walk before Me as your father David walked, in integrity of heart and in uprightness, to do according to all that I have commanded you, *and* if you keep My statutes and My judgments, then I will establish the throne of your kingdom over Israel forever, as I promised David your father, saying, 'You shall not fail to have a man on the throne of Israel.' *But* if you or your sons at all turn from following Me, and do not keep My commandments *and* My statutes which I have set before you, but go and serve other gods and worship them, then I will cut off Israel from the land which I have given them; and this house which I have consecrated for My name I will cast out of My sight. Israel will be a proverb and a byword among all peoples. And *as for* this house, *which* is exalted,

everyone who passes by it will be astonished and will hiss, and say, 'Why has the LORD done thus to this land and to this house?' Then they will answer, 'Because they forsook the LORD their God, who brought their fathers out of the land of Egypt, and have embraced other gods, and worshiped them and served them; therefore the LORD has brought all this calamity on them'" (1 Kings 9:4-9).

God presented all this as a series of consequences in alignment with the promises and threats made in Deuteronomy 28-29, but they were given only as possibilities. It remained up to the king whether he would continue to obey the law or depart from it. At the same time, though, there is a sense of the prophetic about the dream. It is outlining what is likely now to happen.

The dream was saying that the throne Solomon sat on would be cut off if he did not walk from now on in integrity. The biblical record of his conduct showed that superficially, he remained steadfast. He kept the Jewish festivals. The temple was the ongoing focus for burnt offerings and fellowship offerings: he fulfilled the temple obligations. But Solomon did turn away from God. He continued to go through the motions, but he allowed himself to be led astray by his many foreign wives. The turning away was protracted, occurring over many years, but eventually, he was colluding with the pagan practices of worshipping false gods by means of human sacrifice. The dream was a warning given at the right time; but as time passed, the possible turning point faded away. Solomon's heart did not turn back to God.

Immediately after this second theophany, Solomon once again dealt with Hiram, selling him twenty cities in Galilee (which were part of the God-given land and should, therefore, not have been relinquished) for one hundred gold talents;[168] but this time, Hiram was not pleased or honoring regarding Solomon, as if the deal was very one-sided. Scripture provides no reason for Solomon's transaction, but it is likely that the rationale was to procure much-needed additional funds to pay for building works and/or pay for resources for his people.

---

168   1 Kings 9:11; the equivalent to about $4.5 million U.S. today.

Solomon also instituted an Egyptian-style slavery on five different people groups to progress with his additional building works. These works, including chariot cities, were largely military and also intended to build up a trading empire functioning on land and at sea. He also wanted to build a prestigious palace for his Egyptian wife. As Professor. K. I. Parker says, "These three concepts of 'power, prestige and money' typify the new regime, and are indicative of the extent to which Solomon has departed from Torah."[169]

Solomon's taxation system was actually something which sows some of the seeds of the kingdom's destruction. It created and developed resentment in a large part of the population. After Solomon died, the ten northern tribes complained to his son about the king's forced labor and burdensome taxation, stating that they wanted the punishing regime relaxed. This was not forthcoming, and all they got was a threat about an even worse regime coming into being. They then seceded immediately from the kingdom.

Solomon's regime transformed into a strong-arm military empire with ostentatious and extravagant show at its center. Solomon was still able to exercise wisdom; hence, the Queen of Sheba was duly impressed, but her delight was accentuated by the indulgent and decorative luxury of Solomon's elaborate court and all its pageantry. His wisdom had shifted in focus away from the administration and protection of justice (and, therefore, his people) and toward pomp and the accumulation of wealth. Solomon had become far wealthier than any other ruler of his time. There was more to this, though. Using the biblical evidence, a modern estimate of Solomon's comparative wealth at the peak of his power and influence is in the region of $2.2 trillion. This is based on an analysis of gold values and Solomon's trade and taxation regimes. By comparison, arguably the richest American who ever lived, John D. Rockefeller, accumulated a modern net worth of $367 billion. Bill Gates is considered to have achieved the equivalent of a peak net worth of $144

169   K.I. Parker, "Solomon as Philosopher King? The Nexus of Law and Wisdom in 1 Kings 1-11," *Journal for the Study of the Old Testament*, Vol. 17, No. 53 (1992): 84, https://doi.org/10.1177/030908929201705305.

billion.[170] At the time of writing, the wealthiest man on earth, according to *Forbes* magazine, is Jeff Bezos of Amazon. His net worth is estimated at $185 billion according to the BBC article on January 4, 2021.[171]

First Kings 10:14 records that Solomon's annual income in gold was 666 talents; and besides the gold, there was a lot of additional international trade and tribute income, which 1 Kings does not define in numbers or values. If we just stick with the gold, though, 666 talents in weight equates to about twenty-five tons. The current value is, therefore, around nine hundred million dollars. The number, of course, is the same number as the number of man (or the number of *a* man) in Revelation.[172] Together, they suggest that the system Solomon has created is a fallen one, a system which is prophetic of a future man-made and evil trading system. If you are outside of this "beast" system, you cannot buy or sell.

Solomon's wealth was far greater than almost anyone else's throughout history, both before and after his reign right down to the current era. It is a fulfillment of God's promise and prophecy to the king at the very beginning of his reign: "Wisdom and knowledge *are* granted to you; and I will give you riches and wealth and honor, such as none of the kings have had who *were* before you, nor shall any after you have the like" (2 Chron. 1:12).

There is no mention in Scripture that the king used this wealth to benefit the population, care in practical ways for the poor, or even to institute cultural reforms. There was no trickle-down effect. By still exercising wisdom but also departing from the law, Solomon also proceeded to break every law regarding kingship which God had laid down: "But he shall not multiply horses for himself, nor cause the people to return to Egypt to multiply horses, for the LORD has said to you, 'You shall not return that way again.' Neither shall he multiply wives for himself, lest his heart turn away; nor shall he greatly multiply silver and gold for himself" (Deut. 17:16-17).

---

170 "The 20 richest people of all time," Lovemoney.com, April 25, 2017, https://www.msn.com/en-in/money/photos/the-20-richest-people-of-all-time/ss-BBsg8nX.

171 "Amazon's Jeff Bezos: The Richest Man in the World," BBC News.com, January 4, 2021, https://www.bbc.com/news/av/world-53311792.

172 Revelation 13:17-18

These laws were broken with flagrant and extravagant disregard. He took for himself seven hundred wives and three hundred concubines; but on top of that, the wives were invariably from foreign people groups, and they worshiped pagan idols. He also built up incomparable reserves of everything else forbidden in the Torah: horses, gold, and silver. His wisdom was not true, supernatural wisdom any longer. Only the exercise of wisdom in alignment with God's laws amounts to true wisdom.

Solomon was at pains to build up his armed forces to prevent invasion and to level up or surpass the powers around about his empire. This had mainly to do with importing military systems from Egypt—twelve thousand horses, fourteen hundred chariots, and trainers—and then embedding them across the empire in large chariot cities (2 Chron. 1:14; I Kings 9:19). Recent excavations at Megiddo have revealed stables for 450 horses and adjacent constructions to house 150 battle chariots. These were pulled by either two or three horses and held three soldiers (a driver, an archer, and a spear thrower/shield bearer). There is also evidence that Solomon acquired different types of chariots from Egypt for different purposes and that he developed Israelite workshop capacity to service and maintain the chariot force. Solomon's forces possessed at least two very different types: *rekeb*, or war chariots, and *merkābāh*, or royal display chariots. This latter type, heavily decorated in silver and gold, were imported from Egypt and cost him six hundred silver shekels each (1 Kings 10:29).

At the same time, Solomon's horse trading, forbidden by God, brought in animals from Anatolia as well as Egypt.[173] Brief military campaigns by him beyond Zobah (in addition to diplomatic pressure exerted by him at other times) enabled him to acquire territory out toward the Euphrates River on which to build store cities such as Tadmor (or Palmyra). These were used for grain storage but also as relay stations for the horses.[174]

Solomon's offensive military resources were complemented by the building up of a network of fortified towns right across the kingdom, and it

---

173   Deuteronomy 17:16-17, which also forbids the taking of many wives.
174   See Yutaka Ikeda's analysis of Solomon's trading activities set within the wider context of Middle Eastern rulers' trading and gifting of chariots and horses in the Bronze and Iron Ages.

is likely that Phoenician and Egyptian technologies were both used in their construction, the ashlar masonry far stronger than the constructions of Saul's time. Perfectly cut, close-fitting stones made the high walls far stronger and were part of a robust structural system involving trap zones, where attackers would be surrounded by archers on the battlements even if they penetrated an outer wall. Archaeologists have discovered the remains of these structures in locations such as Megiddo and Gezer. The defensive structures are not unique; large portions of the Chinese wall were built with the same types of kill zones included in the construction.

One of the reasons Rehoboam's Judah started off so weak and was completely overrun by Pharaoh Shishak is that Solomon's military computations and predictions were valid only for his time. After his death, the international situation changed, and much of Solomon's defenses became all but useless. The fortresses and chariot cities at Palmyra, Baalath, Hazor, Megiddo, and Beth-horon were all in the wrong places now for his son. If we plot Solomon's principle fortresses on a map, we can see that he perceived all the threats were coming, or likely to come, from the north and northeast, the Aramean boundary of his kingdom. This supposition was proved right by events during his reign but proved disastrously wrong after his death. Shishak had a clear run right through Judah from the southwest, right up and across to Jerusalem and right up north to Megiddo, both of which he sacked. Solomon had overestimated the strength of his alliance with Egypt, and most of the southern border was pretty much unguarded. This was a mistake which Egypt never made. One of its long-term priorities had been to fortify its southern defenses along the Nile against Nubia. At least thirteen separate fortresses were built. Current excavations are revealing just how formidable and intimidating these southern structures were.

Solomon's vast building works were completed at the expense of the people, Israelites and non-Israelites alike, but the latter (such as the remaining Amorites and Hittites) were reduced to the status of bondmen, whose work was their tribute (1 Kings 9:21). Work was part of Solomon's taxation system. Solomon's reign was, in effect, a complete fulfillment of Samuel's prophecy to Israel when they clamored for a king. Through Samuel, God told them what the outcome would be. Because they had rejected God, they wanted a king. Chariots were not used by Israel in any great number until the time of Solomon; the prophecy below is not about Saul or David. It is about Solomon.

> "Now therefore, heed their voice. However, you shall solemnly forewarn them, and show them the behavior of the king who will reign over them." So Samuel told all the words of the LORD to the people who asked him for a king. And he said, "This will be the behavior of the king who will reign over you: He will take your sons and appoint *them* for his own chariots and *to be* his horsemen, and *some* will run before his chariots. He will appoint captains over his thousands and captains over his fifties, *will set some* to plow his ground and reap his harvest, and *some* to make his weapons of war and equipment for his chariots. He will take your daughters *to be* perfumers, cooks, and bakers. And he will take the best of your fields, your vineyards, and your olive groves, and give *them* to his servants. He will take a tenth of your grain and your vintage, and give it to his officers and servants . . . And you will cry out in that day because of your king whom you have chosen for yourselves, and the Lord will not hear you in that day" (1 Sam. 8: 9-15, 18).

Finally, beyond the estimations above, there was something supernatural about Solomon's wealth. It was something so extreme that it can never be recovered or reproduced, no matter how hard people try. At the time, it took people's breath away, even if they had wealth of their own—the Queen of Sheba being just one example. Much of Solomon's wealth, including gold, came from Ophir and Tarshish. No one actually knows for sure where these places were, and anyone subsequent to Solomon who sought to investigate through maritime travel, such as King Jehoshaphat around 860 B.C., was left frustrated. These places were beyond reach.

Scripture points out many times that Solomon's wealth was a one-off acquisition. Nowhere else in history has silver been as commonplace as stones, and if they were products of his unique wisdom, many of his precious objects like his ivory and golden throne were simply irreproducible. We can view it, though, as a misuse of wisdom, something which contributes to a spiritual falling away. Extreme wealth allows Solomon to easily support a harem of wives and concubines, with many of the former leading him away from God.

CHAPTER 24

SOLOMON'S MILITARY AND DOMESTIC OVER-SPENDING

"All our mistakes sooner or later surely come home to roost."

—James Russell Lowell, Romantic Poet
and U.S. Ambassador to Great Britain

When the northern tribes argued with Rehoboam at length, demanding a reduction in taxes, the new king refused this because he was reliant on his military apparatus, funded by the taxation system. His father had left him with nothing. The state coffers were emptied!

In the latter half of Solomon's reign, the pigeons were coming home to roost, but the curse of them landed on his son, not on him. Solomon had made two profound, economic miscalculations throughout his reign. These were both military and domestic.

King David had left his son plenty of gold and silver for the building of the temple. At this point, the state coffers were quite full. Solomon's creative imagination over-extended what David had had in mind, but it is likely that the majority of the costs were still provided for. Solomon's ambitions, though, went well beyond the building of David's temple, since his primary inspiration for how his state should look came from Egypt. While it was languishing in the doldrums during his reign over Israel and Judah, Solomon could see what its military apparatus had been for many hundreds of years. He was also familiar with its vast palace complexes. He wanted the same.

Solomon was determined to achieve military hegemony throughout his realm. This required a very substantial increase in spending on fortifications, chariot cities, expensive horses, and a standing army—far beyond anything his father had created. He wanted his state to be permanently prepared for war. He also did not want to fight any wars. Military campaigns have to be paid for, and they also carry risk. At the same time, though, success in an Iron Age war could mean that the military paid for itself (by looting the vanquished) while also providing a set of circumstances in which conquered people would pay tribute to the king year by year. War could produce income for the state. However, Solomon's ever-growing military complex was simply a financial drain on the state. It protected international trade routes, but it did not furnish the kingdom with any revenue. All of his military had to be paid for with taxation.

At the same time, like other potentates, he also wanted to project his power through the display of wealth. This essentially amounted to lavish domestic building projects, such as his palace complex, and the ostentatious display of personal wealth. The cost of this ongoing wealth projection was extracted by taxation. Solomon's domestic state spending encompassed himself and his retinue, his civil service and the district administration offices, and his wives and concubines. They all had to be housed and fed, as did their many servants, caterers, and entertainers. It is interesting that the Bible contains absolutely no details about Solomon's palace complex, other than the judicial and armory buildings. Logic, though, tells us that it was probably the most opulent and extravagant set of buildings on Earth at the time. Several thousand elite people lived in absolute luxury, surrounded by gold and ivory furniture and luxurious, soft furnishings from India, Sheba, and Phoenicia and enjoyed the finest trappings of power.

The commentator Henri Gaubert implies that the more serious of these errors was the domestic spending spree expedited by slave labor.[175] In his attempts to emulate Egypt, Solomon did not factor in that the land of Israel was not like Egypt. By flooding large tracts of fertile soil every year, the Nile was a wealth-creator in

---

175 Gaubert, 152.

terms of abundant crops and resultant revenues for the pharaohs. Israel had no such geographical resource and, therefore, no such revenue source. His forced labor drew farmers away from their fields for long periods of time to the detriment of crop yields and the taxation regime. They were required to fell trees in Lebanon, work in quarries and mines, bake the bricks, work in regimented logistics and supply operations, and work the furnaces in Ezion-Geber.

In due time, Solomon got into serious debt, most of it to Hiram of Tyre. After Solomon's credit was exhausted, he had to buy the Phoenician off with land—twenty towns close to the border with Phoenicia.[176] This deal only soured the relationship with his banker. When Hiram went to view them after the deal went through, he was dismayed. They did not suit his purposes. Simultaneously, Solomon's laborers were bound to become rebellious. They remembered the stories of how their ancestors had slaved for the Egyptians. The more despotic and removed from them Solomon became, the quicker the rebellion fomented. Through something of a secret service, Solomon was able to nip embryonic rebellions in the bud, but these were only pushed back for a time. Jeroboam, for instance, fled into exile to escape the king's ire.

Solomon's ambitions destroyed the domestic cohesiveness between the twelve tribes which David's statesmanship and openness to God had achieved. Eventually, Solomon's regime deteriorated into thoughtless repression and state control. Solomon simply did not take account of his people's mindsets, especially the many who belonged to the ten Northern tribes of Israel. He also created a merciless class system, perhaps without really meaning to. Below the elite were wealthy landowners. As former farmers left to work in industry and live in industrial settlements and rapidly growing towns, the landowners grabbed up their land at knockdown prices to create large estates for themselves. By the time of Solomon's death, there was a great divide between the exploiters of Israel-Judah and the exploited. There was also a divide between North and South. The kingdom was going to split apart at the seams.

---

176 1 Kings 9:11-13

CHAPTER 25

THE LIBERTARIAN
TOLERANCE OF IDOLATRY

His reign was then so glorious that the moon never decreased, and good prevailed over evil. His control over the demons, spirits, and animals augmented his splendour, the demons bringing him precious stones, besides water from distant countries to irrigate his exotic plants. The beasts and fowls of their own accord entered the kitchen of Solomon's palace, so that they might be used as food for him. Extravagant meals for him (comp. I Kings iv. 22-23) were prepared daily by each of his thousand wives, with the thought that perhaps the king would feast on that day in her house.

—Meillot 11b; Sanhedrin 20b, *The 1906 Jewish Encyclopedia*[177]

Juxtaposed with Solomon's Temple and its effect to remove the power of Israelite pagan high places is the surprising tolerance Solomon had for pagan deities and the worship practices of his pagan wives. Although they were a threat to true worship and although their influence continued to pollute the life of Judah long after Solomon's death, Solomon did not see them as a threat. He was happy to allow his wives their pagan shrines and altars within his palace and in the open air, close to Jerusalem's fortifications and in close proximity to the temple. The implication of altars built outside is that they came with all the trappings of pagan worship: sacrifices and pagan priests.

---

177 Wilhelm Bacher and Jakob Zallel Lauterbach, "Sanhedrin," *Jewish Encyclopedia*, accessed December 8, 2020, jewishencyclopedia.com/articles/13178-sanhedrin.

His wives were representatives of the surrounding nations that Solomon had tied himself to through his economic and trade agreements. These agreements would succeed better if pagan nations saw that their religions, as well as their trade goods, were acceptable to the king. Solomon was extremely confident; he thought that the temple and Jewish religious practice would thrive, despite the presence of all sorts of altars to other gods built in close proximity. His wives were also motifs of international subjugation. Through them, he was making the point that the monarchies they and their servants came from were allied to and subjugated to him.[178] Through his wives, he had permanent influence over the families, dynasties, and tribes they came from. The temple, combined with all his wives, was saying to all emissaries coming to Jerusalem from across the region, "You have journeyed up to the new Garden of Eden and the center of the universe symbolized on earth. It is ruled by Yahweh; His representative on earth, Solomon; and by Israel, Yahweh's chosen people." The temple and wives were a combined political and religious statement. Trade goods and exotic animals served as further incidental flourishes in the capital. "Monkeys and parrots are here, too! This is the center of the world, and all the world is here."

Solomon initially believed that by allowing pagan idol shrines to be built in close proximity to the temple, he was underscoring the supremacy of Yahweh. He was bringing the pagan deities before his God, and in effect, they were paying homage to Him by taking up their secondary positions. They were not allowed to remain in darkness. Yahweh and Solomon could both keep an eye on them and observe what their adherents were doing. If Yahweh found that He disapproved of any, He was easily capable of dealing with them as he had with the Philistine fertility deity, Dagon. After the Philistines had captured the ark of the covenant and placed it in their temple in Ashdod, Yahweh's sudden presence over the ark had thrown the Dagon idol to the

---

178 Carol Meyers, "Israelite Empire: In Defense of King Solomon, *Michigan Quarterly Review,* Vol. 22, No. 3, http://hdl.handle.net/2027/spo.act2080.0022.003:45, accessed December 8, 2020.

ground two nights running, and on the second night, it crashed with such force that its head and hands were severed from its frame.[179] Solomon had very great confidence in Yahweh.

Solomon behaved as he did regarding idols for less important rationales as well. Trade delegations and royal visitors from pagan people groups within Solomon's kingdom and from beyond would see that Solomon could be trusted. After all, he had allowed their deities some recognition adjacent to his central temple complex. He could be considered as good as his word when he signed something. He looked like a ruler who was not conspiring to crush them absolutely or to renege on deals. He seemed tolerant. Yet, there was a psychological propaganda message being communicated as well. Solomon was saying to the many foreign emissaries: just as my God Yahweh is superior to all your gods, I am superior to you, and my kingdom is superior to yours. The least important reason for allowing idols was to appease his pagan wives. By giving minor honors to their idols, he was recognizing their worldviews and showing them that they accounted for at least a little consideration in his sight.

Yet again, Solomon took Egypt as his inspiration for libertarian religious tolerance. Specifically, the Egyptians had allowed Phoenician settlers in Pi-Ramesses to build a temple to their deity, Astarte. This favor was given because the Phoenicians had allowed Egyptian traders living in Byblos to build a shrine to their goddess, Hathor.[180] It was all good for international and domestic relations. It kept the peace. The alternative, at least in Solomon's mind, was to offend his many hundreds of fathers-in-law by not allowing their daughters to practice their religions freely. Solomon's libertarian promotion of idolatry was a direct consequence of his international trade policy and his no-holds barred desire to acquire wealth.

This being so, it is this sin, and not any other, which Yahweh took great exception to: the subtle and gradual turning away from Him and turning instead toward other gods. Solomon made no statement as to his rejection of Yahweh. Yet

---

179   1 Samuel 5:2-4
180   Gaubert, "The Shades of Night."

Scripture does imply that the king's acceptance of pagan gods is at a deeper level than an outward show to placate his wives and their families: "For Solomon went after Ashtoreth the goddess of the Sidonians, and after Milcom the abomination of the Ammonites (1 Kings 11:5).

To understand this, we should spend some time examining his wives, the king's relationships with them, and the demon gods with which they were infatuated. Later, we will consider Solomon's rejection of Yahweh as part of a more fundamental psychological turnaround within the king: his rejection of David, his father.

WIVES, GODS, AND MONSTERS

We know from Solomon's Song of Songs that he loved the company of three categories of females: wives, concubines, and virgins. Song of Songs 6:8 says the last category was without number. These would have been his singers, dancers, musicians, and others, perhaps under consideration as either wives or concubines but undecided on as yet, similar to the position Esther found herself in at the court of Xerxes I.

> But King Solomon loved many foreign women, as well as the daughter of Pharaoh: women of the Moabites, Ammonites, Edomites, Sidonians, and Hittites—from the nations of whom the LORD had said to the children of Israel, "You shall not intermarry with them, nor they with you. Surely they will turn away your hearts after their gods." Solomon clung to these in love. And he had seven hundred wives, princesses, and three hundred concubines; and his wives turned away his heart. For it was so, when Solomon was old, that his wives turned his heart after other gods; and his heart was not loyal to the LORD his God, as *was* the heart of his father David. For Solomon went after Ashtoreth the goddess of the Sidonians, and after Milcom the abomination of the Ammonites. Solomon did evil in the sight of the LORD, and did not fully follow the Lord, as *did* his father David. Then Solomon built a high place for Chemosh the abomination of Moab, on the hill that *is* east

of Jerusalem, and for Molech the abomination of the people of Ammon (1 Kings 11:1-7).

Solomon had relations with at least one thousand women, and the number itself warrants some thought. Did he consider, for instance, that he would be assured of peace by marrying them all, given that in some sense or other, foreign nations might believe that they had representation in Solomon's palace? Did he assume that their idol worship was of no account because his own God was the only true God?

We can infer two kinds of error as to Solomon's approach to the idolatry. First, he tolerated his wives' pagan worship, but then he apparently joined in it himself. The Bible is explicit as to his own participation. But since many of the idols required human sacrifice, did he participate in that as well? Did he sacrifice his children, or did his wives sacrifice their own children behind his back? Is this why only Rehoboam is mentioned as a son of the king, and there is mention of just two daughters, Taphath and Basemath?[181]

It is an interesting omission that Scripture records no other children of the king, unlike many other genealogies, such as the listing of King David's offspring, named and unnamed. It is quite likely that Solomon's many wives were pleased to sacrifice at least some of their children to the idols, placing them on the iron hands before a lever tilted the hands upward, so their small bodies fell backward into the mouth and down into the blazing furnace below. The high-born infants, children of the king, would have been better, more desirable sacrifices than ordinary children. The wives would, therefore, have been more certain of the demons' blessing.

The commentary by Josephus adds some color to the situation and to Solomon's state of mind: "He grew mad in his love of women, and laid no restraint on himself in his lust . . . He also began to worship their gods, which he did to the gratification of his wives, and out of his affection for them . . . Solomon was fallen headlong into unseasonable pleasures."[182]

---

181 1 Kings 4:11, 15
182 Josephus Flavius, *Antiquities of the Jews*, VII, 209.

Scripture says, "For Solomon went after Ashtoreth the goddess of the Sidonians, and after Milcom the abomination of the Ammonites. Solomon did evil in the sight of the LORD" (1 Kings 11:5-6). What was Solomon's attitude toward women, given that he had so many of them? He enjoyed them in a hedonistic way. He had opened himself up to powers which gave him an unusual degree of sexual energy. And what was their attitude toward him? It is very possible that they saw him as a god—the god of women. That is to say, they believed he was Tammuz, the fertility god and "child of the abyss."[183] In other words, he was, in this sense at least, a type of the antichrist and a counterfeit of Christ. Sex with Solomon was an act of worship and part of a pagan cycle of life. They enticed his presence by offering all sorts of exotic foods and by preparing themselves in all sorts of ways, and should he arrive, sexual intercourse might bless them with offspring they could dedicate to the demons they served.

Yet if some of Solomon's offspring were sacrificed to the idols, this was probably not the fate of most. The most likely reason why so few are named or even identified in Scripture is a more prosaic one. Scripture does not tend to include the names of those who are not relevant to God's purposes with the Jews or to His method of salvation. After Solomon's death, Rehoboam's regime was probably very unsympathetic to the wives, concubines, and their offspring. Many wives would have journeyed back to the pagan tribes and nations they had come from, such as Moab, Edom, and Ammon. They would have taken their children with them. As princesses from leading clans and families, they would, in most cases, have reintegrated within the ruling elites. In due course, some of Solomon's children and their descendants would have been adversaries of Israel and Judah. It is possible that some of these are named in Scripture, while their status as descendants of Solomon is unrecorded. For most of his offspring, though, they are not named because they are not relevant to the story of salvation.

Naamah, the Ammonite princess, is the only wife actually named in Scripture. She retained some degree of supremacy, given that her son inherited Solomon's

---

183 Tammuz is generally known as Adonis in the West.

throne. There are also two other identified individuals: the daughter of Pharaoh and the Phoenician princess who eventually replaced her as a primary wife when the Egyptian passed away. Other than these, we merely know of some of the pagan nations from which the consorts came. Most of the concubines, if not all of them, may have been Israelites of non-royal background.

It may be that Solomon applied a rationale to his acquisition of wives which enabled him to believe that their origins did not contradict Jewish law. A careful comparison of the legal injunctions about exogamy recorded in Exodus 34 and Deuteronomy 7 with the examples given in 1 Kings of nations from which his wives derived is worthwhile. Essentially, the prohibition applies (in terms of the letter of the law) to the indigenous population groups—people such as the Perizzites and Jebusites, which Israel was supplanting. Solomon, on the other hand, took wives from pagan nations who were not indigenous to the land of Israel—people such as the Moabites and Ammonites. However, the one exception is the Hittites; and for that exception, Solomon may have judged that they were not indigenous, even though a branch of them had recently settled in the land after their empire had collapsed. Likewise, Solomon may have acquired concubines to obey certain facets of Jewish law, at least in his own mind, separating out sex and marriage as separate activities under the law. For instance, the law (recorded in Deuteronomy 7:3) specifies only an injunction relating to marriage. Nevertheless, if these were aspects of Solomon's rationalization, they do not stack up against the spirit of Jewish law across a range of concerns about the dangers of intermarriage and idolatry.

Other than the sheer number of wives he had, Solomon committed a number of serious errors regarding them. He ignored the law of Moses, which states:

> "And in all that I have said to you, be circumspect and make no mention
> of the name of other gods, nor let it be heard from your mouth . . . You
> shall not bow down to their gods, nor serve them, nor do according to
> their works; but you shall utterly overthrow them and completely break
> down their *sacred* pillars . . . You shall make no covenant with them, nor
> with their gods" (Exod. 23:13, 24, 32).

"But he shall not multiply horses for himself, nor cause the people to return to Egypt to multiply horses, for the Lord has said to you, 'You shall not return that way again.' Neither shall he multiply wives for himself, lest his heart turn away; nor shall he greatly multiply silver and gold for himself" (Deut. 17:16-17).

There is the injunction not to make any covenant with the pagan nations, including that of marriage. There is also the repeated injunction not to worship the false gods of the nations through their idols. In the ways in which he built up his military regime and in his outstanding disregard for the law regarding multiplication of wives, the king would, in normal circumstances, have faced the death penalty many times over. But the king—with his twelve thousand horsemen, chariots, splendor, and wisdom—dazzled people. He was beyond approach and beyond reproach. Yet by creating altars and high places for the worship of foreign gods, Solomon gave the deities and their worship royal legitimacy. The temple was not the only center of worship to command royal allegiance.

The biblical account places Ashtoreth first in the pantheon of pagan gods officially recognized by Solomon. This deity was also known as Astarte and as Ashera. The Zidonians who worshipped her (or to use the Greek term, Phoenicians) had trading colonies in Cyprus, Sardinia, Spain, and along the North African coastline, one of which developed after Solomon's death into the Carthaginian Empire.

Milcom, or Molech, the Ammonite deity, is the next one mentioned. Scripture refers to it as a *shikeitz*, which means "detestable and abominable." Its fire-sacrifice idols were large, bronze constructions, which could be heated up like ovens before children were thrown into them alive. The Ammonite god, Milcom, got a high place outside Jerusalem, perhaps because Solomon greatly valued the Ammonite territory northeast of his capital with its strategic trade routes linking Jerusalem to Damascus and Palmyra. It is also worth noting that Solomon's union with the Ammonite princess Naamah produced the crown prince Rehoboam, who gained the throne in 931 B.C. and who immediately lost most of the empire.

Solomon also built the Chemosh sanctuary, just next to the Milcom idol, high and on open ground near Jerusalem. The idol stared defiantly across the Kidron ravine at the temple. In the Louvre, Paris, there stands the Mesha Stele, discovered in 1868. It is intact and was erected post-Solomon by the king of Moab around 840 B.C. Like so many pagan deities, Chemosh was a receiver of human sacrifice. The stele describes a successful war against Israel by Moab and the sacrifice of seven thousand Jewish men at Nebo to Ashtar-Chemosh. The modern state of Jordan demands the stele's return to where it was found. It is the only example of the Iron Age Moabite language to have been discovered, apart from a few seals, which verified economic transactions and which are stamped with an inscription translated as *Belonging to Chemosh*.

The Bible does not dwell too much on the flood of idolatry spewing into the land because of Solomon's permissive yielding to the religious wants of his many wives, at least during Solomon's reign. Yet many of the citizens were drawn aside to the worship of idols and to profane religious practices. What was good enough for the palace and the elite was good enough for them as well. The deterioration in the land occurred quite swiftly so that by the time Rehoboam came to the throne, there was a situation throughout the land which was completely unacceptable to Yahweh. The book of 1 Kings links the situation directly to the invasion by the new Pharaoh Shishak in Rehoboam's fifth year of rule. Presumably, God had given the new king sufficient time to repent of his father's sins and to steer the nation back toward a better situation.

> Now Judah did evil in the sight of the LORD, and they provoked Him to jealousy with their sins which they committed, more than all that their fathers had done. For they also built for themselves high places, *sacred* pillars, and wooden images on every high hill and under every green tree. And there were also perverted persons in the land. They did according to all the abominations of the nations which the LORD has cast out before the children of Israel (1 Kings 14:22-24).

There are some critics of Solomon, such as Mark Biltz, who condemn him for either sacrificing his own children on the idol shrines, permitting his wives to do so, or both. He is said to have set an example for other rulers who would reign after him, such as Ahab of Israel and Manasseh of Judah, their religious policies aligning with their surrounding pagan trade partners, such as Phoenicia and Assyria. Scripture does record the ritual sacrifice of children in these post-Solomon times. However, Scripture is silent on whether Solomon or even his wives did that. They may well have, but there is nothing in Scripture which backs up the claims of Solomon's arch-critics other than the dark, religious backdrop of pagan shrines.

Solomon ruled over Israel as well as Judah. The same text in 1 Kings describes how the ten Northern tribes also followed in Solomon's apostate way. In their case, the rebellion was even more profound than in Judah. They were destined to never experience a good king, and the initial prophecy by Yahweh clearly stated that Israel would be swept away because their first post-Solomon king, Jeroboam, had been even more idolatrous than Solomon.

After Solomon, idolatry was an ongoing problem for Israel and Judah. The majority of their kings were idolatrous. The idol shrines erected close to the temple stood there for several hundred years after Solomon. And when Manasseh came to the Jewish throne after Israel had been conquered by the Assyrians in about 720 B.C., he focused on building up trade with Assyria, fortified the trade routes, and instituted ritual child sacrifice to Molech. In his efforts to promote an Assyrian-friendly astral polytheism, he built pagan shrines to Asherah and Baal within the temple.[184] It was a trend which led to the temple's destruction by Babylon.

---

184 2 Kings 21

CHAPTER 26

AFTER SOLOMON'S PERIGEE: THE EYEWITNESS

"First Moloch, horrid King besmear'd with blood
Of human sacrifice, and parents' tears . . .
Of Solomon he led by fraud to build
His Temple right against the Temple of God."

—*Paradise Lost* by John Milton, 1667

It is still something of a mystery as to why Solomon's benign reign turned into despotism. We were not there, and we saw neither Solomon's grandeur nor the later effects of his apostasy. There is very little by way of archaeological remains of Solomon's kingdom. His kingdom was not like ancient Rome or Pompeii, where we only have to walk among the ruins to picture how things were. Egypt swept so much away, and Babylon swept away the residue.

But we do have an eyewitness who, although obscure as a figure now, wrote more of the Bible than over a dozen writers of Scripture, including Peter and James. He shows us what went wrong during Solomon's reign and thereafter. He witnessed the destruction of Solomon's kingdom as it split apart in two. In fact, he saw it all, even from the last years of David's reign. Who was he?

Asaph was the eyewitness, and he was a musician and a Levite priest. His life is there as a testimony to how it was and to how he was caught up in it all. He lived from about 1020 to 920 B.C. Therefore, he was a young man when David came to the throne around 1000 B.C., and he lived into Rehoboam's reign after Solomon died. He was so talented that David gave him responsibility for the music played before the ark of the covenant in Jerusalem; he probably also set many of David's psalms to music. He retained this role until after the ark was installed in Solomon's Temple.[185] His brother Zechariah assisted him.

He directly heard David say that God had promised him that David's descendent would be on the throne of Israel forever, and that Solomon was the man. David did not mislead anyone: he reiterated that God's intention was conditional on obedience. But it is understandable that all those present at court, including Asaph, would have focused more on the promise and its security, rather than the condition. David said:

> "And of all my sons (for the LORD has given me many sons) He has chosen my son Solomon to sit on the throne of the kingdom of the LORD over Israel. Now He said to me, 'It is your son Solomon *who* shall build My house and My courts; for I have chosen him *to be* My son, and I will be his Father. Moreover I will establish his kingdom forever, if he is steadfast to observe My commandments and My judgments, as it is this day'" (1 Chron. 28:5-7).

Solomon proceeded to build the temple, and the worship which Asaph officiated over was then incorporated within it. The temple's most sacred place housed the ark. Asaph probably thought that Israel's millennial reign was at hand. He was on the cusp of something akin to a golden era, an earthly realm which evoked something of the perfection and beauty of eternity. For a time, he had before him a false vision of Solomon as the Messiah and, as Clay McLean puts it, "of the glory of Israel filling the whole earth."[186]

There is no role in the modern era, in either Judaism or Christianity, which reflects the kind of function Asaph had in the temple. He was a seer or prophet,[187]

---

185 Richard Thompson, "Who was Asaph?" HFBCBibleStudy.org, May 30, 2005, www.hfbcbi-blestudy.org/index2.php?option=com_content&do_pdf=1&id=482.

186 Clay McLean, "Real God and Real Me," *Nightlight Newsletters, No. 306, November 1, 2018 (Hickory: McLean Ministries)* https://www.mcleanministries.org/uploads/nightlight_news-letters/nov_2018_reg_layout.pdf.

187 2 Chronicles 29:30

and he was a singer and musician at the same time.[188] He stood dressed in white linen at a position just east of the altar, and he was the head of a family of temple singers. Their singing of praises fused with the music of the priest trumpeters and the other priest musicians, and it is this sound which seems to have precipitated the sudden arrival of God into the temple in a cloud.[189] This was an even greater high point for Asaph than when he helped, along with many others, King David bring the ark up into Jerusalem.[190]

Had the renewing song brought Yahweh into the temple? Singing was part of the original creation, and it was a key part of the temple's inauguration. Singing is also part of the consummation of things at the end. The high priest had sprinkled sacrificial blood on the altar in Solomon's Temple on the day of atonement to cleanse the people from sin, the priests' song being heard in the background, a shadow of the true redemption still to come, restoration to God through the Lamb's blood. We know some of the words sung then by the cherubim and elders in Heaven: "And they sang a new song, saying: 'You are worthy to take the scroll, And to open its seals; For You were slain, And have redeemed us to God by Your blood Out of every tribe and tongue and people and nation'" (Rev. 5:9).

For Asaph, though, it all went wrong, and there was a cataclysmic descent from the heights—a personal tragedy which he lives through. After the perigee, darkness began to pour from Solomon into every aspect of the culture. The courts of worship and the government were subject to political intrigue and immorality, along with the occult.

His brother Zechariah was murdered on holy ground, probably by Solomon acting by the hand of someone else, a crime which Jesus refers back to almost a millennium later. Solomon's throne was now one of iniquity and destruction. Jesus castigated the Pharisees and their religious spirit of murder and death, an evil spirit dating back to Solomon's reign and the iniquity brought into the court

---

188 2 Chronicles 5:11-13
189 There are similar examples in Scripture where a fusion of music and prophecy brought about God's presence (e.g. 1 Samuel 10:5-6; 2 Kings 3:15-16).
190 1 Chronicles 15

by his worship of false gods. It killed Zechariah and many other prophets, and in due time, it would kill *Jesus*.

> "Fill up, then, the measure of your fathers' *guilt*. Serpents, brood of vipers! How can you escape the condemnation of hell? Therefore, indeed, I send you prophets, wise men, and scribes: *some* of them you will kill and crucify, and *some* of them you will scourge in your synagogues and persecute from city to city, that on you may come all the righteous blood shed on the earth, from the blood of righteous Abel to the blood of Zechariah, son of Berechiah, whom you murdered between the temple and the altar. Assuredly, I say to you, all these things will come upon this generation. 'O Jerusalem, Jerusalem, the one who kills the prophets and stones those who are sent to her!'" (Matt. 23:32-37a).[191]

The following can be ascribed to Asaph or to his brother shortly before his murder:

> Shall the throne of iniquity, which devises evil by law, Have fellowship with You? They gather together against the life of the righteous, And condemn innocent blood. But the LORD has been my defense, And my God is the rock of my refuge. He has brought on them their own iniquity, And shall cut them off in their own wickedness; The Lord our God shall cut them off (Psalm 94:20-23).

Asaph's lowest point is recorded in Psalm 73. His brother was dead, and Solomon's corrupt and crushing system was growing ever greater. Solomon and his ruling elite were prosperous, undefinably wealthy, and strong enough to eliminate all opposition. But being something of a prophet, he discerned that they and their system would come crashing down, more or less in an instance. He prophesied terror and destruction for those far from God. In an oblique but fairly obvious reference to Solomon and his elite group, Asaph says, "You have destroyed all those who desert You for harlotry" (v. 27). He says later in Psalm 82 that even though Solomon and his elite now ruled like gods, the true God was standing in their

---

191   See also Luke 11:50-51.

midst, and He would see to it that they would "die like men, And fall like one of the princes" (v. 7)—possibly a reference to Satan's fall from Heaven. Then God "shall inherit all nations" (v. 8), including Israel.

Everything was recorded by Asaph. His concern over the splitting in two of the kingdom can be read in Psalms 76 and 80: God now dwelled in Israel and Judah, two separate kingdoms, while Zion was still His focus. The invasion by Pharaoh Shishak is referenced in Psalms 74 and 79, which record actual events during Egypt's invasion of Rehoboam's rump state of Judah. "O God, the nations have come into Your inheritance; Your holy temple they have defiled; they have laid Jerusalem in heaps. The dead bodies of Your servants They have given *as* food for the birds of the heavens, The flesh of Your saints to the beasts of the earth. Their blood they have shed like water all around Jerusalem, And *there was* no one to bury *them*" (Psalm 79:1-3).

During Solomon's later apostate years, his kingdom was built bigger and higher on slavery and taxes. The people complained to deaf ears when they appealed to his son Rehoboam: "'Your father made our yoke heavy; now therefore, lighten the burdensome service of your father, and his heavy yoke which he put on us, and we will serve you'" (1 Kings 12:4). Asaph was pushed to the limit by the oppression he saw, his feet almost slipping from under him. But he placed his faith in God and in the justice he knew would come. He lived long enough to see at least some of it unfold. Solomon's false messiahship was swept away as Asaph clung to God, describing Him as the strength of his heart. Even in his darkest hour, he says, "But *it is* good for me to draw near to God; I have put my trust in the Lord God, That I may declare all Your works" (Psalm 73:28). Asaph says that the evil in rulership had caused him to nearly fall from the path—until he saw the end of the wicked.

In his despair, Asaph's heart was not far from Yahweh. He knew that God was with him during the times when he felt He was not there. Throughout the years following on from Asaph's time, people have drawn on Asaph's cries of despair during their own times of struggle. He trusted in God, and in his lament; he trusted God to carry him through: "Whom have I in heaven *but You*? And *there is* none upon earth *that* I desire besides You. My flesh and my heart fail; *But* God *is* the strength of my heart and my portion forever" (Psalm 73:25-26).

CHAPTER 27

REBELLION

"He was an adversary of Israel all the days of Solomon (besides the trouble that Hadad caused); and he abhorred Israel, and reigned over Syria."

—1 Kings 11:25

Like Pharaoh, Solomon was a builder, but it was *how* he built which became a serious matter for the preservation of his country. After a while, Israelites were forced to experience the kinds of tax and labor burdens that had previously only been applied to foreign and subjugated tribes. The degree to which they would tolerate that was limited, especially in the north of the country. For one thing, they had previously known a high degree of freedom after their captivity in Egypt. They did not have the same mindset as the peasants of Egypt who had endured forced labor for centuries. It is a situation somewhat reminiscent of the antecedents that led to the English Civil War (1642-1651). A tyrant king, Charles I, wanted to dissolve Parliament and step away from the *Magna Carta* and the petition of rights, while at the same time imposing a feudal tax levy.

In addition, Solomon just kept on building—there was no apparent end in sight. After completion of his lavish palace, there was all the building, which formed his extensive country-wide military complex as well as numerous public works such as aqueducts and hydraulic water installations for crop irrigation and city water supplies. We can see now what Solomon's building projects were accomplishing: defense against foreign threats, defense from and control over the domestic population, defense of the trade routes and state revenue, the building up of crop yields, and provision of clean water to all the major cities. Chariot cities, such as the major complex at Megiddo, served two purposes. They were a show of strength for the surrounding people, and they could also provide troops and chariots to reinforce a border citadel under attack from an enemy outside the kingdom. The flaw in all this was that any means were reasonable to Solomon. Israelite citizens were subjected to a never-ending series of labor force requisitions, work they were not trained for and which they would not understand. They would only understand that their labor was their tax to be paid over certain periods of time to Solomon and his state. The returns for this went to Jerusalem, not to Israel. There was also no end in sight.

At the same time, a very real heart of darkness had opened up at the center of power in Jerusalem. 1 Kings 11 may infer that human sacrifices were offered by a large number of Solomon's wives to their idols in close proximity to the temple. They burned incense and offered sacrifices, and it is this which God responded to in anger.

> So the Lord became angry with Solomon, because his heart had turned from the Lord God of Israel, who had appeared to him twice, and had commanded him concerning this thing, that he should not go after other gods; but he did not keep what the LORD had commanded. Therefore the LORD said to Solomon, "Because you have done this, and have not kept My covenant and My statutes, which I have commanded you, I will surely tear the kingdom away from you and give it to your servant. Nevertheless I will not do it in your days, for the sake of your father David; I will tear it out of the hand of your son. However I will not tear away the whole kingdom; I will give one tribe to your son for the sake of My servant David, and for the sake of Jerusalem which I have chosen" (1 Kings 11:9-13).

Solomon was required to battle against a number of rebels from within his kingdom, three of whom are mentioned in Scripture. The first of these was Hadad from Edom, a country which David had subjugated and was now merely a province of Israel. Hadad escaped the Israelite massacre of Edomite males carried out by David's general Joab; and given that he was descended from the Edomite royal household, he and his companions were received favorably by Pharaoh. He was given Pharaoh's wife's sister as a wife, and their son grew up in Pharaoh's court. When he heard that both David and Joab were dead, he successfully asked permission of Pharaoh to return to Edom. It does not seem that he gathered a substantial following there, but he did carry out activities which were detrimental to Solomon, possibly terrorist raids on some of the king's assets. Solomon was unable to capture him.

A second adversary of Solomon was named Rezon. He was more powerful than Hadad, managed to gather a significant enough army, and took Damascus out of Solomon's control. He was one of the reasons why much of Solomon's military apparatus was oriented toward the north and northeast of Israel. Rezon reigned as king over one of the Aramean kingdoms located in the part of Syria from which Solomon withdrew. Rezon's power against Solomon was limited: at no point was he able to overthrow one of Solomon's border outposts. For the most part, the situation was a hostile standoff.

The third and most powerful of all the rebels, though, was Jeroboam, an Israelite from the fortress at Zerada. The present-day location of Zerada is unknown, but it was probably directly to the north of Jerusalem, at least fifteen miles from the capital in the mountainous central area. 1 Kings repeatedly calls Jeroboam a mighty man of valor. Promoted by Solomon from administrator to officer, he oversaw the work being carried out by the tribes of Ephraim (Jeroboam's tribe) and Manasseh. The work involved building the Millo, a military or palace fortification of some kind in Jerusalem,[192] and repairing damage in the city.

A prophet from Shiloh, a walled town near Zerada, approached Jeroboam one day. Shiloh had previously been the sanctuary for the ark before it was placed in Solomon's Temple. The prophet's name was Ahijah, and Scripture records two of his prophecies, his statement to Jeroboam being the first. When Jeroboam was

---

192   The Millo was possibly a tower or citadel.

setting out on a journey from Jerusalem one day, Ahijah approached him wearing a new cloak. The prophet took his cloak and tore it into twelve pieces and said:

> "Take for yourself ten pieces, for thus says the Lord, the God of Israel: 'Behold, I will tear the kingdom out of the hand of Solomon and will give ten tribes to you (but he shall have one tribe for the sake of My servant David, and for the sake of Jerusalem, the city which I have chosen out of all the tribes of Israel), because they have forsaken Me, and worshipped Ashtoreth the goddess of the Sidonians, Chemosh the god of the Moabites, and Milcom the god of the people of Ammon, and have not walked in My ways to do *what is* right in My eyes and *keep* My statutes and My judgments, as *did* his father David. However I will not take the whole kingdom out of his hand, because I have made him ruler all the days of his life for the sake of My servant David, whom I chose because he kept My commandments and My statutes. But I will take the kingdom out of his son's hand and give it to you— ten tribes'" (1 Kings 11:31-35).

Ahijah added that Jeroboam would rule over the ten tribes of Israel and that if he obeyed God faithfully, God would grant him and his house long-term rulership. When Solomon heard about these prophecies, he tried to kill Jeroboam but was unable to have this carried out. Solomon's assassins were not quick enough. Jeroboam fled for safety to Egypt. Given that Egypt was ruled now by the resurgent pharaoh, Shishak, we can place these events in the last few years of Solomon's reign. The new pharaoh was happy to accommodate Solomon's enemies, and we can see that Solomon's alliance with Egypt had already broken down. There was no war yet as Shishak was consolidating his overthrow of the old, weak regime. International trade was continuing, but Solomon had lost Egypt; his son would have to face the consequences.

While Solomon still reigned, Jeroboam maintained contact remotely with his Northern conspirators among the ten tribes. After Solomon's death, Jeroboam headed up a revolt which had been simmering and developing in the North for years. He quickly became king over Israel, a geographical area perhaps twice the size of Judah, while Solomon's son, Rehoboam, his heir-apparent, succeeded him as ruler in Jerusalem but only over the two Southern tribes. Some of the outlying areas in Solomon's kingdom—such as Moab, Edom, and Aram—spiraled out of control and were lost to both of them.

However, Ahijah was not finished with Jeroboam. Years later, he gave a second prophecy to the king. Because he had pursued the worship of idols more than Solomon did, the kingdom was taken from Jeroboam's house; the nation was given up; and the remnants of it were cast into exile beyond the Euphrates.[193] All this came to pass. The Northern kingdom lasted just over two hundred years and was then conquered by Assyria.

In conclusion, we can state that in fulfillment of a prophecy, Yahweh raised up three opponents to battle with Solomon. Yahweh acted exactly as He said He would if Solomon turned his back on Him to worship foreign gods. Nathan's prophecy, given to David, applied to Solomon at times and also reaches forward in places to the rule of Christ after the end of this age. The blows to Solomon from his three adversaries fulfilled part of the prophecy. It was Yahweh Who broke up the Jewish empire, but the rest of the prophecy is still to be fulfilled.

> "When your days are fulfilled and you rest with your fathers, I will set up your seed after you, who will come from your body, and I will establish his kingdom. He shall build a house for My name, and I will establish the throne of his kingdom forever. I will be his Father, and he shall be My son. If he commits iniquity, I will chasten him with the rod of men and with the blows of the sons of men. But My mercy shall not depart from him, as I took *it* from Saul, whom I removed from before you" (2 Sam. 7:12-15).

---

193 1 Kings 14:5-16

CHAPTER 28

GOD'S JUDGMENT ON SOLOMON

So Adam gave names to all cattle, to the birds of the air, and to every beast of the field . . . Then to Adam He [God] said, "Because you have heeded the voice of your wife, and have eaten from the tree of which I commanded you, saying, 'You shall not eat of it': Cursed is the ground for your sake; In toil you shall eat of it All the days of your life" . . . therefore the Lord God sent him out of the garden of Eden.

—Genesis 2:20a, 3:17, 23a

Long before Solomon, Moses wrote the following: "For all our days are passed away in Your wrath; We finish our years like a sigh. The days of our lives *are* seventy years; And if by reason of strength *they are* eighty years, Yet their boast *is* only labor and sorrow; For it is soon cut off, and we fly away" (Psalm 90:9-10).

We could have expected Solomon to live a long time. Moses lived to be 120 years old, and he guessed that a typical human lifespan allowed by God is seventy to eighty years—if the multiple perils of disease, misadventure, battle injury, and famine can all be avoided. Early on in Solomon's reign, when he traveled to the ceremonial high place at Gibeon to offer a sacrifice, God had been pleased with the young king's disposition toward Him over and above the one thousand burnt offerings he offered. The king got as close to God as he could. The temple was not yet built. The king humbly asked God for an understanding heart and wisdom. God replied as follows:

"Behold, I have done according to your words; see, I have given you a wise and understanding heart, so that there has not been anyone like you before you, nor shall any like you arise after you. And I have also given you what you have not asked: both riches and honor, so that there shall not be anyone like you among the kings all your days. So if you walk in My ways, to keep My statutes and My commandments, as your father David walked, then I will lengthen your days" (1 Kings 3:12-14).

God promised four things to Solomon, and the first three were unconditional. The first had already come to pass when Solomon awoke from his dream. The wisdom and splendor of Solomon became so great that many hundreds of years later, Jesus referred back to them, acknowledging what they were—kingly attributes that were unsurpassable until Jesus, Who is greater still. Jesus says, for instance, "The queen of the South will rise up in the judgment with this generation and condemn it, for she came from the ends of the earth to hear the wisdom of Solomon; and indeed a greater than Solomon *is* here" (Matt. 12:42).

God's fourth and last promise to Solomon was conditional. It was given last in the sequence because God knew that Solomon would not fulfill the requirements for the promise to come to pass. This was despite the fact that God made it possible for Solomon to fulfill the requirements. He only had to walk as his own father, David, did. We know, however, from Asaph and from the wider biblical account that Solomon's reign turned evil. God brought his punitive, acquisitive, centralizing plutocracy to an end with his death at fifty-nine or sixty years of age. Solomon's reign was so evil that God pulled his allotted years back to considerably less than what man can reasonably expect. Solomon died, we are told, of natural causes. Many of his latter sayings indicate that he was old and disillusioned before his time. But even in his disillusionment, there is wisdom: "The words of the Preacher, the son of David, king in Jerusalem. 'Vanity of vanities,' says the Preacher; 'Vanity of vanities; all *is* vanity.' . . . *What is* crooked cannot be made straight, And what is lacking cannot be numbered" (Eccl. 1:1-2,15).

What crookedness had Solomon tried to straighten? He had observed the brutal timelines of Egypt to the south and those of the Aramean kingdoms to the north. In all his own empire-building and the creation of a formidable fighting force, he had pursued world trade and the maintenance of a geopolitical peace unlike anything seen before. He had aspired to achieve peace through national self-constraint, the refraining to use destructively the power and wealth he had created. He was always so prepared for war that he never had to go to war.

He was an enterprising and creative genius who even went beyond this when he constructed a vastly expensive temple to centralize and focus his people's faith and worship. In building the temple first before his own palace complex, he had sought to put God first. And it was to be a place of peace which symbolized the national and international peace he had constructed.

But his own crookedness had leached out in all sorts of other ways. His people had, in fact, been trodden down, and he had taken after all sorts of pagan gods hungry for blood sacrifice. He had disregarded a whole swath of Divine prerogatives, and his harem included at least a thousand women.[194] He was wise enough to know that God would hold him accountable for what he had done and for what he had failed to do. He also knew toward the end of his relatively short life that he, as a fallen man, could not actually straighten a crooked way. Only God can do it.

He had become old before his time. Many commentators say in passing that Solomon wrote Ecclesiastes in his old age. Solomon did not experience old age. But his mindset and his awareness of his own tragedy speaks of someone who is old mentally, without the years to go with it. There was nothing else to be done. He had been repeating the same old sins for far too long already. He was aware of humanity's tragic state. He rightly and widely extrapolates from his own life to the lives of all his fellow men. Without God's help, people's lives are vanity and a chasing after the wind.

There was also a strange limitation when it came to Solomon's wisdom. Solomon often pondered on paradoxes and contradictions. He would surely have pondered on the paradox of requiring forced labor from much of the

---

194 Deuteronomy 17:16-17

population to create a super-state which would always know peace in his lifetime. But in a more fundamental way, he came to an awareness of his own contradictory ways of thinking and behaving too late in the day either for him or for the preservation of his kingdom. Essentially, Solomon was either unwilling or unable to reason about his own problems as wisely as about other people's problems. He did not work out what he should do himself from his wisdom regarding what others should do. Solomon's wisdom was world-renowned. The Queen of Sheba and many others were much impressed. Yet although Solomon knew that a son should gain wisdom from a father able to instruct him,[195] he did not instruct his own son, Rehoboam, who tyrannized the people and was unable to rule the kingdom until he was belatedly able to successfully rule the smaller, southern part of it.

Although Solomon knew that happiness was to be found by keeping the law,[196] he comprehensively broke Jewish laws himself in an uncontrolled acquisition of pagan wives and concubines. This phenomenon has now been given a term: *Solomon's paradox*. The phenomenon or condition is the inability or unwillingness to apply to oneself and one's own conduct or decision-making the wiser advice we would give to others if we saw that they were faced with the same choices or possibilities. It has been called "self-others asymmetry." The psychologists Igor Grossman and Ethan Kross have shown that increasing age does *not* improve the self-others asymmetry in wise reasoning, but certain types of cognitive training, such as self-distancing, can.[197] Solomon, in all his wisdom, could not close the gap in his own asymmetric reasoning, since apart from anything else, it is part of the human condition. Yet if social-cognitive scientists can train people to overcome it, surely God could have helped Solomon, if the king had been willing.

---

195   E.g. Proverbs 23
196   E.g. Proverbs 29
197   Igor Grossman and Ethan Kross, "Exploring Solomon's Paradox: Self-Distancing Eliminates the Self-Other Asymmetry in Wise Reasoning About Close Relationships in Younger and Older Adults," *Psychological Science*, Vol. 25, No. 8 (2014): 1571-1580, https://doi.org/10.1177/0956797614535400.

Solomon thought that his wisdom would enable him to *not* suffer the consequences of overindulgence materially and sexually. He thought he was wise enough to circumvent it. He became a hedonist, and he did experience the consequences. Allowing his pagan wives to practice idolatry was bad in itself, but it also led him into his own practice of idolatry. His ever-increasing need for wealth and possessions led him down a road into cruel and adverse industrial relations where rebellion seethed. Tens of thousands of slave laborers in the Northern tribes could see that their grinding poverty was the price they were paying for the king's lavish and exotic lifestyle. The foreign policy initiatives and agreements with foreign powers were more fragile than Solomon thought they would be. Egypt itself was more unstable than he thought it was, and he misdirected his positioning of offensive and defensive weaponry away from the greatest threat on his borders.

The price to be paid for Solomon's misrule, unfortunately, went well beyond all this. Initially, he had helped the Jews to reach a zenith in their approach to God through the creation of a spectacular temple complex. But in the longer-term aftermath, both the splintered kingdoms declined spiritually and militarily. Often at war with each other, their corporate spiritual lives spiraled downward into increasing idolatry, which, to a very great extent, Solomon had initiated. Every king of Israel from Jeroboam onward could now be considered as evil, and many of the kings of Judah were evil, although some were able enough to initiate economic and military innovations.

Scripture makes no mention of how Solomon died. However, in his comparison of Josephus' account of Solomon's life to that of Scripture, C. T. Begg points out that Josephus writes, "Solomon died ingloriously."[198] This is in sharp contrast to the death of his father, David. We do not know whether Josephus referred to a specific set of circumstances or to the general apostasy which had enveloped and swallowed up the king. Scripture (e.g. 1 Kings 11:9-13, 33; Micah

---

198   C. T. Begg, "Solomon's Apostasy According to Josephus," *Journal for the Study of Judaism in the Persian, Hellenistic, and Roman Period,* Vol. 28, No. 3 (1997): 294-313, https://www.jstor.org/stable/24668405.

2:10) records that because Solomon's sin of idolatry was very great, well beyond the sins of Saul and David in severity, the punishment was also very severe: the future destruction of the temple, the immediate destruction of the united monarchy, and the eventual exile of the people.

CHAPTER 29

SOLOMON ON THE COUCH: THE KING'S PERSONALITY

"Wealth is good, and if it comes our way, we will take it;

but a gentleman does not sell himself for wealth."

—H. Rider Haggard, *King Solomon's Mines*, 1885

Solomon did not live to be old as we would consider old age to be. We know, however, that he wrote Ecclesiastes toward the end of his life. It has been described as a book full of world-weariness and skepticism, a standing back from the pursuits of life and observing futility and pointlessness in them. This may be true; but there is more to the book, and it is not written without emotion. Toward its end, in chapter twelve, the main emotional content is depressive.

The last chapter focuses on his failing powers, and its poetic imagery enables us to judge that the king's concerns have to do with sexual impotence. His libido had failed him, and his use of aphrodisiacs had been to no avail. He could not enjoy any of his wives or concubines. Like certain passages in Song of Solomon, the imagery is dream-like. His impotence troubled him so much that he dreamed about it and then wrote the images down in Ecclesiastes. He knew the images had meaning, and he may well have understood the meaning. His wisdom enabled him to interpret his dreams, and the imagery he recorded is sexual. However, he also left it to the reader as to what to make of it.

AN ANALYSIS OF SOLOMON'S DREAMS

"When the grinders cease because they are few, And those that
look through the windows grow dim; When the doors are shut in
the streets, And the sound of grinding is low" (Eccl. 12:3b-4a).

In Solomon's time, grinding of the wheat crop was done between two
millstones. The shut doors represent his wives' sexual organs, which were
effectively closed to him, and they also represent the end of social intimacy. Each
of the millstones had a name. The upper one was called *rekeb* (the rider), and
the lower one was called *shekeb* (the lier-under). These terms have clear sexual
meaning: the grinding had faltered. The grinders also symbolize teeth. Many had
fallen out. Freud saw this dream symbolism as a symbol for impotency.[199] The
meaning of teeth missing is wider than that in dreams; for instance, it can mean
an inability to process information coming to you in your working life; but in
Solomon's case, the Freudian interpretation is correct, since it is in alignment
with other sexual imagery in the text.

"Also they are afraid of height, And of terrors in the
way; When the almond tree blossoms, The grasshopper
is a burden, And desire fails" (Eccl. 12:5).

The almond tree is a sexual image and also a symbol of life and resurrection.
Solomon's female companions still attracted him; they were as beautiful as ever,
but he had lost his strength. His crop of beautiful women was being taken from
him by his lack of strength as if they were being eaten up before him by insects.
The NKJV translation "desire fails" is better translated as "the caperberry fails."
The caperberry is a fruit taken from the Palestinian plant *Capparis spinose*, but it
was the plant's berries, which Israelites and others used to make an aphrodisiac.
The plant is used today in the Middle East for various herbal medicines.

It is very likely that the main meaning of the last chapter of Ecclesiastes
is sexual. The commentator Frank Zimmermann extrapolates convincingly

---

199 A. A. Brill, *The Basic Writings of Sigmund Freud* (New York: Modern Library, 1995).

from the more obvious symbols of impotence to argue that general, somewhat depressive references are also sexual in meaning.[200] For instance, having no pleasure in the days has to do with the absence of sexual gratification. Because the grinding falters, the bird languishes, and the voice falters (because of his sexual failure), the king pretended to disdain the almond tree (his women). His aphrodisiacs failed him. The king was not merely world-weary. He was greatly shocked by his loss of sexual energy.

Apart from Solomon's end section—the whole duty of man, in which he honors God—the king ends Ecclesiastes with the statement: "Vanity of vanities . . . All is vanity" (v. 8). This is also exactly how he starts the book. Therefore, to understand Ecclesiastes, we have to take as its context Solomon's loss of virility, which he describes poetically in its last chapter.

SOLOMON'S CONCLUSIONS

"Let us hear the conclusion of the whole matter: Fear God and keep His commandments, For this is man's all. For God will bring every work into judgment, Including every secret thing, Whether good or evil" (Eccl. 12:13-14).

The king ends, finally, with acknowledgement of Yahweh. Beyond all books and all good and bad decisions of mankind, Yahweh is there. He is the God Who is always there. Solomon's father, David, had ruled through military prowess as well as strength of character. David was also "a friend of God." In contrast, Solomon ruled through wisdom and the persuasive speech emanating from his own strength of character. In his defense, while he may well have desired wealth, he did not ask for the wealth he amassed—or his fame either, for that matter.

THE KING'S PERSONALITY

What can be concluded regarding Solomon's personality? The king began his life as a ruler as someone who felt inadequate to the task. One of the reasons for

---

200 F. Zimmermann, "The book of Ecclesiastes in the light of some psychoanalytic observations," in *American Imago* (December, 1948), 5(4), 301-305.

this is that he had a great father, King David, known throughout the region for his bravery and his exploits in battle. Solomon was merely David's son. When he requested wisdom and an understanding heart from Yahweh, he knew that Yahweh had only shown love toward David. Solomon saw himself as lesser than his father before God, but perhaps God would assist him on that basis because He loved David. So, he approached God as though he were a small child and referred to himself in that way.

Solomon had never assumed he would become king. He had older brothers and younger ones, too. David's loyalties and fatherly love was split across them all; he had great love toward Absalom, who rose up against him, and he had great love toward Solomon's older brother, who died as an infant. Yet Solomon had been acted on by others—David, Bathsheba, and Nathan—and he had been crowned king. He had sufficient wisdom to put Adonijah in his place and had shown strength combined with restraint—not dissimilar to David's approach to challenges—but building up and successfully ruling a kingdom requires a lot more. Solomon allowed himself to be passively made king. Unlike his half-brother, Adonijah, and his half-brother, Absalom, he did not have the drive to rule or the confidence to seek out the kingdom for himself. He felt too inferior, in his late teenage years, to seek his allies out and enter the fray.

We know that God granted Solomon his request for wisdom. But later in Solomon's reign, we find a king whose style of rulership with all its material trappings displayed the outworking of a lot more besides that (i.e. a kingdom generated out of what Solomon really needed). He needed to have power, wealth, and grandeur. He wanted, in reality, to be a bigger and better king than his father, David. The psychoanalytic commentator Zeligs refers to this as narcissism and also as the outworkings of a subliminated sense of inferiority stemming from being just one of his famous father's sons.[201] The grandeur of his kingdom grew and was energized by his attempts to overcome his sense of inferiority. His

---

201 Dorothy Zeligs, "Solomon: Man and Myth," *The Psychoanalytic Review,* 48(1), 77-103 (Spring, 1961) and 48(2), 91-110, (Summer, 1961), http://www.pep-web.org/document.php?id=psar.04 8a.0077a&type=hitlist&num=14&query=zone1%2Cparagraphs%7Czone2%2Cparagraphs%7 Cauthor%2C%22Zeligs%2C+D.F.%22&flash=true.

kingdom was a defense mechanism. Its strength, its chariot cities, and its cavalry enabled Solomon to feel less inferior to David than he would otherwise have felt. But only God can minister to these sorts of things.

God also says this to the king: "And I have also given you what you have not asked: both riches and honor, so that there shall not be anyone like you among the kings all your days" (1 Kings 3:13). God was pleased to also give Solomon what he *could* have asked for but did not. Solomon also wanted these things but did not ask for them, partly because he realized that wisdom had to come first; he knew he needed that gift first and foremost to be up to the responsibility and to achieve anything. Furthermore, he knew that it was not fitting for him to ask. The *Legends of the Jews* says that his natural intelligence determined what should be asked for: "Solomon chose wisdom, knowing that wisdom once in his possession, all else would come of itself."[202]

His speech to God also reveals that he saw himself as important to God only because he was David's son, not because of who he was in himself—another reason to limit his request. But nevertheless, Solomon craved riches, honor, and a long life; he wanted power and a kind of omnipotence. God responded favorably regarding what the king asked for and what he wanted in addition, but the long life was conditional.

We could say that Solomon fought no battles because he feared competition in the same arena as his warlord father. A loss in battle would increase his sense of inferiority. David's battle tally was large, and he hardly ever lost. Battles were best avoided. He competed with his father, David, on his own terms: expanding his father's kingdom and becoming richer than anyone else.

---

202 Louis Ginzberg and Boaz Cohen, *The Legends of the Jews Volume 4* (Charleston: Nabu Press, 2010).

CHAPTER 30
REJECTION OF THE FATHER

"To love many is indeed to love none."

—Dorothy Zeligs[203]

The primary relationship Solomon had within his family of origin was with his mother, Bathsheba, and we can contrast it with his relationships with all his other family members. The relationship became clearer once Solomon had gained the throne. It even determined Solomon's initial display of his God-given wisdom.

His father, David, had a great many sons, initially having six sons when he ruled in Hebron. Solomon was the fourth son born to David in Jerusalem. So, Solomon was merely tenth in line to the throne if rulership operated through a system of primogeniture. Solomon knew he was the promised heir, but this would not have been a fact on the ground which was commonly accepted within the ruling family or even spoken about. David was wiser than Jacob. He did not want nine older half-brothers conspiring against Solomon as Joseph's older half-brothers had done a thousand years earlier. David was content to leave the matter of succession to Yahweh and the prophets.

Many of Solomon's brothers were bold, arrogant, and a lot older than him. If he had expressed his desire or right to rule, it is likely he would have been assassinated by any one of them, but especially by Absalom, who rebelled against David, fighting a major civil war against his father. Absalom had first

203 Zeligs, ibid.

killed his older brother, Amnon, the heir-apparent. Solomon was also well aware of Adonijah, an older brother who admired Absalom but had a more subtle personality and who also nursed a desire for power and the will to attain it by any means. Growing up in the palace, Solomon knew that if he was to live at all, he must live at peace with his brothers and leave his rise to power to the unfolding of circumstances beyond his control. He could dream of power, but he could never talk about it in a charged and fractious home.

Solomon's relationship with David was not so good. Solomon would have been in awe of him as a king, a warlord rich in exploits, and as one whom Yahweh loved and favored. But there is also evidence of mutually felt ambivalence (i.e. a lack of love). The Scriptures record just two interactions between them: a ruler-to-subject speech recorded in 1 Chronicles 22 and the more informal speech recorded in 1 Kings 2. In both interactions, Solomon was silent. An extract of the latter is below:

> Now the days of David drew near that he should die, and he charged Solomon his son, saying: "I go the way of all the earth; be strong, therefore, and prove yourself a man. And keep the charge of the LORD your God: to walk in His ways, to keep His statutes, His commandments, His judgments, and His testimonies, as it is written in the Law of Moses, that you may prosper in all that you do and wherever you turn; that the LORD may fulfill His word which He spoke concerning me, saying, 'If your sons take heed to their way, to walk before Me in truth with all their heart and with all their soul,' He said, 'you shall not lack a man on the throne of Israel.' "Moreover you know also what Joab the son of Zeruiah did to me, and what he did to the two commanders of the armies of Israel, to Abner the son of Ner and Amasa the son of Jether, whom he killed. And he shed the blood of war in peacetime, and put the blood of war on his belt that *was* around his waist, and on his sandals that *were* on his feet. Therefore do according to your wisdom, and do not let his gray hair go down to the grave in peace. "But show kindness to the sons of Barzillai the Gileadite, and let them be among those who eat at

your table, for so they came to me when I fled from Absalom your brother" (1 Kings 2:1-7).

The extract is quite lengthy because it is important to get a sense of the real communication and its psychological significance. It is noteworthy as a speech lacking in warmth or honesty. It was only made at all because David's impending death had confined him into the situation where it had to be made. David did not go as far as giving commands to his son but treated him as an equal. He confided secrets to him: his attitudes and desire toward those who broke the law and those who helped him. He also referred twice to Solomon's wisdom in a way which suggests something akin to manipulation. He was flattering his son through a way of appeal which he thought would work with Solomon. David wanted his son to execute David's will but asked him in a way which suggests either an ailing king's weakness or a weakness which was always there but hidden. It also indicated a former condescending way of relating which has not been straightforward or open and honest. Perhaps it revealed David's distrust of Solomon's qualities, including his natural wisdom. If so, it would only increase Solomon's desire for wisdom. In time, it led to Solomon distancing his rule from that of his father's.

At no time does Solomon fulfill his father's wishes as David had expected. Once in power, he bided his time until he had his own reasons to kill David's enemies. The building of the temple was also a good case in point. As revealed in 1 Chronicles 22, David did absolutely everything he could to construct the temple (short of building it). David used the excuse that Solomon was young and inexperienced, so he could justify organizing the materials. But out of necessity, he was ordering Solomon to build it. We have seen how Solomon built it. He used the materials, but the temple did not comply with his father's ideas. He also substituted alternative and more valuable materials as he saw fit. Did Solomon do this in a reaction against his father?

The psychoanalyst Dorothy Zeligs applies a number of interesting points, standard in the psychoanalytic perspective, to the relationship between David and Solomon. David loved Bathsheba greatly; he committed murder to acquire her. The birth of Solomon, though, would have created complex and mixed feelings for his son. Bathsheba's attention would now be diverted away from David, while at the same time, the son assured David that he has been forgiven by God for his adultery. New life was a blessing. To add to this mix, we have David's poor relationship with his own parents. He was the eighth and youngest son, not considered sufficiently a son for him to be invited to appear before Samuel: "Thus Jesse made seven of his sons pass before Samuel. And Samuel said to Jesse, 'The Lord has not chosen these.' And Samuel said to Jesse, 'Are all the young men here?' Then he said, 'There remains yet the youngest, and there he is, keeping the sheep'" (1 Sam. 16:10-11a).[204]

One of the key emotions David would have felt toward Solomon was jealousy: the son was a rival with him for Bathsheba's affections. It is likely that he suppressed the jealousy and defended his mind against it by projecting an aspect of himself and his ambitions on to Solomon; he should achieve what David could not, and so through Solomon, David could gain God's further approval. It would be as if David had achieved it. Solomon could build the temple Yahweh had told David he was not to build. Therefore, David could obey God and at the same time, or slightly later, be blessed for having achieved the task through his son. In such situations, what the son achieves is never enough for the father. The father's "ego ideal" is always beyond the son's accomplishments toward it, and the son experiences hostility rather than "well done." Solomon, of course, was fixated on accomplishing his father's task, but he also delighted in superseding it. We have to stand back from this analysis and have every sympathy for Solomon. Not only did he accept the task willingly, but he also greatly admired his father. He had thought about how his father reigned, and he, too, wanted—at least at the start—to limit the exercise of raw power with mercy and justice. This was at the heart of what he asked for from Yahweh.

---

204 It is probable that David, unlike his seven older half-brothers, was illegitimate. He says, "In sin my mother conceived me" (Psalm 51:5). Nowhere in Scripture is the name of his mother mentioned. Psalm 51 is penned by David after Nathan has revealed that it is knowledge in Heaven that David committed adultery. Does this bring back to David that he himself is a child of adultery?

The bond between Solomon and his mother, Bathsheba, on the other hand, was very strong. To Bathsheba, Solomon represented God's forgiveness. He was the physical representation and proof of her restitution and favor with God after the death of her first child with David. We also see him honoring his mother greatly; he was loving and protective toward her. Scripture shows us that he honored her in public, bowing down before her. He caused another throne to be brought so that she could sit beside him in the royal palace on his right-hand side.[205] Yet, he was not in awe of his mother. When she communicated his brother's dark request to him for Abishag, he rejected it at once. He was wiser than she and immediately saw the purpose behind the request. He was also operating far above a mindset which might tempt him to shoot the messenger. He was angry only with his brother.

Solomon was also aware that while it was God's will that he be king, his mother had expedited it. David had promised the succession to Bathsheba; and later, she intervened, along with Nathan, to help secure it. She had probably interceded with David at other times for Solomon. She was protective and usually had his best interests in mind.

Solomon very much believed that his mother's love was good and that mothers, in general, are good. He chose the first recorded case of his exercising of his Yahweh-increased wisdom to say that. He showed that even the love of a harlot for her child was genuine and demonstrable. His wisdom struck a chord with the people. They, too, knew that a mother's love counts for much, and they loved his searching for it and his honoring of it.

Solomon's one-on-one conversation with Bathsheba is the only one recorded in Scripture; any other direct speech uttered by Solomon is in a group audience setting, in the context of the palace or court. At other times, we are only made aware that Solomon spoke, but we are not given what he said. The extended interview with the Queen of Sheba is a good example of this. Perhaps God decided that Solomon's wisdom (in relation to the events of his time) was for his time and

---

205 1 Kings 2:19

not for any other. It was not to be communicated to future generations outside of the three books ascribed to him. His judgment over the two prostitutes is retained as an example of the unexpected, fast action of his supernatural wisdom. As an exemplar, it is sufficient.

NARCISSISM AND ITS EMPTINESS

There is a lot of evidence from the biblical record which suggests that Solomon was narcissistic. That is to say, rather than displaying a healthy self-love, Solomon was frequently grandiose and vain. Early in his reign, he demonstrates this when he mentions his own building of the temple. In his dedicatory prayer, for instance, he linked his building of it with strangers or foreigners hearing of it. Solomon wanted all people to know God's name and His power, and he also wanted them to know of Solomon. "Hear in heaven Your dwelling place, and do according to all for which the foreigner calls to You, that all peoples of the earth may know Your name and fear You, as *do* Your people Israel, and that they may know that this temple which I have built is called by Your name" (1 Kings 8:43-44).

His reaching out to strangers and foreigners is not entirely to be dissociated from his acquiring of foreign women as wives and his trade agreements with foreign powers. But his entourage of a thousand women could be considered as the most obvious aspect of a type of "narcissistic supply" as defined by the psychoanalyst, Otto Fenichel. The ever-increasing supply of women could be considered as an attempt to satisfy an excessive need for admiration, interpersonal support, and attention, without any due regard for others' needs. It is also a false proof of achievement.[206] At its root is a hungry and insatiable emptiness. Women cannot actually satisfy it, and so everyone is likely to become frustrated—the narcissist *and* all his women. The wives and concubines are a representation and outcome of Solomon's love addiction, but they were also part of a wider narcissistic supply resource created by Solomon since he was also predisposed to

---

206 Otto Fenichel, M.D., and Leo Rangell, M.D., *The Psychoanalytic Theory of Neurosis* (New York, NY: W. W. Norton and Co., 1996).

surrounding himself with opulent and extravagant wealth. Such a large number of wives and concubines demonstrated his wealth.

None of the wives or concubines appear as central characters in Solomon's story. Although they must have taken up a substantial part of his time, there is no indication that he was too caught up with them. There really is just himself as ruler and judge. His equals may be found among the pagan rulers beyond his territory, but not within his harem. Among the rulers was the Queen of Sheba, a shrewd and beautiful woman who played up to Solomon's narcissism while also being enthralled by his lavish court and his hospitality: "'Your wisdom and prosperity exceed the fame of which I heard. Happy *are* your men and happy *are* these your servants, who stand continually before you *and* hear your wisdom! Blessed be the Lord your God, who delighted in you, setting you on the throne of Israel" (1 Kings 10:7b-9a).

In a spirit of friendly rivalry, the queen tested Solomon with many riddles, and he delighted in answering all of them. He treated her in an honorable way, giving her everything she asked. In fact, this is very characteristic of Solomon. He was keen to honor women. He honored his mother, Bathsheba, even when she asked amiss for a favor his half-brother should not gain. He honored his Egyptian wife with her own palace built alongside his own. He was even led astray by his desire to honor women, building altars to their false gods. Above all else, though, he greatly honored the subject of his song with possibly the most mysterious and powerful love poetry ever written:

Until the day breaks
And the shadows flee away,
I will go my way to the mountain of myrrh
And to the hill of frankincense.
You *are* all fair, my love,
And *there is* no spot in you (Song of Songs 4:6-7).

A TIME OF DEPARTING

Compared to his father, David, Solomon's prayers reveal that he did not have the same level of intimacy with God; there is a lack of joy and delight when

Solomon's prayers are compared to David's psalms. As his reign continued on, his spiritual life decayed from a level below the intimacy David enjoyed with God to a level much further removed from the spiritual life of his father. His intermarriage with every pagan nation known to him diluted his spiritual identity.

The warning as to what was likely to happen was given to Solomon by God when the king was visited a second time, about twenty years after his dream at Gibeon. Unlike the first time, there was no conversation between them. Only God spoke. We have to assume, therefore, that the intimacy which Solomon did know with God very early in his reign had now departed. In its place were narcissistic desires and feelings of omnipotence. In addition, most of the one-way communication was very stark. Even though God had chosen to hallow his temple and focus on it, He would destroy it and turn His people out of the land if the king, or his ruling lineage, committed apostasy and worshipped false gods. The communication was really a prediction, and it marked the start of Solomon's decline as a ruler and spiritual leader, a little over halfway into his reign. He now rapidly descended into the evil of which God had just warned him.

CHAPTER 31

BEYOND NARCISSISM

"Cogito, ergo sum" ("I think, therefore I am").

—René Descartes

In his travels around the world, the analytical psychologist, Carl Jung, met a group of Pueblo Native Americans (Taos Pueblos) in New Mexico. Their chief was called Ochwiay Biano (Mountain Lake). Their religion was secret; Jung was unable to access it directly. Yet, their faith enabled the Taos Pueblos to hold out against the whites. Through elaborate questioning, he found that the Taos worshipped the sun—they were all the sons of "Father Sun"—and all of life came from the mountain and the river pouring down from it. Jung was struck by the chief's serenity.

> "See," Ochwiay Biano said, "how cruel the whites look. Their lips are thin, their noses sharp, their faces furrowed and distorted by folds. Their eyes have a staring expression; they are always seeking something. What are they seeking? The whites always want something; they are always uneasy and restless. We do not know what they want. We do not understand them. We think that they are mad."
> I asked him why he thought the whites were all mad.
> "They say that they think with their heads," he replied.
> "Why of course. What do you think with?" I asked him in surprise.
> "We think here," he said, indicating his heart.[207]

---

207 C.G. Jung, *Travels: America, in Memories, Dreams and Reflections,* Revised Ed. (Visalia: Vintage, 1996).

We need to go a bit further to understand Solomon. The king can only be understood if we infer that a very common head-heart split, as observed by Ochwiay Biano, applied to him. The wisdom Solomon was given deepened and extended many attributes and capabilities of his mind, such as rationality, detachment, creative problem-solving, and project management. In addition, he was given the ability to apply all this to statecraft and the management of vast projects. The king was able to operate at an intuitive level as well—his Song of Songs is a mysterious and transcendent piece of writing. It portrays the movements of lovers' souls in a dynamic, which, at times, is at a purely human level but occasionally transcends it spiritually and emotionally. In other words, he was able to observe, reflect on, and describe reality. His mind was very precise but also creative.

Yet, the king was also in thrall to forces operating at an entirely different level inside him and which could not be controlled or circumvented by the mere application of wisdom. It may not be entirely accurate to conclude that Solomon was a sex addict as the term is understood in the twenty-first century, but he was subject to a condition of that sort. At a mental level, he would probably have rationalized and normalized the hundreds of wives, for many years anyway, as a comprehensive exercise in international diplomacy and connected trade relations guaranteed through sexual relations. Eventually, though, when he comprehended the folly of his choices, he stepped away from any such rationalism.

A more complete wisdom, stemming from inner wholeness, was something which he had failed to grasp, and his life became blighted by the effects of unequal and corrupting marriages. He knew he was unable to come to grips with and comprehend the forces emanating from his own wounded and fallen heart. The wives were the result of it, but they also exacerbated the problem. Trying to satisfy a compulsive addiction by sheer quantity of numbers was not the solution. Solomon knew now that a mind blessed with wisdom was not enough, but he never comprehended that Yahweh could heal.

> I said, "I will be wise"; But it *was* far from me. And I find more bitter than death The woman whose heart *is* snares and nets, Whose hands

are fetters. He who pleases God shall escape from her, But the sinner shall be trapped by her. "Here is what I have found," says the Preacher, "*Adding* one thing to the other to find out the reason, Which my soul still seeks but I cannot find: One man among a thousand I have found, But a woman among all these I have not found. Truly, this only I have found: That God made man upright, But they have sought out many schemes" (Eccl. 7:23b, 26-29).

This is how life had gone for Solomon. He wished it had been different. He was even able to advise others not to do as he did, and he did them a kindness. "Live joyfully with the wife whom you love all the days of your vain life which He has given you under the sun, all your days of vanity; for that *is* your portion in life, and in labor which you perform under the sun" (Eccl. 9:9).

At some point when he still lived in David's palace, Solomon dissociated from the horizontal and vertical jealousies and toxic emotions between wives, between siblings, and throughout David's turbulent family in general. It was his way of coping. He stood back in order to protect himself. Otherwise, he could end up dead. When he became king, there was no time to reflect on why he was really not ready to assume the throne. It was, after all, not like a modern-day job offer. He already had excellent mental faculties; then he was given even more by Yahweh; and so, compared to other heads of state at the time, he was the most fortunate of kings. Right at the start of his reign, though, his inner condition was such that there was an inner propensity or readiness for things to go wrong. In due time, Solomon partnered himself with one thousand women with whom he had very little emotional attachment. Given the sheer number, it was impossible for the relationships to develop. There was not enough time or personal investment for any of the relationships to mature.

Constant sex for Solomon was a retreat from wisdom, a wrong-headed experiment, and, like the accumulation of wealth beyond calculation, a way of bolstering his low self-esteem. Acquisition of wealth and women can involve "many schemes," to use Solomon's words, but it is not wise. The precise reasons for Solomon's obsessions are lost to us. We do not know in detail what happened to him as he was growing up in David's household, but the reasons for his sexual excess began there and exercised a life-long effect on his behavior and choices. He did not understand these things. It was, after all, the Iron Age.

Unlike his father, David, Solomon was cool and detached when it came to the people he ruled over. Dwelling mainly in his palace complex, he was rarely seen by them. Instead, he ruled over them impassively and usually by proxy. His palace and regional officials were employed to be his executive power, enforcing his authority. Although he did have an emotional life, some would probably find him chilling. Much of his time on the throne was spent in the acquiring of wealth and women. Ecclesiastes records the lack of satisfaction and fulfillment that they brought him. It also records his abrogation of narcissism as he objectifies and condemns it. He describes it in a kind of self-parody as he stands beside himself and observes his life and its end results. He was aware that his building works and his possessions did not satisfy and that what he built up would remain after him. He did not really possess them after all! He could not take them with him when he crossed the river of no return. His words are there to help all those who came after him. They are always insightful.

> Then I looked on all the works that my hands had done And on the labor in which I had toiled; And indeed all *was* vanity and grasping for the wind. *There was* no profit under the sun. Then I saw that wisdom excels folly As light excels darkness. The wise man's eyes *are* in his head, But the fool walks in darkness. Yet I myself perceived That the same event happens to them all. Then I hated all my labor in which I had toiled under the sun, because I must leave it to the man who will come after me (Eccl. 2:11, 13-14, 18).

CHAPTER 32

SOLOMON AND THE DJINN

"God also enabled him to learn that skill which expels demons."

—Flavius Josephus

In his *Antiquities of the Jews*, Josephus is at pains to point out that Solomon's wisdom was in no way inferior to that of the Egyptians. We have seen that Solomon borrowed some of his wisdom from them but assimilated it into his more expansive Proverbs. He also spoke in parables and similes about all known trees, animals, fish, and birds, philosophizing about them and investigating them. The scriptural accounts of Solomon's wisdom make mention of this as well.

Yet Josephus is absolutely clear that Solomon also learned how to expel demons. He makes the claim and then recounts how he believed he saw Solomon's wisdom regarding exorcism in action. The events occurred, of course, long after Solomon's death. It is worthwhile to quote Josephus at length in order to evaluate the claim the historian makes.

> God also enabled him to learn that skill which expels demons
> . . . He composed such incantations also, by which distempers are
> alleviated. And he left behind him the manner of using exorcisms,
> by which they drive away demons, so that they never return: and
> this method of cure is of great force unto this day; for I have seen a
> certain man of my own country, whose name was Eleazar, releasing
> people that were demoniacal, in the presence of Vespasian, and
> his sons, and his captains, and the whole multitude of his soldiers.
> The manner of the cure was this: he put a ring that had a root of

one of those sorts mentioned by Solomon, to the nostrils of the demoniac, after which he drew out the demon through his nostrils; and when the man fell down immediately, he adjured him to return into him no more, making still mention of Solomon, and reciting the incantations he composed.[208]

The historian adds some further interesting detail as to the events he says he witnessed in the presence of the Roman emperor, his son, Titus, and others. He recalls that Eleazar then confirmed his magical powers to his audience in a very theatrical way. He set up a basin of water and commanded the outcast demon, seemingly still about the place, to overturn it to confirm to his audience that it had, indeed, been cast out. Josephus states that he saw the basin overturn by itself, and he then waxes lyrical as to the "vastness of Solomon's abilities." The king had, of course, been dead for centuries.

The time and the place of this exorcism are unknown since Josephus does not include them. What is of interest, though, in the story is that, unlike in Scripture, it was Solomon who was applauded as the power behind the exorcism—someone who was not present at Vespasian's gathering—rather than God. Josephus is drawing from a collection of extra-biblical sources and legends to claim that Solomon exercised power over demons. Dennis Duling, emeritus professor at Canisius College, details the range of these in his paper in the *Harvard Theological Review*.[209] Specifically, Josephus draws from Jewish writers from the second century B.C. to the first century A.D. (such as the writers of the pseudepigraphical book, *Testament of Solomon*), who claimed that God's granting to Solomon of wisdom (detailed in 1 Kings 4:29-34) included magical wisdom, such as control over demons, and astrological insights. Solomon ruled over the demons, the spirits of the night, commanding them with the power of his magical ring. Solomon's magical gifts are also referred to well after Josephus in Jewish magical texts such as the *Sepher Ha-Rāzîm* from the third or fourth century A.D. Pseudepigraphical works, spuriously attributed to Solomon, continued to develop in the Middle East

---

208 Josephus, ibid.
209 Dennis C. Duling, "The Eleazar Miracle and Solomon's Magical Wisdom in Flavius Josephus's *Antiquitates Judaicae 8.42-49,*" *Harvard Theological Review*, Vol. 78, No. 1-2, Jan-April, 1-25, 1985.

and the Western world up and into the twentieth century and come under the heading of witchcraft grimoires.

Josephus deviates from Scripture to say to his readers that Solomon was a virtuous, miracle-working, and heroic Jewish king, a man who could interrupt the natural course of events to show God's power, even though he had been dead for many centuries. In other words, Josephus is continuing an already existing mythology being built up by the ancient world around Solomon. Josephus is, after all, writing for an audience: educated Greco-Roman readers. Although the Roman world frowned on the use of "black magic," some of his readers had an interest in "white magic." At the same time, Vespasian had been given the task by Nero of crushing one of the Jewish revolts. Later, Vespasian's son, Titus, sacked Jerusalem and destroyed the temple. As the Jewish-Roman wars were unfolding, Josephus was prepared to draw in anything he could think of to offer as apologetic for his own people, the Jews. A supernaturally endowed but long dead king whose magical power could still be tapped would be helpful.

A Pharisee and Roman sympathizer with imperial patronage, Josephus was also known to deviate from Scripture in order to have impact with his readers of the time.[210] Material in *Antiquities* consistent with references to the king in *Testament of Solomon* about his supernatural powers would appeal to Greco-Roman readers since *Testament* already included Grecian mythological and occult ideas. For instance, it states that one demon said to Solomon that he could transform himself into one of the Greek Titans, Kronos. Another describes Solomon's encounters with seven demon sisters from Mount Olympus—they represent the Pleiades, the companions of the Greek virgin goddess, Artemis. For polemical and political reasons, Josephus tried to authenticate Solomon's inclusion within the ancient world's mythos.

Josephus also frequently de-theologized biblical events; that is, he had a tendency to remove God from the Scripture narrative and replace Him with human speech from prophets giving the word of God to the character—for

---

210 Begg, ibid.

instance, to Solomon when God condemned his apostasy. While God's judgment could have been given via a prophet, Scripture does not say or even hint that it was. Josephus also emphasizes that Solomon mourned when God condemned his persistently apostate actions. Josephus actually plays Solomon's apostasy down, though he admits that Solomon's mourning and grief were to no avail in contrast to David's mourning over his own sins, to which God responded. Yet Scripture does not say that Solomon mourned. Josephus wants his readers to sympathize with and feel for the fallen king.

Did Josephus actually witness the magical event as given? It is likely that he did and that the event was quite well-known among the educated classes. Did the magician-healer Eleazar use Solomon's power of exorcism and demonstrate its success with a proof? By no means. In Jesus' time, the Pharisees claimed they could exorcise demons, but Jesus rejected the claim with this *ad hominem* argument: "And if I cast out demons by Beelzebub, by whom do your sons cast *them* out? Therefore they shall be your judges. But if I cast out demons by the Spirit of God, surely the kingdom of God has come upon you" (Matt. 12:27-28).

How was the basin overturned, though? It could have been overturned by any demon empowering the magician's tricks with the intention to deceive the ruling elite. There is also a kind of fallen, psychic strength which people in rebellion against God can employ, either by themselves or with help. Embrace the psychics and you move further into darkness, embracing the demonic. In such cases, occurrences need not follow the laws of physics. It is possible that Eleazar was operating more at the level of quantum physics but at a soulish or demonic level populated by fallen spirits.[211] If the effect was a demonstrable example of large-scale psychokinesis, it would place Eleazar at the same level as Carrie White in Stephen King's horror novel, *Carrie*, and the character Eleven in the web television series, *Stranger Things*. It seems clear enough, though, that the magical trick attributed to Solomon had nothing at all to do with Solomon.

211 Clay McLean, "The Soul in Prayer," *Nightlight Newsletters,* No. 312, May 1, 2019 (Hickory: McLean Ministries) https://www.mcleanministries.org/uploads/nightlight_newsletters/may_2019_reg_layout.pdf.

CHAPTER 33

TO RECAPITULATE A KING'S FLEETING EMBRACE OF YAHWEH

"The eye that mocks his father, And scorns obedience to his mother,
The ravens of the valley will pick it out, And the young eagles will eat it."

—Proverbs 30:17

Before we go on to consider the far-reaching consequences of his kingdom's collapse, we should spend a bit of time recapitulating the king's life and character. What ultimately is to be said of him? The first contradiction is that although he took no direct action to attain the throne, he did, in fact, long for power and wealth. His kingdom revealed and embodied what the king wanted. On top of this, though, Solomon had the wisdom and creative genius to rule across every department of state and to achieve an impressive, country-wide constellation of military, palace, and religious constructions. He built from a daring and innovative mindset. He did not need to emulate or build on someone else's work. His chariot cities, such as Megiddo, were without precedent in Israel. He developed Jerusalem into an impressive capital city and, overall, had great organizational skill.

Famous for his wisdom, he wrote thousands of proverbs and was highly intelligent, and he was clever enough at international diplomacy and trade to keep his nation at peace while building up a vast fortune. His ivory throne, overlaid with gold, was fixed between two standing lions, and beneath him were twelve lions, two on each side of the six steps down toward those who were before him for judgment. To those among the accused and to the petitioners before the king and who intuited such things, the fourteen lions said together:

You have come to the perfect place of deliverance and salvation.

Fear the Lord.

There is an incarnation and a mysterious salvation greater than this.

Looking back from our vantage point, we can see the throne symbolism realized in history. The fourteen lions symbolize the double perfection of the Lion of the tribe of Judah: the Messiah, Jesus Christ. Solomon divided the sevens by his throne, and he lived within the lineage of Christ as Matthew records it in his gospel. From Abraham to King David is fourteen generations. From King David, then Solomon, to the exile is another fourteen. From the exile to Joseph, the man who accepted Jesus as his son, another fourteen.

The fourteen lions each say: "Fear the Lord." Solomon ensured that fear of the Lord was emphasized fourteen times in his proverbs: "The fear of the Lord *is* the beginning of knowledge . . . Then you will understand the fear of the Lord, And find the knowledge of God" (Prov. 1:7a; 2:5).

The Israelites knew that God delivered Israel at the Passover on the fourteenth day of the first month. On the same fourteenth day of the first month, Jesus, the Lamb of God, was crucified outside Jerusalem to save humankind from sin. All those who believe in Him are saved from death and the second death. His death was a double completion of seven—symbolized by fourteen. His death completed His earthly ministry and also ended all need for animal sacrifices. Solomon on his dazzling throne, collectively symbolizing Yahweh and His plan and method of salvation, would have been an enthralling and fearful sight.

Even the wisest human ruler is a poor imitation of Christ, but having said that, Solomon can be considered as a forerunner of Christ in a number of respects. This is possibly best represented in the *Kebra Nagast*, which distills a number of key accomplishments of Solomon's life to compare them with Christ's ministry. This holy book indicates that Solomon's rule contains a series of advanced acting-outs, very imperfectly, of Christ's saving work. The temple in Jerusalem is compared to Christ's body in the same way that Christ compared it:

> So the Jews answered and said to Him, "What sign do You show to us, since You do these things?" Jesus answered and said to them, "Destroy this temple, and in three days I will raise it up." Then the Jews said, "It has taken forty-six years to build this temple, and will You raise it up in three days?" But He was speaking of the temple of His body (John 2:18-21).

The *Kebra Nagast* also states that Solomon's love of many foreign pagan wives is prophetic of Christ's love of foreign nations, those who were beyond the salvation offered first to the Jews. As Solomon did before Him, Christ saw their beauty. As Solomon gathered his wives into his palace, "He gathered them all into His heavenly kingdom by His Flesh and Blood."[212] We could even say that just as for Solomon, "so Christ gathered together from alien peoples those who had not the Law, but who believed on Him. And there was no uncircumcised man to Him, and no pagan; and there was no slave, and no Jew, and no servant and no free man."[213] [214]

Regarding Solomon's statecraft, we can conclude that Israel was far greater and more solid than any modern day kleptocracy. It was far more akin to a plutocracy (literally *wealth-rule*), similar in functioning to certain Greek city-states; Carthage; Italian merchant-states, such as Venice and Genoa; and eighteenth-century France before the revolution of 1789. All these states were ruled by a few people of very great wealth. The countries they govern tend not to last because the greed and hedonism displayed by the top one percent of the population engender class conflict fueled by despair and need. The poor rise up from within. An alternative fate is that the plutocracy is attacked from without

---

212   E.A.Wallis Budge, transl., "Concerning the Prophecy of Christ," in *The Kebra Nagast* (Scotts Valley: CreateSpace Independent Publishing Platform, 2014).
213   Ibid.
214   See also Galatians 3.

by opposing and more militaristic forces. In the case of Solomon's son, both these fates occurred in quick succession.

Solomon's reign declined throughout most of its second half. Scripture does not dwell on it. Some of the key facets of the decline are mentioned but only briefly and in such a way that it is difficult to imagine or work out the severity both of the fall and of its many consequences. It is defined in this way:

> But King Solomon loved many foreign women, as well as the daughter of Pharaoh: women of the Moabites, Ammonites, Edomites, Sidonians, *and* Hittites— from the nations of whom the LORD had said to the children of Israel, "You shall not intermarry with them, nor they with you. Surely they will turn away your hearts after their gods." Solomon clung to these in love. And he had seven hundred wives, princesses, and three hundred concubines; and his wives turned away his heart. For it was so, when Solomon was old, that his wives turned his heart after other gods; and his heart was not loyal to the Lord his God, as *was* the heart of his father David. For Solomon went after Ashtoreth the goddess of the Sidonians, and after Milcom the abomination of the Ammonites. Solomon did evil in the sight of the Lord (1 Kings 11:1-6).

We do not know to what extent he participated in the grotesque pagan worship practices his wives' pagan deities required (such as child sacrifice and cult prostitution) but at the very least, he gradually turned away from Yahweh and entertained a worshipful and respectful stance toward these entities. Therefore, God removed the kingdom from Solomon's dynasty, temporarily leaving two of the twelve tribes under its rule. How can we understand this apostasy and its etiology?

Solomon wanted to be omnipotent but was sufficiently in touch with reality to know that he was not and never would be. He also wanted power and was able to realize that to a considerable extent without the realization of it warping into megalomania. There was a limit to the degree of narcissism that Solomon's personality embraced. Why the apostasy, though? To at least partially understand it, we should consider his family of origin and its dysfunction.

As one of many children of many wives, Solomon would have had an ambivalent attitude toward his father, the king, but a close relationship with his mother, who was also invested strongly in her son out of love and also, perhaps, a desire to retain power and influence through a new role of dowager queen or mother of the king regnant. Out of necessity, Solomon often needed to relate to his father through Bathsheba, and in turn, it was her influence and hand on events, which catapulted Solomon up into kingship. Solomon admired his father and took cognizance of David's standing before Yahweh, but Solomon was also ambivalent toward his father. He did not love him.

In the first half of Solomon's reign, he embraced his father's desires and goals sufficiently to carry out his commands, albeit in Solomon's own time and with the addition of many Solomonic temple alterations and embellishments. Later, though, in the second half of his reign, Solomon deviated away from his father and his father's faith and interests. He was unable to fully integrate them into his own long-term wishes. He was not ultimately identified with them. They were of his father, not of him. He did not love his father, and so he was unable to fully identify with David's desires and especially his devotion to Yahweh. Solomon's faith began as childlike, but it was unstable and quite shallow, and he had not brought it into his core personality. Neither had his faith grown in adversity. There were no bears and wolves to defend his sheep against, no real giants to fight. He never took flight in fear of his life. He never had to depend on Yahweh for his very existence, alone and on the run. In the end, the waves of pagan idolatry and his desire to honor his pagan wives and their deities washed his faith in Yahweh away. His faith was secondary to whom Solomon really was and with what he identified.

Throughout the second half of his reign, Solomon rebelled against his father—not as Absalom did with force of arms, but in the realm of faith and religious practice and also in the deliberate breaking of multiple injunctions. He *did* have horses; he *did* have chariots; he *did* have gold and much else besides. His ambivalence toward David included genuine anger, and so he was compelled by psychological forces to rebel and chase after the forbidden things. The anger had been latent. As a younger son, he had many people with whom he contended, especially his older half-brothers and their claims on the throne. For Solomon growing up in the palace, David was an afterthought, not relevant to his survival and usually not accessible anyway. The anger and ambivalence, however, were there. Now, it was expressed in a turning away from David's temple, from David's priests, from David's prophets, and from David's God. Solomon overthrew him.

At the center of Solomon's rebellion were the myriad of pagan wives. With them, he regressed away from monotheism and into idolatry, sexual excess, and even, we suspect—though there is no concrete literary evidence—child sacrifice. The activity was a sign of a narcissistic and internal disintegration, while the women were also an excuse: "It was not me. They made me do it, and they are responsible." The woman was always powerful for Solomon. Bathsheba caused him to rise to power, and now, all those women combined to precipitate his fall. In due course, Solomon's rebellion and personality disintegration resulted in the destruction of the dual Israel-Judah monarchy, followed by catastrophe for his people.

Solomon's evil consorts sped up the inevitable collapse of the kingdom Solomon had built up. It would have collapsed anyway, even without those women coming on board. Given that humankind is fallen, everything we create— whether it be bridges, computers, kingdoms or complex financial systems—is prone to fall as well. This is because imperfect, spiritual creatures build imperfect artifacts and structures. In addition to that, though, the god of this world can infect and destabilize anything in it, corrupting it so that its disintegration inevitably follows. God never wanted Israel to have a king other than Himself. In wanting one, they rejected Him. Instead, they wanted a fallen man to rule them and be subject to his fallen system of government. They wanted to be like everyone else. All man-made kingdoms rise and fall, but the onboarding of so many evil consorts made Solomon's kingdom a very unstable and fractious place. Its fall was inevitably going to happen quickly after that.

We can admire Solomon for his genius, his mastery of wisdom and poetry, his attempts to create a system of regnal justice, and his statecraft. We can wonder at his all-too-brief moments reigning with the God of the miraculous sending fire from Heaven and appearing in the smoke within the temple. The kings and queens of the Earth ran to Solomon because he was so favored by the God Who reigns from highest Heaven. Yet even then, Solomon stood on a brazen scaffold, a man-made structure, ruling amidst a governmental system which was prone to fall. We should not follow in his footsteps from the scaffold downward into apostasy.

CHAPTER 34

THE AMBIGUITY OF SOLOMON

"When R. Eliezer was asked for his opinion of Solomon's future life, he gave his pupils an evasive answer, showing that he had formed no opinion concerning it."

—Rabbi Emil Gustav Hirsch[215]

How are we to sum up the king? Was he a good king or a bad king? Was he a good king who went bad? The ambiguity of Solomon is perhaps the most critical reason as to why he is often ignored by preachers and Christian writers alike. Yet he is ambiguous because the biblical narratives make him so. Solomon's story is told with discretion—God, through the writers, has overseen and managed his inscrutability. Scripture allows us to see him through the palace windows and the temple door, but though we try, we cannot view him close up. We are not allowed to. Solomon is a biblical mystery, protected by God.

Take his wealth, for instance. As one of the wealthiest men who ever lived, was the attainment of this status a fulfillment of God's promise to him at Gibeon to give him riches beyond any other, or was it a direct contravention of the Jewish Law governing the conduct of kings: "nor shall he greatly multiply silver and gold for himself" (Deut. 17:17b)? It would seem to be the former, since God did not condemn him for his riches.

God only condemned his idolatry after he married hundreds of foreign pagan wives. He contravened the first part of the same legal clause: "Neither shall he multiply wives for himself, lest his heart turn away" (Deut. 17:17a). The

215 Hirsch, ibid.

king ignored the injunction, perhaps thinking that being wise, he would avoid the reason for it. He could marry many foreign wives in the understanding that he would take all steps necessary to avoid falling into idolatry through them. If he did not become idolatrous by worshipping their idols, there was no reason not to marry them. The key error made by Solomon, then, was failing to appreciate that by becoming one with them, he would be unable to avoid their corruptive influence on his soul. The power of the demonic overflowing from his wives and into him overwhelmed his best intentions to remain loyal to Yahweh. It is similar to a driver who exceeds the speed limit on the understanding that his senses and reflexes are quick enough for him to avoid all misfortune. Therefore, there is no need to obey the speed limit. The rules are there for lesser men, lesser kings, but not for him.

Solomon attempted to bring forth God's kingdom through materialistic construction. This effort was going to fail. When the time was right, after a long period of exile, God was incarnated as Jesus Christ. Solomon's kingdom was of this world, but Christ's kingdom is not. When He was walking on the Earth, Christ sometimes thought of Solomon. He may have been thinking of the king when He said, "Assuredly, I say to you that it is hard for a rich man to enter the kingdom of heaven. And again I say to you, it is easier for a camel to go through the eye of a needle than for a rich man to enter the kingdom of God" (Matt. 19:23b-24).

The king had a destiny to fulfill. He was to be a man of peace much loved by God (Yedidyah). For a time, Solomon fulfilled that destiny. He sought and secured peace on all sides of his kingdom, and he constructed a temple, which God then blessed with His presence. Then the unexpected happened. He kept on marrying foreign pagan wives and fell into idolatry; in other words, he betrayed Yahweh. He became *Not Solomon* in his inner life.

In his commentary on the Hebrew text, Steven Weitzman of Stanford University indicates that this is alluded to in a pun on the king's name contained in 1 Kings 11:14—the king's heart was "not full (*shalem*) with the Lord his God."[216]

---

216 Steven Weitzman, ibid.

THE AMBIGUITY OF SOLOMON   283

Solomon has deviated from his destiny. The kingdom was flawed by the king's departure from what he could have been. It was up to God Himself to bring about the birth of a future Son of David, a truly Messianic Man of Peace. Solomon had the potential, given by God, to be a forerunner of the Messiah. Yet his inner life brought about his apostasy and his untimely end at the age of fifty-nine or sixty, divorced from his destiny and ruling over a kingdom which, like Ahijah's robe, would be split apart.

Commentators such as Steven Weitzman put forward the perspective that Solomon's life and rulership were essentially ambiguous. He was neither a good king nor a bad one but displayed both aspects. We could add that this followed a pattern or curve with a trajectory of good toward bad. Because he had been given supernatural wisdom, some decisions he took were prophetic of Christ, yet his life and kingdom also became prophetic or symbolic of a supernatural wickedness still to emerge in the world and, compared to Solomon's empire, far into the future. Ecclesiastes essentially says that perhaps even with wisdom, the best efforts of humankind will end in frustration and pointlessness without Christ's redemptive power and influence.

Can we, in the end, reconcile Solomon's wisdom with the way he led himself astray into idolatry through all his relationships with pagan women? It would seem that we have two opposing forces, with one trumping another, a wisdom affecting the mind and decision-making being overtaken frequently by a passion which routinely conquers it. Solomon, though, was aware of the potentially destructive effects of sexual passion and enticement and records his warnings in Proverbs. Yet he did not take his own advice and heed his own warnings. One of the ways this can be understood is to consider the possibility that Solomon, at times, misused his wisdom.

God makes it clear in Deuteronomy that the reason why an Israelite king must not take too many wives for himself is that if he does, he will turn aside and into the great offense of idolatry.[217] In his wisdom, Solomon would understand that,

---

but he may well have reasoned that given this understanding, he could, in fact, take many wives and also hold before himself the need to refrain from idolatry. In his case, the one need not lead to the other. This was a presumption—that his wisdom removed the need to comply with the usual standard boundaries and limits set on humankind by God for our own good.

The ambiguity of Solomon was a reality throughout much of Solomon's life and carried on even to his death. We do not actually know if, toward the end, he repented of his sins or not. Is he now in Heaven or in Hell? Like the rabbis, we do not know! On the one hand, there is no actual record of his repentance and no evidence in Scripture that he pulled down any of the idol shrines. On the other, we have a number of rueful comments attributed to his later days on Earth. Are they evidence of repentance or a world-weariness and regret which, in their omission of reference to God, fall short of it? "Then I looked on all the works that my hands had done And on the labour in which I had toiled; And indeed all *was* vanity and grasping for the wind. *There was* no profit under the sun" (Eccl. 2:11).

The Armenian church retains intriguing Scripture translated from Greek into Armenian. The work states that Solomon repented in tears and that he commanded most of his written work to be burned. Some extracts of this extra-biblical text are included below:

> Solomon took for himself many wives, seven hundred. And because he was not satisfied by this, he had recourse moreover to the Gentiles and took three hundred concubines from the unclean heathen . . . to the scandal of his soul and to the contempt of the multitude of his pure wives who were gathered to him on account of his wondrous wisdom . . . For he was deceived on account of his wisdom and he permitted his thoughts to go in the paths of the women who planned together for the undoing of his soul, until he set up images upon the mountains and worshipped idols openly opposite the Temple. And he meditated remembering his father David's commandment, "For you to go," he had said, "in the ways of the Lord and in the Law of Moses his servant." When he remembered this his father's commandment and the time of David's death, he wept from the

depths of his heart until he had bedewed his room and his bed . . . Solomon, indeed, having fallen into great sadness on account of this great number of sins, in despair summoned his grand chamberlain and commanded (him) to burn the multitude of his writings which he had pronounced by the grace of the spirit. And he carried out the commandment. Then Solomon asked, "What did you see?" and he said, "An immeasurable light with a flame ascended to heaven." And he wept on account of this from the depths of his heart.[218]

---

218 "Commentary on the Paralipomena Concerning the Penitence of Solomon," in "Concerning the penitence of Solomon," trans. Michael E. Stone, *Journal of Theological Studies*, Vol. 29, No. 1 (1978), 1-19, https://www.jstor.org/stable/23960252.

CHAPTER 35

THE COLLAPSE OF
THE KINGDOM

"When Solomon sat upon the carpet he was caught up by the wind, and sailed
through the air so quickly that he breakfasted at Damascus and supped in
Media. The wind followed Solomon's commands, and ensured the carpet would
go to the proper destination; when Solomon was proud, for his greatness and
many accomplishments, the carpet gave a shake and 40,000 fell to their deaths.
The carpet was shielded from the sun by a canopy of birds."

—Hirsch[219]

Solomon's kingdom collapsed immediately after his death, and no other
king in the Northern or the Southern kingdoms could bring it back in terms
of geographical territory, grandeur, or influence. From the point of Rehoboam
coming to the throne of Judah right until Judah's defeat by Babylon, the two
competing rival Jewish kingdoms were at loggerheads with each other and
with the surrounding kingdoms and territories. The time of peace and stability
was over.

Solomon had not considered that Ezion-Geber, just a few miles from the
Egyptian border, combined with his maritime trade route down the Red Sea,
would be suspiciously viewed from over the border. Egypt viewed the Red Sea
as theirs. A new pharaoh, Sheshonk, came to power, and he decided to base
his throne in Bubastis, the center of worship of the fierce cat goddess Bastet.

219 Hirsch, ibid.

Backed by Bastet, lioness goddess of warfare, he was prepared to go to war, but he also did not want Egypt to do it alone. He ensured that Edom would attack Israel-Judah from the southeast, while he would attack from the southwest. Just five years into his reign, Rehoboam was required to hand King Solomon's three hundred gold shields to Sheshonk as part of war reparations to Egypt to be replaced by shields cast in bronze.

Much of Rehoboam's potential defensive and offensive capabilities were located too far north to be any use at all when Egypt invaded. But to compound the problem, the rebellion by the ten Northern tribes stole this military capability and infrastructure away. Solomon had believed that the main military threats would come from the north and northeast from neo-Hittite, Aramean, and Hurrian entities, such as Geshur (within Solomon's territory) and Aram-Damascus (lost by Solomon and outside his territory). Solomon did accurately perceive what these threats were. For instance, as soon as Israel rebelled against Rehoboam, Geshur rebelled against Israel and aligned with Aram against it.[220] Yet he had no perception of the residual power which Egypt could exert in battle if a new hostile dynasty took over.

Rehoboam realized very soon after taking the throne that Egypt had become an adversary. Desperately, he tried to build up his southern defenses, probably building out of little or nothing that Solomon had done on the southern frontier. He also fortified towns in the Judean heartland—a total of fifteen fortified towns and cities. Unfortunately, he had made an enemy of Israel, and so he was fortifying against dangers from the South and the North simultaneously. He thought about armaments and supplies for all of the towns and their garrisons (2 Chron. 11). The efforts were in vain. Pharaoh Shishak invaded with a huge international army and chariot force, sweeping through Rehoboam's defenses and up to Jerusalem.[221] The king was forced to empty the city of treasure to save his kingdom by offering tribute.

---

220 See the overview of these kingdoms and entities summarized by Mark W. Chavalas in *The Age of Solomon: Scholarship at the Turn of the Millennium*, Lowell K. Handy, ed., (Leiden: Brill, 1997).

221 According to the triumphal hieroglyphic relief and stelae of Shishak's invasion and victory, Amun Temple, Karnak, c. 925 B.C.

Taking the long view, the effect of Solomon's reign was to reverse the progress Israel had made from the time of Abraham, in the years around 1800 B.C., to David's expansion and consolidation of the state (1010-970 B.C.) forged in war by Saul. The combined effect of the patriarchs such as Jacob, Joseph, Moses, and Joshua (between Abraham and David in the Israelites' timeline) was to give the people a purpose and a developing focus on Yahweh. After the appearance of a zenith of spiritual development under Solomon, this and all the progress prior to him were reversed. Solomon's undermining effect on state unity led to the splitting of Israel and Judah in the first few months after the king's death.

Israel and Judah then went to war with each other frequently and were also victims of invasions, the first one fought by Pharaoh Shishak and his Edomite allies against Judah. Ruled by a series of evil kings,[222] Israel was overrun completely by the Assyrian Empire in 721 B.C. and its entire people deported. The Northern ten tribes of Israel then vanish from the historical record, absorbed into Sargon's territories. There are many tales today as to what became of them, and a number of tribes and people groups in countries such as Ethiopia, India, and Kurdistan claim descent from the ten tribes, their claims backed by long-preserved Jewish customs.

Judah lasted longer, and its spiritual life benefited from the ministry of Isaiah (active from 740 B.C. to 686 B.C.) and then by the edicts of a righteous King Josiah (649 B.C. to 609 B.C.). At the same time, though, idolatry held sway in the Southern kingdom with people extravagantly expanding Solomon's idolatry across the land in an idol-worshipping spree (1 Kings 14:22-24). Like Israel, Judah's spiritual trajectory went downward from 931 B.C. until it, too, was overrun in 586 B.C. by Babylon. Jerusalem and its temple were destroyed and the gold, the broken-up pillars, and the other materials carted off to Babylon.

The kingdom of Judah did have ambitions and thought it would survive. It is only in very recent times that archaeological evidence has been uncovered as

---

222 Not one king of Israel worshipped Yahweh or ruled in a just way. Its first king, Jeroboam, decided to create golden bulls for the people to worship. His rationale was to use them to prevent Israelites returning to Jerusalem to worship Yahweh. He was intent on preserving his rule by means of idolatry (1 Kings 12:26-30).

to the kingdom's feigned strength and also its spiritual apostasy. In Lachish, for instance, southwest of Jerusalem and the second most important city in Judah, a palace complex has been uncovered which was three times the size of Solomon's palace complex.[223] It was probably built by King Asa and developed further by King Jehoshaphat. Yet this great city and fortress fell twice to sieges by the Assyrians and then the Babylonians. Another palace complex just east of Jerusalem at Ramat Rachel was about the same size as Solomon's complex. It has been identified as belonging to Athaliah, the daughter of King Ahab and Queen Jezebel of Israel, who instituted Baal worship in Judah. Archaeologists may well have uncovered the House of Baal mentioned in 2 Kings 11:18.[224]

The pagan idols Solomon gave permission to be erected outside the temple remained in place for about 350 years. By the time they were removed and destroyed by King Josiah around 621 B.C., the damage was done, and God's will to have Jerusalem destroyed was decided.[225] The abominations which Solomon was accountable and responsible for were swept away. The book of 2 Kings is kind, though, to Solomon and attributes God's irrevocable decision not to Solomon's actions but to those of Manasseh, who reigned afterward in Jerusalem and who had multiplied the idols and practiced child ritual sacrifice so much that an explicit record of it is recorded in Scripture.

In exile, the Jews remembered Solomon and his greatness, his gold and ivory throne, the glorious temple in Jerusalem, and a time when Israel was an equal with the nations surrounding it, even superior in its wealth and military power. Those born in exile had never experienced Solomon's forced labor, only the privations wherever they lived. They did not know that the ostentatious show of wealth was merely that of a tiny elite and that it hid from casual view the oppression and poverty of the many. There was a recounting among themselves and to their children of a lost golden age, and around it, myths about Solomon were spun. He flew on a huge, magic carpet sixty miles long and sixty miles wide, made of

---

223 Garfinkel, 203.
224 This is according to the lead archaeologist, Yigael Yadin, who also served as Israel's deputy prime minister from 1977 to 1981.
225 2 Kings 23:13-14

green silk and with a golden weft. He had magical powers, and he controlled the demons, getting them to do his will. Imaginary tales helped the Jews survive.

For a time, Solomon's kingdom existed as a summit of Jewish religious life and experience. However, the king's falling away had a catastrophic and long-term effect on his people. The collapse of both the later Northern and Southern kingdoms led to ongoing exile for the Jews, a revisiting of the exile of Adam and Eve from the Garden of Eden. Leaving the symbolic Garden of Eden—the temple—behind them, the Jews were exiled by Babylon to the East. From that time to now, Jews have largely lived a life of exile. Often persecuted, they have gone from place to place, a witness and a mystery to the nations. In only the last few years has the number of Jews in Israel risen to approach parity with the numbers living in other countries. Even now, though, just forty-four percent live in Israel. So far, they do not have a third temple.

We noted much earlier that Solomon was one of the richest men who ever lived. What became of his wealth? Will all or much of the gold be rediscovered sometime? These questions have already been addressed by the Bible scholar and Egyptologist Kenneth Kitchen. A meticulous researcher, he realized some time ago that most of Solomon's wealth disappeared into Egypt, taken off by Pharaoh Shishak. Just a year or so after Rehoboam lost his father's fortune to Shishak and his army, Shishak's son, Osorkon I, started to donate what amounted to four hundred tons of gold (fourteen thousand talents) to the Egyptian temples and their gods. This was donated over a period of four years of rule.[226] Shishak died just months after his successful and brutal campaign against Judah and Israel ended. Osorkon's reign, however, was known for its length and prosperity. In due course, this wealth flowed through conquest or tribute out of Egypt and into Assyrian and Persian hands and, from there, to Greek and Roman ones.

---

226 Kenneth A Kitchen, "Sheba and Arabia," *Age of Solomon* (Leiden: E. J. Brill, 1997), 126-153.

PART 4

IS THERE ANYTHING NEW UNDER THE SUN?

BY: ARCHIE W. N. ROY

THE FOCUS NOW SHIFTS SOMETHING like three thousand years from Solomon's rule over Israel into the modern era of the twentieth and twenty-first centuries A.D. In doing this, we jump over a long period of time when, for the most part, the people of Israel lived in exile, thrown out of and then kept out of their homeland in the Middle East by the Gentile nations.

In exile, God enabled the Jews to preserve their unique national identity, their customs, religious schools, and the deepest of faiths expressed in the Jewish annual festivals. When they had settled in a place, they usually thrived in the trades they were permitted to follow by the Gentile nations which ruled over them. These trades were typically at a lower rank, such as keeping shops or working as peddlers. Sometimes, however, Jews were permitted to operate in banking and through their networking, industry, and ingenuity, often outwitted and outperformed their competitors. Yet whatever societal strata they were permitted to operate within, Gentile authorities would all too often turn against them. Throughout their diaspora history, Jews were often on the run in large numbers, fleeing the pogroms in Russia, Spain, Germany, England, and many other jurisdictions. All too often, they did not escape. When they did, it was to repeat the cycle of the refugee, industrious worker, and persecuted somewhere else, in another strange land.

One of the inspirations which helped to keep them going through all this time of flight and persecution was Solomon, not just in all his glory but in all the mystique which the rabbis chose to spin around the reality of his kingdom: his flying carpet, his masterful conversations with the djinn, and his majestic, imperial throne with all its animal automata so far ahead of anything else of its time. His was a time of Jewish rulership, untold wealth, and dominant military power. His was the temple. His was Jerusalem, another inspiration.

For most of us, Israel has been a life-long fact, a nation existing in the Middle East since its formal declaration of independence in May of 1948. We need to remember, though, that this national rebirth is nothing short of a miracle. It is the only time in history when a nation has come back from such a long period of exile to re-establish a nation state, a language, a distinctive culture, and a presence that is strong enough to require every other nation on Earth to consider it very carefully, in order to work out how to deal effectively with it according to national interests. We will consider in many of the chapters which follow different aspects of this miracle, particularly the military and scientific ones.

In doing this, we are merely bringing up to date to the present time our consideration of King Solomon's empire. Although it began as such, this empire is not just a historical Iron Age one. The empire was never extinguished. Jews forced into exile took its memory with them. They focused on it, re-imagined it, embellished it. The empire lived on in hearts and minds, but it is now back, in reality. Israel is a force to be reckoned with in the Middle East. Every nation on its borders knows that it is not just inferior to Israel in a military sense but that any Arab alliance against Israel has been proven to be weaker than the Jewish state.

As time continues to move forward toward Christ's return, we see more and more of Solomon's kingdom also coming back. In all things of Earth, as opposed to Heaven, "there is nothing new under the sun" (Eccl. 1:9). Solomon knew this, but we typically do not. We see things re-appear and think they are new. Israel has fought many wars since 1948, each one a war of national survival. But it did that before, prior to King David establishing the kingdom Solomon would inherit. Israel has been required to do it again, to repeat the past. We see Israel borrowing liberally from Solomon's books of military and geopolitical strategies to establish a new, but not new, rule that is peaceful. The Jewish state is confident in its endeavor because, for one thing, Solomon has shown Israel that peace is possible. "What has been will be again" (Eccl. 1:9), and we will consider some of the strategies in the chapters which follow.

In the outgoing days of the Republican administration through 2020 and 2021, the United States facilitated a number of peace accords between Israel and Arab states such as Morocco, Sudan, and the UAE. These built on prior peace treaties between Israel on the one hand and Egypt and Jordan on the other. The Egyptian and Jordanian treaties have lasted well, and they are better than a "cold peace." There is multi-faceted cooperation between these states, much of it not discussed in the public domain. At the time of writing, it looks as if

Saudi Arabia will also join the American and Israeli peace efforts. Time will tell. There is a push to establish a comprehensive and lasting peace between Israel and every surrounding nation. There is also a long-considered plan to re-establish the temple in Jerusalem, and we will take a look at that, too.

We will also reconsider Solomon's pursuit of women and the issue of polyamory. We will see that there have been many instances in the current era as well as recent history where this obsession has come to the fore again. The context has usually been either imperial rule or a cultic focus on sex, which can be either hedonistic or sublimating (i.e., channeling sexual desires into behaviors which are more socially acceptable to the life and mores of a cult). We will focus on just a few of these. At the same time, we will explore additional manifestations of polyamory in criminality. These are not mutually exclusive categories. It is possible to have polyamorous, cultic practices which are criminal in a twenty-first century legal sense.

CHAPTER 36

APOSTASY AND HOPE

"Acknowledge the otherworldly character of faith . . . believers will not be able to escape the tension between 'this world and the next.'"

—Garrett Green[227]

The character of Solomon, along with his rule and his kingdom, prefigure the last years of the present age in a number of respects. There is currently, for instance, a significant slide into apostasy within Western Christianity. This follows a much more energetic and successful phase throughout the nineteenth and early twentieth centuries when missionaries went out across the world and evangelized, cared for the poor, and committed to staying on to lead wherever they were and to educate and look after those they had met. They systematically taught people to obey everything Christ had commanded. Many missionaries never returned to their homelands. They had no wish to, and in some cases, when they left their homelands, they took their coffins with them.

The anxiety balanced by faith with which Asaph was familiar is a mindset also familiar to many Christians in the early twenty-first century. Asaph's situation and mindset creates hope in us: we are to pray for Christ's kingdom to come, even to hasten its coming through prayer. At times, we see that prayer brings about victory. People get free of whatever was weighing heavily on them. People experience justice, even through a human system that is so often

---

227 Garrett Green, "Chapter 4: Imagining the Future" in *The Future as God's Gift Explorations in Christian Eschatology* by David Fergusson and Marcel Sarot (London: Bloomsbury Collections, 2000).

arbitrary and flawed. Often, it is prayer activated by an imagination used well. We can imagine what the future will be like or, at least, *could* be like given our understanding of God's will as it has been revealed to us. We have Christ's actions, words, and prayers recorded for us in Scripture. All these can inform how we choose to pray.

Solomon imagined and then built the temple as a spiritual space where Heaven met with Earth. The space was a re-creation of the start of human time, a re-imagining of the Garden of Eden, a beautiful place where a man, a woman, and God walked in intimacy. Although it was replaced with an Earth full of groaning, we can only take hold of hope when we imagine the future, a millennial reign followed by an eternity of communion with God in a new Heaven and a new Earth. God came to the temple; He walked on Earth in the person of Christ; and He will return to us. When we think about His coming again, we can trust Scripture, and we can set critical reason aside without wading into overly concrete interpretations of exactly how and when it will occur. Somehow, it will happen as He said it will. Until then, one of the gifts which can help us is an active Christian imagination. The theologian Professor Garret Green of Connecticut College calls this the "inescapable duality of the Christian life."[228] We can rightly imagine a world to come, a new Heaven and a new Earth incompatible with the world as it is. This is better by far than the false imagination stemming from fallen theories of man and the fanciful, yet all-encompassing, visions offered up by many of the cults. All of these earth-bound efforts block heavenly glory from view.

In the meantime, God's grace is sufficient for us as we continue to live through a time when we long for justice. We hope because we are sure of a guaranteed and positive outcome: creation delivered from corruption, decay and death, and entrance into glorious freedom. We are mortal *now,* but Christ will transform this type of being into immortality. We live in a kind of anxious anticipation, especially if we are weary of the world's systems. God is with us as we groan,

---

228 Ibid.

and He is likewise with the world as *it* groans. All creation is groaning, waiting for its deliverance. It has been a long time since Christ secured His victory over the enemy on the cross, but He is intent on saving all He can. Then all enemies, including death itself, will be crushed under His feet.

The international peace and prosperity engineered by Solomon was a false one based on the selective breaking of Jewish laws. In amassing such wealth alongside the one thousand pagan consorts as well as the horses and chariotry from Egypt, his tendency was to flout the law laid down for Israelite kings. Scripture prophesies that another lawless one will arise and build the third temple in Jerusalem. He will also flout the law but in a far more egregious way. He will enter the temple and proclaim himself to be God (2 Thess. 2:4). Like Solomon, he will be a narcissist, but unlike Solomon, he will not get beyond it. For him, there is no possibility of redemption. Believers at such a time will need to hold fast as Asaph did and cry out in their distress, "Beloved, now we are children of God; and it has not yet been revealed what we shall be, but we know that when He is revealed, we shall be like Him, for we shall see Him as He is" (1 John 3:2).

CHAPTER 37

JESUS AND HIS VICTORY

"The queen of the South will rise up in the judgment with this generation and condemn it, for she came from the ends of the earth to hear the wisdom of Solomon; and indeed a greater than Solomon is here."

—Matthew 12:42

There has been no other king like Solomon. Many have sought to emulate him and to acquire his power and the respect he enjoyed. Many have, in fact, sat on thrones and attempted to re-create Solomon's throne. The Mughal (and later Persian) peacock throne, Great Britain's Coronation Chair (or King Edward's Chair), and the Byzantine emperors' throne in Constantinople with its moving birds, lions, and beasts automata are all examples of these.[229] There has been so much striving after Solomon's power, wisdom, greatness, and mastery over the Earth. Yet Solomon, as a son of David, prefigured Someone greater than him, not less—likewise a kin descendent but One Who can fulfill the prophecies about the eternal kingdom and remain free from sin. The masterful and wise Iron Age king of kings who reigned for a time prefigures the true King of kings, the Son of God, Who reigns forever.

"There is nothing new under the sun" (Eccl. 1:9) when it comes to the horizontal realm of humankind's dealings with each other and with the Earth.

---

229 Mary-Lyon Dolezal and Maria Mavroudi, "Theodore Hyrtakenos' Description of the Garden of St. Anna and the Ekphrasis of Gardens,"in *Byzantine Garden Culture*, A. Littlewood, H. Maguire and J. Wolschke-Bulhman, eds, (Washington, DC: Harvard University, 2002), page 128.

But on the vertical plane, the birth, death, and resurrection of Jesus has brought us into a new era, here on Earth and in the hereafter. It has changed the destination of our spirits when we die. Before Christ's death, all human spirits went to Hades, the realm of the dead; but when He descended into that place, Christ freed the spirits of the righteous dead and enabled them to rise to be with Him in Heaven. In this current era, after Christ's resurrection, the righteous go immediately to be with Jesus when they die.[230] He has set the captives free—those who were righteous but in Hades and those living who feared death. King David, for one, looked ahead to such a time: "I have set the LORD always before me; Because *He is* at my right hand I shall not be moved. Therefore my heart is glad, and my glory rejoices; My flesh also will rest in hope. For You will not leave my soul in Sheol, Nor will You allow your Holy One to see corruption" (Psalm 16:8-10).

Christ's victory does not just enable Him to free those who are captive in Hades. His victory is over Hades itself. Revelation reveals that at the last judgment, He will cast Hades into Hell, the lake of fire, along with all those who are not found recorded in His Book of Life.

In his article, "Solomon as Philosopher King," K. I. Parker concludes, "Isaiah predicts the coming of a messiah who is to be endowed with wisdom and an ability to rule in accordance with Torah and who will usher in the new age . . . In this way, the severing of wisdom from Torah, which led to the ultimate failure of Solomon, is reversed as wisdom and Torah are reintegrated, both eschatologically and ontologically, in the person of Jesus."[231] This is a good observation, but we also need to be able to see something of the astonishing transformation in humanity's fortunes brought about by this Messiah Who reintegrates Divine wisdom with the Torah and Whose rule will exemplify both. Solomon's flawed rule ushered in the crushing demonic forces sometimes pictured in iconography, such as the bulls of Bashan.

Behind the iconography are real, spiritual personalities and entities, demon powers who were worshipped at, among other places, Mount Hermon, currently

---

230 2 Corinthians 5:8
231 Parker, ibid, 87-88.

lying partly in the far north of Israeli control and partly in Lebanon. It was here, according to the extra-canonical book, Enoch, where certain demons (fallen angels) descended to Earth and interbred with the daughters of men. The demons were known as the Grigori, or watchers, and their half-breed offspring were known as Nephilim. The Grigori were worshipped in early Mesopotamian religions and are worshipped today in some wiccan systems and in Italian witchcraft.[232] It was on Mount Hermon that Christ was transfigured before Peter, James, and John (Matt. 17). Christ was keen to take the demonic territory back, and He showed that he could. He had also just said to His disciples that He and His Church would overcome evil. He mentioned the gates of Hell because this is where He and his disciples were, close to Mount Hermon:

> He said to them, "But who do you say that I am?" Simon Peter answered and said, "You are the Christ, the Son of the living God." Jesus answered and said to him, "Blessed are you, Simon Bar-Jonah, for flesh and blood has not revealed *this* to you, but My Father who is in heaven. And I also say to you that you are Peter, and on this rock I will build My church, and the gates of Hades shall not prevail against it" (Matt. 16:15-18).

The demonic forces fought back, and they surrounded Christ as He was dying on the cross. They know who He is; they saw His transfiguration on Hermon, and they know about the prophecies (of King David) concerning His conquering of evil generally and them, the Bulls of Bashan, in particular. He will bring people out of their territory and into freedom.

> A mountain of God *is* the mountain of Bashan; A mountain *of many* peaks *is* the mountain of Bashan. Why do you fume with envy, you mountains of *many* peaks? *This is* the mountain *which* God desires to dwell in; Yes, the LORD will dwell *in it* forever. The Lord said, "I will bring back from Bashan, I will bring *them* back from the depths of the sea, That your foot may crush *them* in blood." O God, *You are* more awesome than Your holy places. The God of Israel *is*

---

232 Grigori are associated with solstices and equinoxes.

He who gives strength and power to *His* people. Blessed *be* God! (Psalm 68:15-16, 22-23a, 35).

Then from the cross where Christ's victory over evil was won, we read:

My God, My God, why have You forsaken Me? *Why are You so* far from helping Me, *And from* the words of My groaning? Many bulls have surrounded Me; Strong *bulls* of Bashan have encircled Me. They gape at Me *with* their mouths, *Like* a raging and roaring lion. For dogs have surrounded Me; The congregation of the wicked has enclosed Me. They pierced My hands and My feet; I can count all My bones. They look *and* stare at Me. They divide My garments among them, And for My clothing they cast lots. Save Me from the lion's mouth And from the horns of the wild oxen! You have answered Me (Psalm 22:1, 12-13, 16-18, 21).

Solomon's Temple was built from uncut stone. The true Church is now the temple of living stones. The Cornerstone is Christ. The Church exercises God's power in Christ's name through prayer and the use of God's gifts. We are here on Earth, and we may groan as Asaph did, but we can also enter Heaven's throne room when we come to God in prayer. There will be a new Heaven and a new Earth. Praise God. And after the Gospel has been taken to every tribe and nation, the end will come. Then we will dwell with Him forevermore. "Then *comes* the end, when He delivers the kingdom to God the Father, when He puts an end to all rule and all authority and power. For He must reign till He has put all enemies under His feet. The last enemy *that* will be destroyed *is* death" (1 Cor. 15:24-26).

CHAPTER 38

SOLOMON'S LIFE AS PROPHECY

"That which has been is what will be, That which is done is what will be done,
And there is nothing new under the sun."

—Ecclesiastes 1:9

At times, even when Solomon acted through his human wisdom and before he received Divine wisdom, there is an end times dimension to his actions. In particular, he established his kingdom by killing his enemies—executing his brother, Adonijah, and the other individuals, such as Joab, whom his father had condemned but not killed. The Presbyterian preacher Dale Ralph Davis comments that this is a similar account to the one expounded by the last Davidic King, Jesus. There is a final death for the enemies of the kingdom so that the kingdom can be fully established. He Himself says this to his disciples and prophesies how it will be at the end of the age:

> "Therefore as the tares are gathered and burned in the fire, so it will be at the end of this age. The Son of Man will send out His angels, and they will gather out of His kingdom all things that offend, and those who practice lawlessness, and will cast them into the furnace of fire. There will be wailing and gnashing of teeth. Then the righteous will shine forth as the sun in the kingdom of their Father. He who has ears to hear, let him hear" (Matt. 13:40-43).

Solomon's prayer for wisdom at Gibeon prefigures much of New Testament and, later, Christian experience. Jesus would often seek solitude at night in

305

order to pray. We are encouraged to pray to the faithful God, Who responded so generously to Solomon. He will give us what we need, and He is all we need. We should pray in such a way that we please God, as Solomon did, and ask for the sake of others, especially on behalf of family and the Church.

In the current day, Solomon's wisdom is only matched by Christians filled with the Holy Spirit who exercise wisdom in situations as God inspires us. It is a rare thing to witness or experience, but it is not unknown. Charles Spurgeon, for instance, exercised the gifts of prophecy and wisdom from his pulpit on at least twelve different occasions, pointing out visitors to his meetings and admonishing them for their recent decisions and actions, which he could not have possibly known about by natural means.233

Since 1948, the re-emergence of Israel as the greatest power in the Middle East has been something to behold. In some extraordinary ways, it would seem that Solomon's life as king, especially the latter half of his reign, was prophetic of recent and current times. We can divide this prophecy of action and decision into several areas:

- His military strategies and achievements
- His domestic and financial ambitions
- His focus on the arts and sciences

There are different levels and types of prophecy. The Jewish sage Maimonides (c. 1135-1204 A.D.), laid out twelve levels of prophecy, and it would seem that Solomon's life was that of a prophet—at least at the most basic level of prophecy as defined by the sage: inspired actions.234 It would also include the second level: inspired words—for instance, in the book of Proverbs. These are actually the least clear levels. Before Solomon's drift away from God, he was granted prophetic insight at Maimonides' level seven: audio-visual dream revelations in which God is the Speaker. In contrast, Moses was given the highest level of prophetic awareness: audio-visual waking revelation in which God speaks.

233 Sam Storms, "When a Cessasionist Prophesies, or, What Are We To Make of Charles Spurgeon?," Enjoying God Blog, October 25, 2013, https://www.samstorms.org/enjoying-god-blog/post/when-a-cessationist-prophesies--or--what-are-we-to-make-of-charles-spurgeon.
234 Moses Maimonides, *The Guide for the Perplexed* (New York: Cosimo Books, 2007).

In the chapters which follow, we will take a look at recent Israeli history and also take into account Jewish intellectual and artistic life in different parts of the world. It is our view that Solomon's actions and decisions prefigure much of what has come about in the twentieth and twenty-first centuries A.D. in the Middle East in a number of respects. To some extent, this is because Solomon's wisdom and success directly inspired some of the key Jewish players responsible for Israel's successful striving in recent times for regional military supremacy. Yet there is also a wider interplay of forces, all ultimately allowed or constrained by God, Who continues to fulfill His purposes for humanity. We are also at a particular moment in history; and beyond Israel's current resurgence and confidence as a nation state, there is more to come before Christ's return. Other dimensions of Solomon's life as prophecy will continue to unfold in these last days. There will be a more comprehensive peace accord involving Israel and all the surrounding nations. This will emulate Solomon's achievements again in the modern era. There is the biblical prophecy that a new Jewish temple *will* be built in Jerusalem. For Judaism, this must be on the site of Solomon's temple. It can be built nowhere else!

CHAPTER 39
MILITARY STRATEGY

"Today we have a shield and what a shield it is. Israel will do whatever it must do to defend . . . the Jewish future. Our hand is extended in peace to all our neighbors. Thank you very much, one and all."

—Benjamin Netanyahu, Prime Minister of Israel[235]

Solomon's earthly kingdom and the borders of modern Israel are contiguous up to a point, with the main exception being the expanded territory Solomon governed, which now lies in Syria and Jordan. In the twenty-first century, Israel is defending less land at a time when it is possible to invade foreign territory very quickly by land and air. At the same time, the modern borders of Israel in the south and southeast are more or less as they were in Solomon's day. To the west is the Mediterranean Sea.

In essence, Solomon's military strategy was to develop parity with the most powerful neighboring kingdoms as fast as possible and then to exceed it. He did this through alliances with Egypt and Tyre, and his standing army, with a chariot force of fourteen hundred chariots and twelve thousand horses (spread across his chariot cities and the capital), deterred all but a few skirmishes with hostile powers. Solomon's policy was one of deterrence through force of arms. In an early reflection of modern-day strategies, Solomon's military strategy included, for instance, strategic defense prioritization with no further territorial

---

235 Benjamin Netanyahu, "Remembering the Holocaust, Fighting Antisemitism," Speech, The World Holocaust Forum, Yad Vashem, Jerusalem, Israel, January 23, 2020.

ambitions and the seeking of peace agreements with neighboring powers, such as Egypt.

These strategies have returned and are employed by modern-day Israel. Its forces are called the Army of Defense for Israel, or *Tzahal* (צה״ל). It has had nuclear weapons since 1967, but this, of course, is not the only way it exceeds what Solomon created. Solomon quickly gained military superiority by buying in a very substantial amount of Iron Age weaponry from Egypt. This approach is somewhat like the high-spend, quick-fix development strategies which some Middle Eastern powers utilize now. These countries expend substantial shares of their gross domestic products on military acquisitions from the United States, the United Kingdom, and other major arms producers. In Israel's case, the modern state has, at times, emulated Solomon's quick acquisition of state-of-the-art military hardware. For instance, Israel recently acquired from the United States up to seventy-five Lockheed Martin F-35I Adir[236] stealth fighter aircraft. Israel has based them at Nevatim in the center of the country, something a little akin to Solomon building a huge chariot city at Megiddo and placing a substantial military resource there. When some of these state-of-the-art planes were flown over Tehran, Iran, in March of 2018 to photograph Iranian air defense systems, Iran failed to detect their presence.[237]

Modern-day Israel, however, is much more innovative than merely being a purchaser of foreign arms. It has, of course, a more developed military defense strategy than Solomon had, and it is also far more creative. Israel both improves its bought-in military technology where it can and has its own major military industry. Turkey, Russia, Cyprus, and China buy military equipment, such as drones, from Israel; and in 2009, India agreed to purchase an advanced air defense system from Israel. Israeli defense contractors, such as Soltam Systems in Yokne'am, a few miles west of Nazareth, actually sell military equipment to the United States. But consider the most advanced combat aircraft currently operational in the world, the F-35, a stealth multi-role fighter with a top speed

236 Adir means "mighty."
237 Dario Leone, "Israeli Air Force's F35 Stealth Fighter Went into Iran's Airspace: Report," The National Interest.org, July 22, 2019, https://nationalinterest.org/blog/buzz/israeli-air-forces-f-35-stealth-fighter-went-irans-airspace-report-68352.

of 1.6 Mach or 1,200 mph. Its wings are delivered to the United States by Israel Aerospace Industries (IAI). They are made by Israelis, and on September 26, 2019, IAI delivered the one-hundredth F-35 wing to Lockheed Martin.[238] This is scheduled to increase to eight hundred wings by 2034. The technology IAI uses to create these very advanced composite material structures is classified.

In all this, we can see the mindset of King Solomon, who created a formidable military state but also one which was essentially defensive in posture. He achieved this through trade alliances which had a military technology aspect. He imported and exported chariots and horses, investing greatly in any superior military technology from outside his kingdom. Modern-day Israel has, at times, invaded territory well beyond its frontiers, but this has been a reaction to attack by surrounding nations; and it has, at times, also bought into the idea of land-for-peace, withdrawing its forces out of Egypt and Lebanon. Israel's military, or defense, strategy is really the same as the one adopted by King Solomon: one of deterrence. It is part of Israel's Defense Forces (IDF) multi-year "Gideon Plan." The unclassified version was published in Hebrew in 2015, but this has been translated into English by academics at Harvard University.[239]

---

238 "IAI Inaugurates New Line for F-35 Wing Skins," Lockheed Martin.com, , December 24,2018, https://www.lockheedmartin.com/en-il/israel-news/iai-inaugurates-new-line-for-f-35-wing-skins.html.

239 Lieutenant General Gadi Eisenkot, "Israel Defense Forces Strategy Document," Belfer Center. org, August, 2015, https://www.belfercenter.org/israel-defense-forces-strategy-document.

CHAPTER 40

SHALHEVET AND THE BOMB

"For love is as strong as death; Jealousy as cruel as the grave:
Its flames are flames of fire, A most vehement flame."

—Song of Songs 8:6

David Ben-Gurion, the first of Israel's prime ministers, probably saw the Jewish survivors every day of his life after he first met them at the death camps. It is hard to know what shocked him the most—the half-living skeletal people or the dead, buried in the mass grave at Bergen-Belsen. He made the visit in October of 1945. He stood there and wept, and afterward, he met survivors, among whom were some distant relatives from Plonsk, his place of birth in Poland. They all spoke to him at once, crowding around him, and he made notes about their experiences as best he could. From that point, his ideas developed quickly. The Jews needed to be set free from an anti-Semitic Europe, and they needed a homeland, their own sovereign state. After the Jews won their war of independence and the state was created in 1948, he then decided, in the face of a perceived ongoing threat from all around of extermination, that they also needed nuclear weapons. The evidence from his diaries suggests that this thought, however, had first occurred to him in 1945 after the first use of nuclear weapons and during his visits to Dachau and Belsen. No nation would seriously contemplate annihilating the Jews if they possessed a nuclear option as an ultimate deterrent. His existential dread born of his experiences in Germany was shared by many other Jews.

As time went by, it became clear to Israel that the Americans were only going to be useful up to a point. A nuclear agreement was signed with them in 1955, and through this, the United States provided a small reactor for a site near the Mediterranean coastline at Nahal Soreq, a few miles south of Tel Aviv. The reactor, a twenty-sided geometrical structure, is built next to an inner courtyard surrounded on all four sides by concrete columns. Completed and opened in 1960, the complex looks like a modernist, brutalist-style ancient temple. It was strictly intended to be a training and research site for medical and industrial scientists. Today, it is overseen by the International Atomic Energy Agency. Back in the 1950s, Ben-Gurion thought that it was a step forward, but he also wanted a "real reactor." He wanted the bomb.

In 1955, his defense ministry director-general was Shimon Perez, and he instructed Perez to travel to Paris, the City of Lights, capital of the short-lived French Fourth Republic (1946-1958). His task was to push for as much military cooperation as possible: weapons and a nuclear reactor. The reactor, along with provision of enriched uranium, was agreed upon by the Republic in 1956 and again in writing in 1957. This agreement was unique and remains so to this day. Aspects of it are still classified.

More than three-quarters of the Fourth Republic's territory lay in Africa (French Algeria), and it was seen by the French governments of the time as absolutely integral to France. The Republic was unstable in many different ways. It had twenty-one prime ministers in twelve years, and it lost extensive colonial territory between 1954 and 1956 in Africa (south and east of Algeria) and Indochina. The Republic lurched from one foreign policy crisis to another. At the same time, the Republic built France's economy, military, and social institutions up again in the period of time immediately after the war. In time, Israel began to perceive Algeria as a French problem on which it could capitalize. Both states also perceived Egypt as a significant problem. Algerian terrorist activity against French targets had begun in 1954, and the Republic viewed Egypt's President Nasser as a key instigator. It discovered that many of the arms confiscated from dead Algerians originated in Egypt. France needed intelligence about Nasser, which Israel had, and Israel needed weapons.

At this point, something fundamental happened between the Republic and Israel. There was a meeting of minds at an intellectual level, and at the same time, something of an emotional connection was established. Nasser's bellicose rhetoric reminded them of Hitler, their common enemy. He was going to throw the Jews into the sea and throw the French out of Africa. It reminded the French, too, of how they had behaved toward the Jews. They capitulated to Hitler when during the occupation, they abandoned them and even hastened most French Jews toward their fate in the East. Now there had to be a balancing of the books. The French knew that they owed the Jews. Occupied France and the Vichy regime had both participated in the Holocaust.

The window of opportunity for Israel in the last years of the Fourth Republic allowed for massive acquisition of weaponry: almost one hundred Mystère jet fighters, armored cars, two hundred tanks, forty thousand artillery shells, and much else besides were secretly shipped to Israel.[240] Indeed, it was a time when France was intent on developing its own nuclear deterrent in order to maintain its status as a world power. In due course, its initial nuclear tests were conducted at Colomb-Béchar in Algeria. While all this was going on, Israel was paying a lot of money but also giving the French vital intelligence concerning Nasser's orders to the Algerian underground militant cells. Israel had cracked the Egyptian codes.

The written 1957 agreement with the Republic led to ten intensive years of Franco-Israeli collaboration at Dimona. By 1968, Israel had its nuclear deterrent, while at the same time, the nuclear technology enabled it to develop rapidly as a scientific and technological power, giving it a strategic superiority over its neighbors in the Middle East. This had been Ben-Gurion's overall vision. The nuclear dimension would eliminate fear of annihilation. It would also trigger a range of other domestic and scientific advancements, and together, they would give Israel its long-term advantage.

---

240 Michael Karpin, *The Bomb in the Basement* (New York: Simon & Schuster, 2007).

SHALHEVET FREIER

His parents called him Shalhevet. The name means "fire," or the "flame of the Lord" and is taken from Solomon's Song of Songs. Hardly anyone has heard of him. He lived in the twentieth century, but because of his extreme humility and desire to avoid any public attention, no matter how trivial, there are almost no photographs of him. He was absolutely committed to the cause of Israel acquiring nuclear weapons, and during the short-lived years of the French Fourth Republic, he was Israel's nuclear emissary to France. He was a scientist, mystic, musician, and philosopher who was exceptionally talented. Shimon Perez, whom he collaborated closely with during these days, said of him: "The open and the hidden functioned within him together and at the same time."[241]

He was born in 1920 in Eschwege, a small town in central Germany. His father was a rabbi to the Jewish community in Berlin, and during the Nazi era, he found sanctuary in London. His mother was a courageous and committed Zionist, and she enabled several thousand Jewish children to escape the Holocaust through her Youth Aliyah organization, which operated in Germany prior to World War II. She, too, escaped and emigrated to then-Palestine.

Shalhevet seemed to inherit both her courage and her creativity. In 1936, he escaped to England, and in 1940, he made aliyah himself and fought in the British Army in North Africa and Italy. After the war, he was quick to join the Jewish underground movement, Haganah, and managed (while impersonating a British officer) countless clandestine operations which sent Jewish refugees, stolen British Army trucks, and munitions to Israel via Italy and France. One operation alone involved over a thousand refugees and thirty-five trucks.[242]

He started his education in physics in 1947, but it was his clandestine career that was meteoric during the late 1940s. He created a powerful spy network within the British Army to furnish Haganah with the most detailed plans about British withdrawal from Palestine; the intelligence enabled the Jews to move

---

241 Karpin, 96.
242 Maayan Shalhevet, "This Is the Way It Was," Palyam.org, http://www.palyam.org/English/IS/Freier_Shalhevet_Uri.pdf (accessed March 12, 2020).

into each British security installation as soon as it was abandoned. Then, after 1948 and the War of Independence, Shalhevet became the very effective head of Mossad in Europe. In that role, he performed many tasks, but the main one was to oversee the nuclear pact between Israel and the Fourth Republic and to ensure that nuclear reactor parts were delivered and that Israeli scientists were trained in the new French nuclear centers. A key aspect of this task was concealment: to hide the location of the Dimona site, which he had helped to set up, and its construction from the world (and especially from the Americans) behind the lie that it was a textile factory. Another aspect of his work was openness. During the 1950s, he signed a number of explicit agreements between Israel and the French Commission for Atomic Energy. In 1957, the French technical specialists and advisers started to arrive at Dimona. The Jewish scientists working in France were in awe of him. He was urbane, astute, dependable, diplomatic, and very knowledgeable, a velvet glove around a steel hand. In each top-secret report which he sent to Perez from his office in Paris, he would begin with a verse from Proverbs or Psalms or the Talmudic Ethics. Did Shalhevet perceive nuclear armament to be a holy project?

Shalhevet's work and that of others has led to a current situation where it is estimated by the U.K. and the United States that Israel produces ten atomic bombs a year. This accords with its estimated output in plutonium at Dimona. At the same time, Shalhevet's complicated thinking around nuclear weapons has led to a very strange scenario. On the one hand, like Ben-Gurion, having met with the emaciated and desperate survivors of the Nazi death camps, he was convinced that the Jews needed their own homeland and that they absolutely required their own ultimate nuclear deterrent. This was a moral imperative, and it was justifiable because of the events in Germany. Israel must become a defensive fortress—essentially, the same military strategy pursued by Solomon. Yet, later on, as director of the Israeli Atomic Energy Commission, he developed a more complicated policy.

This includes, on the other hand, the policy of nuclear ambiguity. It is a policy doctrine and a national posture which only works if a number of Shalhevet's own personality characteristics are adhered to by the Jewish state. For instance, it must be extremely modest and also extremely disciplined. Never boast about nuclear weapons. Never even admit you have them. Be absolutely prudent, even if the enemy is at the gate. If you are always ambiguous about it, your enemy does not feel beholden to try to take it from you or acquire it as well. At the same time, why would an enemy risk a major conflagration with a supposed nuclear power? Having it makes you confident. Not boasting about it, though, not even admitting it, makes you seem prudent and responsible to your friends. Could the policy not have been written by Solomon and appear in Proverbs? Based on reason and logic, it is a policy doctrine formulated by Shalhevet, who has been inspired by the king.

Shalhevet's policy framework also included complete nuclear disarmament for Israel. Strangely, he also became chairman of the Israeli Pugwash Group,[243] a satellite of the important international disarmament entity known as the Pugwash Conferences on Science and World Affairs, founded in 1957 by the British philosopher Bertrand Russell FRS and the Polish Jewish physicist Sir Joseph Rotblat. Israel has believed in nuclear disarmament ever since Shalhevet framed the doctrine. His doctrine states that Israel opposes nuclear proliferation and that its defensive deterrent can and should be removed after peace is achieved. This peace must be proven and be beyond doubt. This peace will be achieved via separate treaties with each and every Middle East power. Shalhevet's policy opposes disarmament as a stage toward peace. Peace must happen first, and the motivation for peace must be seen to be from pure motives. Shalhevet worked out a careful multi-step process toward this peace, and it involves many incremental confidence-building and mutual trust measures. The signing off on a nuclear-free Middle East zone would be the last stage. The deterrent can then be discarded. Shalhevet's thinking is in alignment with other great minds he met at international Pugwash conferences—for instance, Bertrand Russell.

---

243 Pugwash, Nova Scotia, Canada, was where the committee was founded, following the Russell-Einstein manifesto for nuclear disarmament and world peace.

The books of Daniel and Revelation are not straightforward, and the prophecies within them as to the last days can be interpreted in different ways depending on the reader's eschatological viewpoint and leanings. A commonly understood reading, though, of Daniel and Revelation is that in the last days before Christ's return, Israel will be attacked in at least two different wars, the latter one involving all nations.[244] This happens after an international peace treaty has been signed by Israel.

We know that Israel is desperate for peace. Yet why would attacks occur in the last days when Israel has presumably continued to add to its nuclear deterrent year by year? Clearly, the prophetic passages are invoking a time when Shalhevet's peace policy has been worked through and fully implemented. Israel will think there is a peace deal of the quality required by its disarmament doctrine. It is happy to sign up, and then, of course, it has no deterrent when the double-cross comes along.

---

244 Daniel 11; Revelation 16:16

CHAPTER 41

ISRAEL'S RED SHEET KILLINGS: A STATE POLICY OF ASSASSINATION

"You killed him with the sword of the Ammonites. Now, therefore, the sword will never depart from your house, because you despised Me and took the wife of Uriah the Hittite to be your own."

—Part of Nathan's prophecy to King David, 2 Samuel 12

The topic of assassination is close to King Solomon and the nature of his kingship. After all, his father had ordered the assassination of his mother's first husband, Uriah the Hittite. Uriah was murdered by proxy, abandoned by Israel's army during their siege of an Ammonite city. Then, on attaining the throne, Solomon was quick to assassinate his half-brother, Adonijah. Solomon employed his righthand man, Benaiah, an assassin, to carry out the act. David's army commander, Joab, was next in line for a "red sheet" killing, a term we will explain soon. Shimei was assassinated after that. There are almost certainly other victims of Solomon's targeted assassination policy. It is probable that Asaph's brother, Zechariah, was assassinated by Solomon through the use, again, of an assassin. The reason was to silence a critic of Solomon's adoption of pagan gods and the construction of their idol shrines outside the temple.

In a recent book, the journalist Ronen Bergman makes the claim that Israel has, for many years now, employed assassins to conduct targeted killings, far more executions than targeted, individual killings organized by any other Western or Western-allied power.[245] It is an unusual use of state power, but like the Israeli acquisition of nuclear weapons, the extent to which Israel will go in its policy of extra-judicial killings and assassinations is caused by both very great fear and very great determination. At any time since 1948, it has perceived threats which are existential in their severity. It is determined to thwart another holocaust at *any* cost, whether it be financial, military, or moral. The sword of assassination has not left Israel's house. Solomon took it up and used it many times. Israel uses it today.

Ben-Gurion circumvented the absence of a death penalty in Israeli law by giving himself permission to order assassinations: covert special operations behind the enemy lines. The carrying out of this stratagem today is shrouded in many types of false appearance, and its aim is primarily to weaken enemies so that all-out warfare is avoided. Like Solomon's Israel, modern Israel avoids all-out international warfare, but it is also more robust: pin-point attacks and the hunting down of individual enemy leaders are pursued with great determination. Captured by Mossad and Shin Bet agents in Argentina in the 1960s, Adolph Eichmann, the leading Nazi, is a good example of this. The Israelis hanged him in June of 1962 at Ayalon Prison. This followed a drawn-out judicial process, but often the killing of enemies has been much more covert.

OPERATION WRATH OF GOD

In 1972, the Israeli assassination campaign called *Wrath of God* focused on Mahmoud Hamshari, who was living in Paris.[246] The hit squad had first killed Wael Zwaiter, a cousin of Yasir Arafat, in Rome that October. This killing was the first in a campaign to kill off everyone who had been involved in the Munich Summer Olympics massacre of eleven Jewish hostages. After their success in Rome, they moved on to Hamshari, a terrorist leader they tied to the Munich incident and many other attacks—such as the bombing of Swissair Flight 330, which killed

---

245 Ronen Bergman, *Rise and Kill First: The Secret History of Israel's Targeted Assassinations* (London: John Murray, 2018).
246 Bergman, ibid.

forty-seven people—as well as failed attacks on Jews. The assassination squad put Hamshari under close observation and discovered that he was often at home with his wife and daughter, and when he wasn't, he would be at meetings elsewhere in Paris, usually in crowded public venues. The Israeli prime minister at the time, Golda Meir, was fine with killing people in Europe, but she insisted that no French lives were taken and also that the wife and daughter were spared. The assassination had to be clean-cut. Just the target, no one else. She signed off the Red Sheet kill order, known as such because it was typed on red paper. Former and later prime ministers of Israel would do the same.

The procedure went like this: agents broke into Hamshari's apartment when the family were out. They photographed everything, especially around the target's home office area, and sent the photos to Mossad's technical unit in Israel. These were studied carefully with attention focused on the marble base on which Hamshari's telephone sat. Mossad then constructed as identical a marble base as possible, cramming it with explosives.

A Holocaust survivor by the name of Nehemia Meiri then gave him a call. Nehemia had been born in Poland in 1927; and when he was twelve, Nazis rounded up his entire village along with him, made them dig their mass grave, and shot them all dead. Nehemia had jumped into the pit a fraction of a second before the shooting started; and when the Nazis left, he clawed his way up through the bodies. He was covered in their blood. In 1972, he had been a member of Shin Bet for some time.

On the phone, he told Hamshari that he was an Italian journalist named Carl and that he'd like to interview him the next day in a nearby café. Hamshari was happy to oblige, and when he was out, the assassination squad entered his apartment again and swapped the marble bases. When Hamshari got home, his phone rang. He picked up the receiver; and when he confirmed he was Hamshari, the marble base blew up, almost cutting his body in half. Like many others in Mossad and Shin Bet, Meiri believed in something recorded in the Jewish Babylonian Talmud, Tractate Sanhedrin, Portion Seventy-two, verse one: "If someone comes to kill you, rise up and kill him first." How could he not, given what he had seen?

THE KILLINGS IN TUNIS

Israeli assassination projects have sometimes involved far more considerable firepower, even if the main objective has been to kill one enemy operative. They have been military as well as intelligence-led operations, and they have also had a political dimension. The killing of Khalil Ibrahim al-Wazir in April, 1988, otherwise known as Abu Jihad, is a case in point.

Until his untimely and violent death in Tunis at the age of fifty-two, Abu Jihad was Yasser Arafat's righthand man. He led numerous attacks against Israeli military and domestic targets. In one attack, known as the Coastal Road Massacre, a bus was hijacked, and thirty-five Israelis were killed.[247] In a targeted retaliation, ten McDonnell Douglas F-15 fighters flew to Tunis along with two Boeing refueler aircraft and two Hawkeye spy planes, which jammed radar right across the northern coast of Africa. The F-15s hit all their targets with GBU-15 guided bombs, killing sixty PLO fighters and Tunisians and wounding another seventy. Abu Jihad heard the bombs exploding but was not injured, and this angered Mossad, which then drew up a pinpoint strike for Tunis. By this time, assassinations were called "negative treatments." Prime Minister Yitzhak Rabin signed the order, and Ehud Barak oversaw the mission as IDF deputy chief of staff.

It was decided that just like Hamshari, Abu Jihad would be killed at home. He lived in a lovely and quiet, isolated house close to the beach, and the beach could be the entry and departure route for the assassination team. Mossad also thought that a home killing could have a much wider negative psychological effect on terrorists: they would feel safe nowhere. Mossad got to know the beach area. Over many months, Israeli spies walked all over the place, examining possible routes while dressed as Arabs. They examined Abu Jihad's movements and activities closely as well, and they came to like the fact that he

247 *Wikipedia, s.v.,* "Khalil al-Wazir," December 4, 2020, https://en.wikipedia.org/wiki/Khalil_al-Wazir.

was a good family man and a genuine leader and that he was an accomplished and persuasive writer. Still, he had to get the negative treatment. And what about his neighbor, Mahmoud Abbas, living in another lovely villa close by? Negative treatment for him as well? No, they decided. Too complicated. Just get the flotilla of commandos in and out.

An advance team of six with bogus Lebanese passports arrived in Tunis on four separate flights. They acted as drivers of hired cars and lookouts and ferried the kill team from the beach to the residence and back. The kill team came in on five missile boats, one of which carried a mobile hospital. An Israeli submarine escorted them, while a military Boeing 707 provided communications from above. Some F-15s were also flying around to offer assistance if required. Seven commandos landed on a deserted beach after swimming the last third of a mile. Then, another twenty-six men came ashore. A number got changed in order to pose as locals out for walks.

Abu Jihad had just returned home shortly after midnight. The family was all home: Jihad, his wife, his sixteen-year-old daughter, and his baby son. The daughter told him a dream she'd had: she had been in Jerusalem, but then some Israeli soldiers had chased her and her friends out of the city. Then when she was outside the city walls, she saw her father. She asked him, "Where are you going?" He replied that he was going to Jerusalem and would get around the Jewish soldiers by riding a white horse. The dream had ended. Abu Jihad took off his glasses and looked at his beloved daughter. Oh, yes, he said—he was going to Jerusalem.[248] He then picked up the phone, which had been ringing. An aide told him he had purchased him a seat on the night-time flight from Tunis to Baghdad. It would leave in a few hours' time.

His phone, of course, was tapped. The Israelis needed to go in right away, and they got a green light from Tel Aviv. The sentry outside the home was shot in the head. One operative used a hydraulic jack to force the front door open. The hit team shot dead a bodyguard in the basement before he could open fire.

---

248 Bergman, ibid.

Abu Jihad rose from his desk and got his gun from a cupboard. He saw two Israelis dressed in black coming rapidly toward him, and he pushed his wife further back into their bedroom. Both Israelis shot him, and he died at once. His wife rushed to his body, and an Israeli hauled her off, pushing her hard against a wall so she would not die as well. Another two Israelis arrived and shot at Abu Jihad's corpse. Then a third. His wife and daughter looked on, held at bay by a gun pointed at their heads.

As Ronen Bergman says, it is "very hard to predict how history will proceed after someone is shot in the head."[249] Initially, Israel saw Abu Jihad's assassination as a great success. They had been after him for twenty-three years, ever since Golda Meir had signed off his initial Red Sheet. All the Israeli hit team got out without incident. They left three abandoned hired cars on the beach. His death left a gaping hole in the Palestine Liberation Organization (PLO) leadership, and the number of attacks orchestrated by them against Israel fell away for a time. Yet relatively speaking, Abu Jihad had been a moderating influence on Yasser Arafat. Without him, more radical elements were pitched forward, and in due course, Hamas consolidated its power base at the expense of Fatah and the PLO. Covert operations, while very successful most of the time, have not led to cessation of hostilities, and they have sometimes aggravated them. They have not led to a stable peace. Was assassination as a strategy ever really wise?

---

249 Ibid.

CHAPTER 42

CULTIC POWER AND THE QUEST FOR A SEXUAL UTOPIA

"And then, in the midst of the still-encompassing dream,
he felt himself master of Shangri–La."

—James Hilton[250]

There is little direct evidence of harem stratification by rank order among Solomon's wives and concubines, but it seems clear that there was still something of a ranking system. While Pharaoh's daughter is never seen to be ruling alongside Solomon as empress, she is given priority in focus, partly because she became Solomon's wife very early on in his reign and was given her own palace. Egypt was the first and most strategic of all Solomon's early international alliances. When she died, her position was not taken up by any of Solomon's other wives or concubines but given in marriage to the daughter, a Phoenician, of the King of Tyre.

Beneath this queen were an unknown number of other wives, senior in rank, who were powerful enough to have frequent access to the king. We can determine this—as researchers such as Brady Cook have done—from Solomon's writings. There were wives, for instance, whom Solomon did not get on with but whose status and consequent access to him provided him with emotional problems, and these are reflected on by him in writing: "A foolish son *is* the ruin of his father, and the contentions of a wife *are* a continual dripping. *It is* better

---

250 James Hilton, *Lost Horizon* (London: MacMillan, 1933).

to dwell in a corner of a housetop, Than in a house shared with a contentious woman" (Prov. 19:13; 25:24).

Likewise, there were other wives who were a delight to him. He writes frequently of them as well. There is the romance of Song of Songs, but there are also other frequent allusions to "good wives" elsewhere in his writings—wives who brought life and joy and sometimes contrasted with tiresome ones: "Let your fountain be blessed, And rejoice with the wife of your youth . . . An excellent wife *is* the crown of her husband, but she who causes shame *is* like rottenness in his bones . . . *He who* finds a wife finds a good *thing*, And obtains favor from the LORD" (Prov. 5:18, 12:4, 18:22).

There has been no real focus at all, though, in the literature about Solomon on the harem of wives and concubines; there is merely a mention of attributed motivations as to their acquisition: lust for women and lust for power through political alliances. It would be helpful to try to make better sense of the situation in two different ways: what exactly was the motivation, and what can we determine, if anything, about the situation of the women? It would seem sensible to start in ancient times and focus on other empire harem structures by way of comparison, even when it comes to basic dimensions and features such as size and stratification. Just how unique or distinctive were Solomon's domestic arrangements?

IRON AGE COMPARISONS

We have characterized Solomon's kingdom as an empire, and it is to other early empires we need to turn if we want to look at some comparison data.

Ancient China saw a number of dynasties with similar cultures in certain respects to Iron Age Israel. One of these was in allowances for a myriad of wives and consorts at the emperor's palace complex and court. The *Rites of Zhou*, a bureaucratic work from the Chinese Warring States era (c. 403-250 B.C.), defines the harem ranking system and defines a possible eventual total of 121 wives and consorts as the maximum and ideal number in an emperor's sexual and domestic utopia. At the top is one empress only; at the second level are three wives; and at level five, the lowest consort level, there are eighty-one women.

Just as the Chinese specified an ideal number for a sexual utopia, it may be that Solomon acquired one thousand partners because of the meaning and significance he attributed to the number. He mentions it, for instance, in Song of Songs regarding both his vineyard and his armory (4:4; 8:11), and he saw the number as a perfect number. When he sacrificed to Yahweh at the altar of Gibeon, he offered up one thousand burnt offerings (1 Kings 3:4). In fact, he would have perceived the number as a link between Earth and Heaven and as the fullness of heavenly blessing according to the Scriptures with which he was familiar (emphasis mine):

- "The faithful God who keeps covenant and mercy for a **thousand** generations with those who love Him and keep his commandments" (Deut. 7:9).
- "Remember His covenant forever, The word which he commanded for a **thousand** generations" (1 Chron. 16:15).
- "He remembers His covenant forever, The word *which* he commanded for a **thousand** generations" (Psalms 105:8).

It may be that although love for women was certainly a factor (a stated factor in Scripture[251]) and likewise political alliance-making through marriage, it was Solomon's perception of Divine blessing through the construction of an ideal sexual utopia which was the primary driving force for his collecting of wives and concubines. It is the only driver which explains the exact number. At the end of his reign, even the perfection of one thousand had paled for the king: "Even if he lives a thousand years twice—but has not seen goodness. Do not all go to one place" (Eccl. 6:6). Yet for most of his reign, wealth, women, and the favor of Yahweh dance through his mind. They were all inextricably linked in the mystical number of blessing. "Solomon had a vineyard at Baal Hamon; He leased the vineyard to keepers; Everyone was to bring for its fruit A thousand silver coins. My own vineyard *is* before me; You, O Solomon, *may have* a thousand, and those who tend its fruit two hundred" (Song of Songs 8:11-12).

---

251   The outworking of Solomon's inordinate love for women disobeyed clear scriptural commandments for Jewish kings (e.g. Deut. 17:17).

In China, later emperors ignored the *Rites of Zhou*. During the Han Dynasty, no ceiling number was put, at least during *some* of the Han reign, on the number of consorts an emperor could have. The number of women at the palace rose to around twenty thousand for two successive and corrupt emperors reigning from 146 to 189 A.D. The first, Emperor Huan, died at age thirty-five or thirty-six without a son to ascend the throne, while the second—the son of a marquis, Emperor Ling—died even younger, at either age thirty-two or thirty-three.

The easiest biblical comparison between Solomon's wives and concubines to anyone else's domestic situation would probably be to King Ahasuerus, ruling over the Achaemenid, or Persian, Empire. This is, in all likelihood, Xerxes I, the son of Darius the Great. The events in the Book of Esther focus on the plight of the Jews living within that empire and their rescue by Esther, the Jewish queen who took the place of the deposed Queen Vashti, a Persian.

King Ahasuerus is known to have had a number of wives and concubines, including Esther, and his empire was very wealthy with, of course, a much greater land mass than anything Solomon acquired. Yet the architectural evidence surrounding palace buildings associated with the women suggests that the number of partners was relatively limited, perhaps to less than a dozen. This concurs with genealogical information about the emperor's named offspring, along with limited cultural records about limitations placed on the early Achaemenid rulers' domestic arrangements. It is interesting, though, that the number of the Achaemenid emperors' concubines increased to such an extent with each successive ruler that by the time it was conquered by Macedonia, the emperor had acquired 329 concubines, according to General Parmenion's inventory,[252] which he created for Alexander the Great. Among their other skills and qualities, all 329 could play musical instruments. Parmenion got the impression that they were used to sleeping all day so that they could be awake and lively at night.

---

252   Leslie T. Shear, *Trophies of Victory: Public Building in Periklean Athens* (Princeton: Princeton University Press, 2016).

THE QUEST FOR SEXUAL UTOPIA IN ANTEBELLUM AMERICA

The period leading up to the American Civil War included a number of sudden attempts by different unorthodox millennial groups to create communitarian utopias. They varied greatly among themselves as to how they re-imagined sexual relationships within their communities, but they were all formed in reaction to a turbulent and chaotic civil society, especially in New York, to which they were opposed. At least one has survived to this day, though not in its original form, while others have died away completely, sometimes quite quickly. In terms of Solomon and his domestic arrangements, perhaps they can all be placed on a continuum. We will start with an example which could be considered to be diametrically opposite to Solomon's palace life in their envisioning of a sexual utopia and then consider other antebellum polygamous cults, which at least in one case, was inspired by him as well as less acquisitive polygamous patriarchal rulers described in the Old Testament's account of them. Perhaps some of this will shed a little light not just on Solomon but also on his sexual utopia: what it and some of its human dynamics were like.

We will just consider three examples, but all are communities where certain ideas about sex and the millennium were taken to their logical conclusions, albeit working from very dubious and unorthodox theological starting points. The first of these were the Shakers, who believed that Christ's second appearing had occurred in 1770 in the form of Ann Lee, their founder. Since then, the final heavenly kingdom was on Earth, but people—namely, Shakers—had to work toward its realization. Their *modus operandi* included absolute celibacy, since as Christ said, human beings existing in their resurrected state neither marry nor are given in marriage. Rejecting the Christian doctrine of the Trinity, they were very comfortable with the idea that God had manifested His dual and balanced sexual nature by incarnating first as a man and then as Ann Lee. Their unique vision of utopia included the abandonment of all sex and all procreation.

Initially, the Shakers were very successful, spreading out across New England, New York, and west of there; and their communities reached a membership peak of about four thousand members in 1830.[253] Their success inspired other antebellum cults after them, though none of them adopted the Shakers' monastic approach to living out the millennium of Christ's reign on Earth. Yet very soon, internal tensions and divisions caused their zeal and their membership to slip.

Then from 1837, a remarkable ten years of extreme Shaker charismatic phenomena ensued. In this ten-year period, charismatic Shaker girls, mainly ten to twelve-year-olds, exhibited remarkable manifestations which were initially accepted as revitalizing and useful by the leadership who hoped that the phenomena would propel the movement out of the doldrums. The girls would shake, whirl around rapidly, and then sing unknown songs, which they said came from Heaven. The new hymns quickly amounted to several hundred previously unknown songs, and they were sometimes accompanied by ecstatic dancing. Those who danced would sometimes gyrate very rapidly and then fall to the floor. They would then remain on the floor, absolutely still like corpses, for several days. They might then get up again as if nothing had happened and continue to dance. They said they had seen visions of angels and, sometimes, of Ann Lee, who had died fifty years prior. Many entered into a trance state, usually in meetings, though occasionally it would be known to happen to a few of the men working in the fields. These phenomena, sometimes gentle and sometimes violent, spread across almost all the Shaker communities. Sometimes, the phenomena were very disturbing; some young Shaker boys in one community, for instance, would fall to the floor and scream in agony as if their souls were in torment. Many members in the meetings would receive individual communications "from the spirit world" through the girls.

Although they were seen initially as inspiring and encouraging, the charismatic phenomena were later viewed as disruptive and too challenging of the leadership team by Shaker leaders who moved to subvert and then shut down the activity. The whole Shaker movement then declined rapidly. There was no

---

253 Lawrence Foster, *Women, Family, and Utopia: Communal Experiments of the Shakers, the Oneida Community, and the Mormons (Utopianism and Communitarianism)* (Syracuse: Syracuse University Press, 1991).

renewal from within the movement, given the rule of celibacy, and for those outside, there were many other churches and cults from which to choose. The Shakers had almost entirely disappeared by 1896, but their creative output lives on to some extent. One of their most famous hymns, the beautiful dancing song "Simple Gifts" from 1848, is well known in its own right, but it gained more prominence when Aaron Copland incorporated its melody twice, first into his "Appalachian Spring" and later into his "Old American Songs." The Shaker tune was also adapted by Sydney Carter in 1963 for his hymn, "Lord of the Dance." The first four lines of the original Shaker dancing song read:

> 'Tis the gift to be simple, 'tis the gift to be free
> 'Tis the gift to come down where we ought to be,
> And when we find ourselves in the place just right,
> 'Twill be in the valley of love and delight.[254]

The year "Simple Gifts" was published also saw the advent of another strange religious group in New York, which became known as the Oneida Community. It did not grow as large as the Shakers, numbering at the most about 250 adults at its peak, but again it sought to create a sexual utopia, albeit a very different one. Its founder, John Humphrey Noyes, was an itinerant theology student who lost his license to preach after declaring himself "perfect." When his travels through New England failed to bring in converts to his unorthodox religious and sexual views concerning "complex marriage," he created a community at Oneida, New York. For a time, this community practiced polygamy combined with polyandry, in that each adult community member was considered married to everyone else of the opposite sex. This was combined with a set of control mechanisms, which included absolute opposition to monogamous sexual relations (judged to be worldly and antisocial in a communitarian sense); a status hierarchy of "ascending and descending fellowship," which depended on individual conduct and which could limit sexual contacts; and a method of male continence practiced to subordinate the sexual impulse in favor of the

---

254 Joseph Brackett, "'Tis the Gift to Be Simple," Public Domain.

showing of affection. This extreme form of community life lasted until 1879, and the community was dissolved in 1881, driven apart by a combination of internal schisms and external pressure.

Scholars such as Lawrence Foster believe that this strange type of intimacy combined with distance was an effort to recreate Noyes' experiences within his own family of origin. It was only possible because he exhibited a drive and possibly a type of psychopathy which drove him to impose his views and brook no opposition. Those who opposed him left. Like the Shakers, Noyes and his followers believed that they were to realize the millennium and the Kingdom of God on Earth.

Perhaps there are echoes here of Solomon's sexual utopia. If one has, after all, one thousand wives and concubines, is that not a way of balancing intimacy with distance? Perhaps one of the drivers propelling Solomon in his acquisition of so many sexual partners was his internalization of dysfunctions within David's household—itself a polygamous household no doubt full of fractious competition and jealousy. At the same time, a second desire also sought to hold sway. This had to do with the creation of the Kingdom of God on Earth—a palace utopia in Jerusalem, the center of the world, where all nations were represented and impacted by Solomon, God's representative on Earth, united with him through sexual love. We have already three different, but sexual, outworkings of this cultic kingdom perception: celibacy, complex polyamorous marriage, and extreme polygamy. As for the women who joined, they would feel they were leaving a fallen and dangerous world behind to be part of God's kingdom on Earth. They would feel secure and supported. In the case of Noyes, as well as Solomon, there was God-like authority. With the former, though, there is also written evidence from community members of the downside to a cultic life founded on heresy. The psychosomatic and psychiatric illnesses, along with suicide attempts, are most clearly referenced in the book, *Free Love in Utopia*, by Lawrence Foster, as well as in earlier summaries of the cult (1991, 1997, 2001).

A third group, the one whose founder adopted polygamy in an extreme way, in contrast to the other antebellum groups, was the Mormons. Roger Patterson summarizes the polygamy of Joseph Smith. It amounted to the accumulation of forty or more wives, but Patterson also details something of the additional complexity of this arrangement. While some were married to Smith, others were "sealed to him" in Mormon ceremonies. They would become his wives in eternity, if not on Earth. At least fourteen of the forty or so were already married to other men when they were married to or sealed to Smith.[255]

It is interesting to take this relatively recent example of polygamy and reflect back to Solomon's substantially greater acquisition of wives and concubines. It brings to light that it does not follow that Solomon had sexual relations with all of his seven hundred wives, especially when the marriage was solely to do with the forging of political and economic alliances. There may also have been different wedding ceremonies for different kinds of marital relationships. It is also possible that some of his wives had other sexual partners, either formally or informally, especially those who had very little or next to no access to the king. Somewhat related to that, it also does not follow that all Solomon's wives lived in an extended harem palace in Jerusalem. There is no architectural evidence of a palace of anything like that size. It is more likely that although a substantial number did live in the royal complex in Jerusalem, others lived throughout Israel and Judah and occasionally beyond its borders. A cluster of wives and concubines would also travel with the king alongside his additional military and domestic retinue. They would be as itinerant as he was. While this is speculative, it is possible that we see in the early Mormons of Illinois in the 1840s something of a repetition of some ways in which powerful cultic leaders chose to follow through on and develop domestic polygamous utopias for themselves.

From the 1850s until 1890, polygamy was celebrated by the Mormons in Utah and nearby areas as the highest type of marriage, after which they reverted to a much more conventional outlook and practice. Having said that, offshoots of the Mormons—some would say fundamentalist Mormon groups—often still

---

255   Roger Patterson, *Mormonism, World Religions and Cults, Vol. 1,* Bodie Hodge and Roger Patterson, eds. (Green Forest: Masterbooks, 2015).

practice polygamy, with leaders sometimes having in excess of twenty wives.[256] Their reasoning casts back to Joseph Smith and his claims that an angel appeared to him to insist he practice plural marriage. To the sceptic, this statement by Smith could suggest that the claim was either a lie or a fantasy used to paint a religious veneer over unrestrained lust, especially when one learns that at least one or two of Smith's wives were teenagers. There is, though, a more complex scenario. It does seem the case that Smith did have a strong sex drive, but he also shared in the millennial zeal which inspired a number of the other groups. His group would escape a corrupt and dying world and institute a restoration of right living, inspired by the polygamous patriarchs and, surely, Solomon as well. It could also be the case that Smith suffered from some kind of psychological mania, which could possibly account for the religious visions at such odds with orthodox belief as well as his heightened sex drive.

There was also the idea of marriage blessing. It is possible that Solomon believed that a perfect number of one thousand in his sexual utopia would bring him ultimate Divine blessing. Joseph Smith and other Mormon leaders believed something not entirely dissimilar, although the Mormon belief system is very idiosyncratic, and it is also from a different time and place. They believed that through polygamous marriage, a powerful kinship group could be established, both useful and comforting when an outside world is opposed to your beliefs and practices. Yet this kinship group created on Earth was created to extend into the spiritual realm and be useful in it. Mormon temple "marriage sealings" for eternity created kinship groups which last forever. United for eternity, they would conquer new worlds and become like gods. In Smith's thinking, sexual union and procreation had celestial significance. The stars in the sky and the stars beyond them. Polygamy as a way to godhood. Perhaps an idea born out of mania. Emma Smith, Joseph's first wife, had other ideas, though. When she was

---

256 Nate Carlisle, "The Mormon polygamists who believe Missouri is the 'promised land,'" The Guardian.com, Jan. 7, 2019, https://www.theguardian.com/world/2019/jan/07/the-mormon-polygamists-who-believe-missouri-is-the-promised-land#:~:text=The%20Mormon%20polygamists%20who%20believe%20Missouri%20is%20the%20'promised%20land',-Flint%20Laub%20and&text=The%20Laubs%20live%20in%20a,a%20few%20cows%20and%20chickens.

asked by a visitor where she thought her church had gotten their idea of spiritual wives from, she replied, "Straight from hell, madam."[257]

MODERN CULTIC AND CRIMINAL QUESTS

Like antebellum America of the 1830s and 1840s, the more modern-day America of the 1960s was also a time of uncertainty, societal upheaval, and searching for an alternative utopia separate from mainstream culture. Many groups and communal cults formed at this time in order to explore "free love" and free expression: Drop City, Gorda Mountain, Black Oak Ranch, Peoples Temple Ukiah, and the Perry Lane cabins, to name just a few. Perhaps the cult which focused on sex the most, however, was yet another millennialist group, the Children of God, formed in 1968 at Huntington Beach, California. It was later renamed as The Family, and it exists to the present day with an estimated nine thousand core members living in communal homes in over ninety countries.[258] At the time of writing, Jeremy Spencer of Fleetwood Mac still has an association with the group. Other celebrities, such as Rose McGowan and Susan Justice, grew up in the cult but left and have been successful. Others—including a few celebrities such as River Phoenix, who referred to the group as "disgusting" in a March 1994 interview for *Esquire Magazine*[259]—have not been able to get beyond the psychological trauma caused, in part at least, by the group and, sadly, have ended their lives.

This group lies well outside mainstream Christianity in both theological beliefs and social structure. Their founder, David Berg, was descended from Mennonite settlers, German Jewish immigrants to Pennsylvania, and died in 1994. His parents were itinerant evangelists, eccentric but relatively mainstream. Yet, David developed a hatred early on for mainstream churches. It seems that, like Solomon, David Berg rejected the God of his father. He also rejected all authority, anyway, dismissing the world's system of laws and governments

---

257 Foster, ibid.
258 Douglas E. Cowan and David G. Bromley, *Cults and New Religions: A Brief History* (Oxford: Wiley Blackwell, 2015).
259 Tad Friend, "River, With Love and Anger," Esquire Magazine online, March 1, 1994, https://classic.esquire.com/article/1994/3/1/river-with-love-and-anger.

with the pejorative term, *the Romans*. Instead, he turned to "spirit guides" for information, channelling them. We do not know if Berg knew much, if anything, of the Oneida Community and its history, but it was as if he took their sexual ideas as a starting point and then pushed them much further within the Children of God in terms of polygamous marriage. In addition, he advocated sex as a device to empower missionary activity with people outside the group, a strategy he named "flirty fishing," arguably a modern reinvention of Canaanite and Phoenician cult prostitution. First-hand accounts, such as his daughter Deborah Davis' autobiography, describe a horrible extended family life at the cult's core, a multi-partner family riddled with jealousy and in-fighting and over which Berg would rule like a despot. We do not think that Solomon was consumed by bitterness in later life, but according to Davis, her father certainly was after he was dismissed by a church he had helped to found as a young man, the charge against him being sexual misconduct. Davis argues that her father never matured beyond adolescence.

David Berg alluded explicitly to Solomon and also to King David. Like the great kings, David Berg was an exception to God's prescription of monogamy for humanity and for the church. Polygamy was justified through a spurious and homespun philosophy of Divine exceptions for God's great kings and prophets, with Berg self-defined as the last prophet before "the end." Such kings and prophets could ignore the Mosaic Law. The Children of God became a classic cult, often drawing in disillusioned youth looking for a home and some degree of certainty but finding instead a gospel of rebellion, an institutionalized hatred of God and of true family cloaked by false religion and a prophetic persona. Davis' account describes her father's rapid descent into a consuming lust, which fueled incest, child sex, adultery, and the weaving of false, and often sexualized, doctrines. Over time, the cult has been forced to pull back from much of this and to reinvent itself several times. It has often been on the run from national and international authorities, relocating according to opportunity and expediency. In its original form, though, it is a distinctive and disturbing example of the manipulative exercise of power, false and cunning authority, and psychopathy.

And what of Solomon's many wives and concubines? Why would they all join? Can they be compared in any way with the dropouts who saw something in the Children of God and which appealed to them? Something in it for themselves which they thought was desirable—status, protection, a predictable and more comfortable life? Did some of them even view Solomon in Divine terms?

It is possible that in the Oneida Community, the early Mormons, and the early Children of God members, we see something being outworked which relates to Solomon's sexual utopia in a political sense. The shift away from monogamy and the reorientation of sexual relationships through polygamy can be viewed as a strategy to solidify the group or cult as a whole; in Solomon's case, it was a strategy to unify the kingdom. Every tribe and nation in Solomon's orbit would have at least one emissary at court, sometimes within earshot of the king, and from time to time, in bed. In more recent times, the strategy has led to exploitation and abuse. It has also tended to fail. The polygamous, sexual utopias we have considered have all been short-lived, although the organizations which adopted them have sometimes survived in a different form. The antithetical approach is also flawed and sometimes short-lived. The Shakers did not survive, and monastic ecclesiastical cults can also be toxic nests of abuse and victimization by seeking to suppress a God-given, natural, and very powerful drive.

There are other examples, of course, of both historical figures and very recent figures who sought to create sexual utopias. Genghis Khan, for instance, had one principal wife "who he loved dearly," five wives of lesser status, and five hundred concubines.[260] Usually, only one wife would accompany him on a military campaign. In recent times, not all examples have to do with unorthodox and extreme religious cults focused on the millennium of Christ. A secular example of someone who thought he could pursue the idea outside the law and that he was an exception to it—someone not entirely dissimilar to David Berg—was Jeffrey Epstein.

---

260 "Five Things to Know About Ghenghis Khan," Discovery Place online, December 19, 2016, https://science.discoveryplace.org/blog/five-things-to-know-about-genghis-khan.

Starting out as a math and physics teacher, Epstein liked to be thought of, in later life, as a philanthropist, and he had the resources to give large amounts to institutions such as Harvard. Epstein's focus was young and often under-age girls between the ages of fourteen and sixteen.[261] His parents had been Lithuanian and Russian Jewish refugees fleeing Nazi persecution. Growing up in New York, he quickly displayed prodigious talents in both math and music. He could also spot easy-win business and property deals of which he took advantage. Women were part of that mix from the start. One story is that he got into Bear Stearns as a twenty-three-year-old trader (without qualifying from college or university first) by dating the chief executive's daughter, Lynne Greenberg. No one is sure why Epstein was required to resign five years later, although it was probably to do with regulatory infractions. (Deana Pollard Sacks describes the offense as "financial chicanery."[262]) But he still walked away with a lot of money. From there, he started his own financial consultancy firm, and his *modus operandi* was to work only for the super rich (i.e. billionaires) and help them to avoid paying their taxes.

Unlike Solomon, Epstein never married any of the many hundreds of girls and women with whom he had sexual relationships. It also has to be clarified that many of the girls could not be said to be in a relationship with him at all, given the brevity of the association. These were usually the ones procured for Epstein under false pretenses by a few of his older former girlfriends. Newly acquired ones replaced other ones known for just weeks in what Sacks, a law professor in Texas, alludes to as "a flow of girls."[263] Epstein's sexual utopia was complex and international. From early on, he had enjoyed acquiring property and business contacts, and he used them to fly in teenage girls from many different jurisdictions for "modeling work."

Vicky Ward, a British investigative journalist, had this to say of Epstein's New York mansion for her beautifully crafted 2003 article in *Vanity Fair*: "You feel

---

261 James Patterson, John Connolly, and Tim Malloy, *Filthy Rich: The Shocking True Story of Jeffrey Epstein The Billionaire's Sex Scandal* (New York: Grand Central Publishing, 2017).

262 Deana Pollard Sacks, *The Godfathers of Sex Abuse, Book 1: Jeffrey Epstein* (Saint Louis, MO: Stonebrook Publishing, 2019).

263 Sacks, ibid.

you have stumbled into someone's private Xanadu. This is no mere rich person's home, but a high-walled, eclectic, imperious fantasy that seems to have no boundaries."[264] In 2003, when the article appeared, subtly associating the subject with the New York-born confidence scammer Tom Ripley in its title, Epstein's estate also included a seventy-five-hundred-acre ranch in New Mexico, one of the smaller Virgin Islands in the Caribbean but still around seventy acres, a large mansion in Florida, and several aircraft.

When finally placed under legal scrutiny, Epstein acted for years like the typical sex offender profiled by Anna C. Salter, writing well before his case became all too public. For instance, he finally admitted to just one misdeed, while denying everything else in his entire offending history, displaying profound lack of empathy for his victims. Salter's analysis also shows that Epstein's offending was well within the typical data range regarding his number of victims when viewed alongside empirical evidence about sex offenders and their multiple victims.[265] He was, despite his mystique and utopian property estate, one example of a type. This narcissistic and compulsive type of criminal sex addict does not develop deep emotional ties with anyone. But Epstein viewed himself as an exception, as David Berg did. Rules don't apply to them. In 2019, Epstein was rearrested in New York under federal sex-trafficking law and in August that year was allegedly found dead in his high-security prison cell.

As wily and manipulative sex and power-obsessed egomaniacs, David Berg and Jeffrey Epstein merely lived out grotesque parodies of Solomon's sexual utopia, under the guise of religion or not. They also lived lives well beneath Solomon, full of smoke, mirrors, and illusions. Solomon always dealt with and commented on the nature of reality. Yet perhaps we get a glimpse through their lives of Solomon's own narcissism and underneath that, a psychological state of felt inadequacy and lack of self-esteem. He, too, considered himself an exception, someone who could flout the rules and live out a life well beyond them.

264 Vicky Ward, "The Talented Mr Epstein," Vanity Fair online, March 1, 2003, https://www.vanityfair.com/news/2003/03/jeffrey-epstein-200303.
265 Anna C. Salter, *Transforming Trauma: A Guide to Understanding and Treating Adult Survivors of Child Sexual Abuse* (Thousand Oaks: Sage, 1995).

There is also the question of whether Solomon himself was a sex addict, someone for whom no number of women was enough. Like Epstein, did Solomon keep having to refresh the human livestock in his harem? Was there a frisson like the one experienced by Epstein caused by a powerful, connected, and wealthy man pursuing the freshness and inexperience of youth? Salter would say that this situation is gratifying to the rich man because it feeds his ego.[266]

None of these protagonists are completely evil, of course. Epstein could be generous. He organized the modification of a submarine to accommodate the disabled scientist Stephen Hawking and his wheelchair so that he could view an alien landscape underwater. Yet their lives reveal that the actualization of a sexual utopia, when it is possible, is a misdirected ambition. There will always be many victims. In all cases, it is a chimera which is there for a moment and then collapses. It is one of the few matters on which the world and God agree. A sexual utopia, created out of mass polygamy, is a bad thing.

266 Ibid.

CHAPTER 43

DOMESTIC AND FINANCIAL AMBITIONS

Jesus looked around and said to His disciples, "How hard it is for those who have

riches to enter the kingdom of God!" And the disciples were astonished at His

words. But Jesus answered again and said to them, "Children, how hard it is for

those who trust in riches to enter the kingdom of God! It is easier for a camel to

go through the eye of a needle than for a rich man to enter the kingdom of God."

And they were greatly astonished, saying among themselves, "Who then can be

saved?" But Jesus looked at them and said, "With men it is impossible, but not

with God; for with God all things are possible."

—Mark 10:23-27

In 2018, *The Times of Israel* reported that five Jews were included in the newly released *Forbes* list of America's top ten wealthiest people. Mark Zuckerberg of Facebook ranked at number four, followed by Larry Ellison of Oracle at number five; and Google co-founders Larry Page and Sergey Brin were numbers six and nine. Michael Bloomberg came in at number ten.[267] This is a striking result, but it is not just about the money. It is just as much about business acumen, innovation, and perhaps something which is not easy to define but is still there.

Jewish thinking today emulates King Solomon to some extent: it is good to build up one's wealth and property while at the same time impacting the world

---

267 TOI Staff, "5 Jews make Forbes' list of top 10 wealthiest Americans," The Times of Israel. com, October 6, 2018, https://www.timesofisrael.com/5-jews-make-forbes-list-of-top-10-wealthiest-americans.

to elevate it to a higher level. As part of that, mankind is to be creative and should enjoy the world. This thinking, though, usually stops short of hedonism, and it is balanced by responsibility and an injunction not to destroy that which is enjoyed. Mankind can then create new worlds and new life out of the old. The Midrash says, "All that was created during the six days that God created the world still requires work."[268] The accumulation of wealth is also balanced, to some extent, by injunctions toward charity (through tithes and lending to those in need) but which do not amount to the redistribution of wealth within society.

It is also good to strive for high educational achievement. The pan-religion survey figures pulled together by Barry Kosmin and Ariela Keysar reveal that across the United States, the Jewish population has the lowest high school underachievement result when compared to all other religious and non-religious groupings and the highest achievement result for university graduates (undergraduate degrees and higher degrees).[269] This demonstrates a desire to persevere and achieve and reflects a more long-standing Jewish intellectualism. At the same time, a minority in the Jewish community (for instance, Hassidim) have a disdain for secular education similar in its effects to the disdain shown by some Protestant sects such as the Brethren. The Jewish community also ranks first in income level in the United States, easily outstripping all other religious and non-religious groups. This community is successfully leveraging educational attainment into wealth accumulation.

In Judaism, private property rights are sacrosanct: thievery can be perceived as being somewhat akin to murder. King Ahab lost his throne and was killed because he stole a vineyard and because he murdered its owner by the hand of his pagan wife, Jezebel (1 Kings 21:17-19). The rights are also absolute. To be sovereign over property is to rule in harmony with God, acting as God's creative partners. In addition, accumulating wealth is seen as good, as long as the means used are honest ones. Wealth achieved through hard work and the turning of ability into

268 Joseph Isaac Lifshitz, *Welfare, Property and the Divine Image in Jewish Law and Thought* (Abingdon: Routledge, 2008).
269 Barry A Kosmin and Ariela Keysar, *Religion in a Free Market: Religious and Non-Religious Americans Who What Why Where* (Ithaca, NY: Paramount Market Publishing, 2006).

achievements is affirmed greatly within Judaism. On the other hand, poverty and becoming a burden on the state or on others around is to be avoided. Christian teaching does disagree with this position and some of the premises behind it (for instance, that righteousness is to be equated with wealth and never with poverty) but not absolutely, particularly regarding Protestant thinking.

This particularly Jewish goal of pursuing both wisdom and wealth is a constant which goes right back to Old Testament times. As Cosimo Perrotta observes in his magnum opus, *Consumption as an Investment*, it is God who directs the Jews to a promised land full of resources in the first place. From there, wealth will be given them *if* they trust in Him.[270] For instance, if they obey the Sabbath rest, as commanded, famine will cease, and they will gain a surplus and the wealth of other nations as well.[271] Wealth also exists alongside wisdom as per the iconic King Solomon and his achievements—the former can be a reward for the correct exercising of the latter. Wealth achieved through hard work is a good thing. In contrast, wealth obtained too easily and too quickly is to be distrusted, since it is unstable and undeserved and so will not last; luxurious wealth obtained at the expense of the poor is also condemned: "Wealth *gained by* dishonesty will be diminished, But he who gathers by labor will increase" (Prov. 13:11). "The LORD will enter into judgment With the elders of His people And His princes: 'For you have eaten up the vineyard; The plunder of the poor *is* in your houses. What do you mean by crushing My people And grinding the faces of the poor?' Says the Lord God of hosts" (Isa. 3:14-15).

Wisdom and wealth will come together again in the future when the Messiah creates His millennial kingdom. The wealth revealed in 1 Kings and the approach of the Queen of Sheba with her retinue to Solomon are prophetic of a time still to come when the rulers of the Earth come to visit the Messiah reigning from Jerusalem. Solomon is living out a prophecy of the Messiah ruling and judging in Jerusalem in a time still to come—the Millennial Age—even before some of the

---

270   Cosimo Perrotta, *Consumption as an Investment (Routledge Studies in the History of Economics)* (Abingdon: Routledge, 2004).
271   Isaiah 58:13-14; Isaiah 60

Jewish prophets, such as Micah, foretold it. Solomon, writing at a time when he was still focused on Yahweh, also writes prophetically, directly linking his reign and his meeting with the Queen of Sheba with the future reign of Someone greater still. Then there will be a recreation of her visit from the very same places from which she hailed. The actors, both the ruler and the reigned-over, will be different, though.

Psalm 72 is a remarkable and prophetic work. It seems to have been King David's last—or among his last—oral works at a time when he was unable to formalize or even write down his thoughts. It was written down and edited by Solomon, who formalized David's song into a psalm. The following are some extracts of the psalm:

- "Give the king Your judgments, O God, And Your righteousness to the king's Son" (v. 1).
- "They shall fear You As long as the sun and moon endure, Throughout all generations" (v. 5).
- "He shall come down like rain upon the grass before mowing, Like showers *that* water the earth" (v. 6).
- "The kings of Tarshish and of the isles Will bring presents; The kings of Sheba and Seba Will offer gifts" (v. 10).
- "Yes, all kings shall fall down before Him; All nations shall serve Him" (v. 11).
- "And He shall live; And the gold of Sheba will be given to Him" (v. 15).
- "His name shall endure forever; His name shall continue as long as the sun" (v. 17).
- "And *men* shall be blessed in Him; All nations shall call Him blessed" (v. 17).
- "Blessed *be* the LORD God, the God of Israel, Who only does wondrous things! And blessed *be* His glorious name forever! And let the whole earth be filled *with* His glory. Amen and Amen" (vv. 18-19).

Dale Ralph Davis reminds us that the Queen of Sheba will be there at the final judgment. She had less light than we do—merely the flawed light of

Solomon. But she saw his wealth and the blessing it revealed, and she heard his wisdom, sparked by a transcendent reality from above and beyond this world. It was enough for her. Jesus warned those around Him that she will appear to them and condemn them if they do not accept that One greater than Solomon had now appeared and spoken to them face to face. They had received much greater revelation, and so they had much greater responsibility. He would not stoop to their level and perform magical party tricks for them. He required faith, but He knew that some would not believe he was the Son of God, even after he rose from the dead.

CHAPTER 44

SOLOMON'S FOCUS ON THE ARTS AND SCIENCES

"The fig tree puts forth her green figs, And the vines with *the tender grapes*
Give a good *smell. Rise up, my love, my fair one, And come away!"*

—Song of Solomon 2:13

One of the most intriguing and prophetic aspects of Solomon's achievements is his focus on the arts and sciences. We are told that Solomon composed three thousand proverbs and 1,005 songs, and much of this accomplishment would have included some degree of empirical observation. To get a sense of the grand sweep of this and its worldwide impact, we refer again to the book of 1 Kings.

> And God gave Solomon wisdom and exceedingly great understanding, and largeness of heart like the sand on the seashore. Thus Solomon's wisdom excelled the wisdom of all the men of the East and all the wisdom of Egypt. For he was wiser than all men— than Ethan the Ezrahite, and Heman, Chalcol, and Darda, the sons of Mahol; and his fame was in all the surrounding nations. He spoke three thousand proverbs, and his songs were one thousand and five. Also he spoke of trees, from the cedar tree of Lebanon even to the hyssop that springs out of the wall; he spoke also of animals, of birds, of creeping things, and of fish. And men of all nations, from all the kings of the earth who had heard of his wisdom, came to hear the wisdom of Solomon (1 Kings 4:29-34).

Is it possible that when God blessed Solomon with this type of wisdom, he was blessing the Jewish people? Solomon was, after all, their representative. Yahweh is a generous God, and He rarely removes what He has given. We also know that God has blessed the Jews, His chosen people, anyway. The blessings of an eternal God are themselves eternal, and they are for individuals as well as a whole people. They include the miraculous regathering of His people in modern times:

> "Thus says the LORD, your Redeemer, The Holy One of Israel: 'I *am* the LORD your God, Who teaches you to profit, Who leads you by the way you should go'" (Isa. 48:17).

> "Fear not, for I *am* with you; I will bring your descendants from the east, And gather you from the west; I will say to the north, 'Give them up!' And to the south, 'Do not keep them back!' Bring My sons from afar, And My daughters from the ends of the earth" (Isa. 43:5-6).

How would this blessing on Jewish individuals and their efforts outwork itself in modern times? We would need to consider modern-day worldwide recognition of achievement in the arts and the sciences. Since 1901, this has been the prerogative of the Nobel Foundation and its committees.

If we look at the numbers of Nobel Prize winners by country, the top two are the United States (375 prizes) and the United Kingdom (131 prizes) at the time of writing, with Israel achieving a modest eighteenth place (twelve prizes). If we re-examine winners by country *per capita*, Israel rises to twelfth place. However, what if we reconsider prize winners by ethnicity? After all, less than half of the 14.5 million Jews actually live in Israel. In 2017, about 6,451,000 Jews lived in Israel, compared to 5,700,000 living in the United States. Then there were the 456,000 living in France, and so on.[272]

Jews number less than 0.2 percent of the world population, but they account for twenty-two percent of all Nobel Prizes.[273] This includes Israelis as well as Jews living in the diaspora, often in the United States and European countries such as

272 *Wikipedia, s.v.* "Jewish Population by Country," Last modified December 14, 2020, https://en.wikipedia.org/wiki/Jewish_population_by_country.

273 Ruth Schuster, "Why Do Jews Win So Many Nobels?," Haaretz.com, https://www.haaretz.com/jewish/why-do-jews-win-so-many-nobels-1.5347671.

Belgium, the home of Francis Englert. Englert is a Jewish scientist, who, together with Peter Higgs, predicted the elementary "God particle" later discovered by the Large Hadron Collider. Beyond some spectacular examples, though, Jews have won prizes in all Nobel categories.

It is as if, no matter what is thrown against them, the Jews will succeed because even if many of them are not currently on God's side, God is still on theirs. As God's chosen people, they are blessed, and they will prevail in the times to come. It could be said that King Solomon was an early example of this. Turning his back on God, his life and works still flourished. Including their flaws, his life and musings still speak to us today. They have come down to us in the perfect Word of God.

Albert Einstein, the Nobel Prize winner for physics in 1922, is a more contemporary Jewish example. He was, in his own words, a "deeply religious nonbeliever" and did not believe in an afterlife.[274] For him, this present life was quite enough. As to the reason why so many Nobels are awarded to Jews, there are a few naturalistic and sociological theories which are somewhat unconvincing, so much so that even Richard Dawkins is confused about it. When asked about it, he said, "I haven't thought it through. I don't know. But I don't think it is a minor thing; it is colossal."[275] In the year he said that, half the new Nobel laureates were Jewish.

Solomon was the wisest of sages, but his sage-like Jewish descendants have been all around us for many years. Though all lesser than Solomon, there are many of them. We need only think of Sigmund Freud, Albert Einstein, and other greats, but I remember fondly my German Jewish psychology professor H. Rudolph Schaffer. Born in Berlin in 1926, he arrived in London in 1939 on a kinder-transport train with next to nothing, and like so many Jews, he excelled regardless of the difficult situation. For many years, he was the professor of psychology at the University

---

274   *Wikipedia, s.v.* "Religious and philosophical views of Albert Einstein," Last modified January 8, 2021, https://en.wikipedia.org/wiki/Religious_and_philosophical_views_of_Albert_Einstein.

275   Zach Pontz, "Richard Dawkins Perplexed by Number of Jewish Nobel Prize Winners," The Algemeiner.com, October 29, 2013, https://www.algemeiner.com/2013/10/29/richard-dawkins-perplexed-by-high-number-of-jewish-nobel-prize-winners.

of Strathclyde. He had a brilliant mind and so much enthusiasm for his subject: the significance of early human relationships and the intricacies of mother-infant interaction. He saw something in me and offered me a scholarship, which I was glad to accept. As a teenager in England, he saved up his pocket money. He wanted to bring his parents to England, but they both died in concentration camps. How much has anti-Semitism robbed the human race of the benefits of Jewish minds and spirits?

Also, consider the astounding number of Jewish artists and actors who have excelled in the arts in recent times: Bob Dylan, Carole King, Barbra Streisand, Paul Simon, Felix Mendelssohn, Yehudi Menuhin, Harrison Ford, Dustin Hoffman, Paul Newman, and so many more. In the series *Star Trek*, both Captain Kirk and Science Officer Spock were played by Jewish actors, who, once in a blue moon, would refer back to their Jewish roots. The Vulcan hand sign ("live long and prosper") was the Jewish priestly blessing offered in the synagogue, representing the Hebrew letter *Shin* and signifying "Almighty God" and "Shalom." Star Trek scripts also occasionally had Jewish references. For instance, this one is from the Jewish screenwriter, David Gerrold:

> SPOCK: They (tribbles) remind me of the lilies of the field. They toil not, neither do they spin. But they seem to eat a great deal. I see no practical use for them.
>
> MCCOY: Does everything have to have a practical use for you? They're nice, soft, and furry, and they make a pleasant sound.
>
> SPOCK: So would an ermine violin, but I see no advantage in having one.[276]

---

276 *Star Trek: The Original Series,* "The Trouble With Tribbles," Directed by Joseph Pevney, Written by Gene Roddenberry and David Gerrold, Desilu Productions, Norway Corporation, December 29, 1967.

CHAPTER 45

THE THIRD TEMPLE

"Let no one deceive you by any means; for that Day will *not come unless the falling away comes first, and the man of sin is revealed, the son of perdition, who opposes and exalts himself above all that is called God or that is worshiped, so that he sits as God in the temple of God, showing himself that he is God."*

—2 Thessalonians 2:3-4

Solomon's Temple was the first of three temples to be built on the threshing floor on Mount Moriah, which King David bought from Araunah the Jebusite and where the avenging angel of the Lord was seen to sheath his sword. Two temples have passed away—Solomon's Temple and the smaller temple built later by Zerubbabel and completed around 515 B.C. but enlarged, only to be destroyed by Titus in 70 A.D. The third is yet to come. It is the temple which the Antichrist is prophesised to enter in order to declare himself to be God (2 Thess. 2:3-4).

In the present age, Masonic temples also have two wooden pillars at their entrances, but these are positioned *inside* the buildings. Also called Jachin and Boaz, one is colored red and the other white. Masons ascribe multiple levels of bogus meaning to these terms and to the pillars—such as the sun and the moon, light and dark, zodiacal signs, and so on. It is pointless to dwell on such things. There is a reason, though, to focus on the temple still to be built.

Years before its destruction, Jesus predicted the complete destruction of the second temple, which had been built over Solomon's Temple. The prophecy is recorded by both Matthew (24:1-2) and Mark: "Then as He went out of the temple, one of His disciples said to Him, 'Teacher, see what manner of stones and what buildings *are here!*' And Jesus answered and said to him, 'Do you see these great buildings? Not *one* stone shall be left upon another, that shall not be thrown down'" (Mark 13:1-2).

We have two lost temples, the one built by Solomon and destroyed by the Babylonians and the one built by a number of architects, though usually referred to as Herod's Temple, and destroyed by the Romans. Yet this era we live in is one of returns. From their dispersal throughout the nations, the Jews have returned to their homeland in sufficient numbers for Israel to be a nation again for the first time since 1947.[277] Since then, Israel has increased in strength and is now, as in Solomon's day, arguably the most powerful nation in the Middle East.[278] In addition, there are very advanced plans to rebuild the temple exactly where Solomon's Temple and the second temple stood. This is very important in both Jewish and Christian eschatology. The Jews refer to this third Messianic-era temple as the בית שדקמה הׁשילישיׂ, or *Beit haMikdash haShlishi.* Translated literally into English, this reads as "The House, the Holy, the Third."[279] Jewish organizations, such as the Temple Institute, have as their goal the building of the third temple, and the policy is supported by the Israeli government.

Until now, the main stumbling blocks have been the Muslim structures located on the Temple Mount, but a further blockage has been a disagreement as to the exact location of the lost temples. The third temple—and the Holy of Holies in particular—must be built on their footprint. A majority view has been that the second temple's only visible remains are seen when one approaches the Wailing Wall or Western Wall (Kotel). Yet this view contradicts Christ's prophecy concerning that temple: that from His vantage point when He gave the prophecy, some way off, all traces of the temple would be gone because of its complete destruction. It also contradicts eyewitness accounts such as that of Josephus, who says that he would not have believed the temple had ever existed, had he

---

277 *Britannica, s.v.* "United Nations Resolution 181," accessed March 14, 2021, https://www.britannica.com/topic/United-Nations-Resolution-181.

278 Egypt and Turkey are sometimes seen as more powerful than Israel in military terms according to a number of metrics, but both are non-nuclear powers.

279 *Wikipedia, s.v.* "The Third Temple, Last modified January 5, 2021, https://en.wikipedia.org/wiki/Third_Temple.

not witnessed its destruction personally.[280] Although we cannot say for sure, historians and researchers believe that the true site is likely to be a quarter-mile south of the Temple Mount at the Gihon Spring, which rises up to this day within a cave, with the temple remains completely buried.

A number of eye witnesses from the Greek and Roman eras reported that the temple had a spring, an essential source of fresh water to cleanse a site used for animal sacrifice. Yet the Temple Mount site has no natural spring. In addition, Solomon's Temple was built on a threshing floor. The Temple Mount, located at the very top of a sharp elevation, is inconvenient for threshing and the other work associated with that. A site lower down from the peak would make use of the prevailing wind but would also be a lot more accessible.

The Western Wall may actually be the only visible remains of the Roman Fort Antonia, built to house up to ten thousand personnel: a *tagma,* or legion, of six thousand men, plus support staff. Such a large and sprawling structure would have dominated the landscape and would surely leave remains viewable today. If this theory gains further traction and is accepted by the Israeli authorities, then the obstacles to building the third temple fall away. The Western Wall, or Kotel, may actually be the remains of the fort and praetorium site where Jesus was condemned to death by Pilate.

We can imagine, though, what would occur when the third temple is built. While the Jewish religious authorities will seek to reinstitute animal sacrifices, this will not go down well with animal rights campaigners, vegans, and other interest groups.[281] It is likely that the Antichrist will capitalize on these kinds of disputes and intervene for his own ends—to elevate himself and formalize a one-world religion. Paradoxically, the country with the highest percentage of vegans is Israel: five percent of Israelis claim to be vegan, while another seven percent are vegetarians.[282]

---

280 Robert Cornuke, *Temple: Amazing New Discoveries That Change Everything About the Location of Solomon's Temple* (Lifebridge Books, 2014).

281 Tzvi Freeman, "Are You Really Planning to Bring Back Those Animal Sacrifices?," Chabad. org, https://www.chabad.org/library/article_cdo/aid/2942/jewish/Animal-Sacrifices.htm (accessed October 17, 2019).

282 Ben Sales, "Israelis growing hungry for vegan diet," Jewish Telegraphic Agency online, October 15, 2014, https://www.jta.org/2014/10/15/lifestyle/israelis-growing-hungry-for-vegan-diet.

CHAPTER 46

WORSHIP AND APOSTASY
IN THE CURRENT ERA

"They lived at the end of an epoch, when everything was dissolving into a sort of
ghastly flux, and they didn't know it."

—George Orwell[283]

Scripture predicts that in the last days, there will be a great apostasy or falling away. The apostle Paul may be saying in 2 Thessalonians 2 that this includes the majority of individuals and cultures and even the majority of the professing Church. This should be taken to be *the* falling away. It is unlike any prior straying from revealed truth, and it is a process—presumably a global process—which occurs immediately prior to the short period of time known as the Great Tribulation and thereafter the Millennial reign of Christ on the Earth. These are all global events. There is a lot of evidence which, taken together, suggests that we are well into this time of apostasy. While it can be argued that no nation really ever adopted an entirely Christian approach to government, there was a significant Christian influence in Western countries until early on in the last century. This is no longer the case, and instead, we can see a remarkable decline gathering pace through the last one hundred years in religious adherence. Christianity has very largely been replaced by humanism, atheism, and multifaith. A recent pan-European study by Professor Stephen Bullivant of St. Mary's University, for instance, revealed very low Christian

---

283 George Orwell, *Coming Up For Air* (New York: Mariner Books, 1969).

adherence numbers in young adults across the continent, using data from the European Social Survey.[284]

The Book of 1 Kings makes explicit the fact that the apostasy which Solomon instigated involved, after a time, cult prostitution. This type of apostasy has seen a return in the twentieth century through the re-emergence of types of ritual sex. The best-known cult to practice it has been the Children of God, but there have been a number of others as well. In 1989, for example, a neo-pagan high priestess and former Mormon in Los Angeles, California, Mary Ellen Tracy, did an extensive interview. She said that through revelation her husband received, she was to re-establish a cult of Isis. At the time the report came out, she had since forgiven the sins, she said, of about one thousand men while they had sex with her.[285] Sex is part of the cult's scared rites.

Idolatry became intrinsic to the brief civilizations experienced by the northern and southern Jewish kingdoms after Solomon, albeit with brief remissions in the South. In the North, for instance, the prophet Amos rails against female cultists when he says: "Hear this word, you cows of Bashan, who *are* on the mountain of Samaria, Who oppress the poor, Who crush the needy, Who say to your husbands, 'Bring *wine*, let us drink'" (Amos 4:1). It is likely that the cultists' syncretistic Asherah and false-Yahweh bull worshipping activities were similar to the spirit operating in much more recent and current cult activities.

To return briefly to the building of the third temple still in the future, could its construction, inauguration, and the first priestly sacrifices trigger a final apostasy? As soon as the temple is ready, we are right into a new and probably very brief era of ritual animal sacrifice. One aspect of this is the ritual slaughter of a "red heifer," according to God's commandment in Numbers 19 and also the rabbinic oral law known as the Mishnah. Use of its ashes is an absolute requirement for temple service. The details of these combined biblical and rabbinical commands make

---

284 Stephen Bullivant, "Europe's Young Adults and Religion: Findings From the European Social Survey (2014-16) to inform the 2018 Synod of Bishops," distributed by St. Mary's University Twickenham London: Benedict XVI Centre for Religion and Society, 2018, https://www.stmarys.ac.uk/research/centres/benedict-xvi/docs/2018-mar-europe-young-people-report-eng.pdf.

285 Jack Alexander, "Church Uses Sex to Save Sinners!," *Weekly World News,* June 6, 1989, 17.

this animal something of a biological anomaly, but at the same time, there are considerable efforts being made to search for it but also to genetically engineer it.

Thinking more generally about animal sacrifice, though, it is currently becoming more controversial with some veterinary associations, vegetarians, and secularists opposed to it, particularly if traditional methods are used and the animals are not stunned beforehand. We are now in an era of animal rights but also at a time when anti-Semitic forces sometimes rail against Jewish ritual requirements. Nazi Germany, for instance, outlawed Jewish ritual animal slaughter in 1933, misrepresenting it while also elevating animal rights to an unprecedented level.[286] The Nazis banned animal vivisection, and acts of animal cruelty could be punished by the perpetrator being sent to a concentration camp. It is not too far a stretch to imagine a future Antichrist figure banning the newly reinstituted sacrifice procedures in favor of temple worship focusing on him alone: a man, yes, but a self-declared god, the true representative of a new divine humanity, the final master race. Those still alive at that time should look up and expect the Messiah:

> And from Jesus Christ, the faithful witness, the firstborn from the dead, and the ruler over the kings of the earth. To Him who loved us and washed us from our sins in His own blood, and has made us kings and priests to His God and Father, to Him *be* glory and dominion forever and ever. Amen. Behold, He is coming with clouds, and every eye will see Him, even they who pierced Him. And all the tribes of the earth will mourn because of Him. Even so, Amen. (Rev. 1:5-7).

This then will be the final fulfillment of the prophecies in Daniel and Isaiah, who predicted events associated with the building in Jerusalem of the third temple. "He shall bring an end to sacrifice and offering. And on the wing of abominations shall be one who makes desolate, Even until the consummation, which is determined, Is poured out on the desolate" (Dan. 9:27b).

---

286 David B. Green, "This Day in Jewish History | 1933: Nazi Germany Outlaws Kosher Slaughter," Haaretz.com, October 4, 2018, https://www.haaretz.com/jewish/.premium-1933-nazis-outlaw-kosher-slaughter-1.5437764.

It will also be the fulfillment of Jesus' prophecies concerning the end of the age and His return. Jesus linked His second coming to Earth with a rebuilt Jewish temple. He specifically mentioned events to do with "the holy place," and these require the existence of a Jewish temple. The Roman Empire's destruction in 70 A.D. of the temple Jesus was looking back at—He had just left it—when He prophesied entails a still future building of a third temple in order for all His words to be fulfilled. Jesus predicted the complete annihilation of the second temple while at the same time also prophesying as to events within a future temple. We will conclude with Jesus' teaching in which He reassured His disciples that when the (third) temple is desecrated, there is but a very short time before His return.

I have been selective as to the words quoted below, but please read the entire section in Matthew's gospel to gain a complete overview of what is being said. Jesus is quoted as He walks with His disciples from the temple to the Mount of Olives and then, as He sits there, gazing down at the magnificent buildings. He tells them what they and we need to know about its destruction and the end of the age we live in.

> Then Jesus went out and departed from the temple, and His disciples came up to show Him the buildings of the temple. And Jesus said to them, "Do you not see all these things? Assuredly, I say to you, not *one* stone shall be left here upon another, that shall not be thrown down." Now as He sat on the Mount of Olives, the disciples came to Him privately, saying, "Tell us, when will these things be? And what *will be* the sign of Your coming, and of the end of the age?" "For nation will rise against nation, and kingdom against kingdom. And there will be famines, pestilences, and earthquakes in various places. All these *are* the beginning of sorrows. Then they will deliver you up to tribulation and kill you, and you will be hated by all nations for My name's sake. But he who endures to the end shall be saved. And this gospel of the kingdom will be preached in all the world as a witness to all the nations, and then the end will come. Therefore when you see the 'abomination of desolation,' spoken of by Daniel the prophet, standing in the holy place" (whoever reads, let him

understand), "then let those who are in Judea flee to the mountains. Let him who is on the housetop not go down to take anything out of his house. And let him who is in the field not go back to get his clothes. Then if anyone says to you, 'Look, here *is* the Christ!' or 'There!' do not believe *it*. For false christs and false prophets will rise and show great signs and wonders to deceive, if possible, even the elect. See, I have told you beforehand. Therefore if they say to you, 'Look, He is in the desert!' do not go out; or 'Look, *He is* in the inner rooms!' do not believe *it*. For as the lightning comes from the east and flashes to the west, so also will the coming of the Son of Man be" (Matt. 24:1-3, 7-9, 13-18, 23-27).

CHAPTER 47

REAL LIFE AND THE END TIMES

"Only Christ can be the perfect friend. He says to his disciples—'I have called you friends.' It's a most moving and beautiful picture. He is our friend. He is our reason for working. He is our reason for being."

—David Robertson[287]

One of the impressions we are left with regarding King Solomon is his loneliness. To paraphrase what the psychoanalyst, Dorothy Zeligs, said, having one thousand women is to have no women at all.[288] Solomon's loneliness is best exemplified in his later work in Ecclesiastes: "I saw vanity under the sun: There is one alone, without companion: He has neither son nor brother. Yet *there* is no end to all his labors, Nor is his eye satisfied with riches. *But he never asks,* 'For whom do I toil and deprive myself of good?' This also *is* vanity and a grave misfortune" (Eccl. 4:7b-8).

In his wisdom, Solomon identifies not just one of our enemies—loneliness—but something of the fallen nature of things, of the kinds of lives that we are destined to pursue without Christ. He was aware of the deluded futility, the pre-programmed and fallen, sin-based nature of life. One can hardly call it being. It is more about a grim and futile survival, which pits us competitively against our fellow creatures and which is destined to end all too soon. We can expend all our

---

287 David Robertson, "Ecclesiastes 4 and the cure for loneliness: the cord of three strands," Christian Today online, February 2, 2018, https://christiantoday.com/article/ecclesiastes-4-and-the-cure-for-loneliness-the-cord-of-three-strands/125282.htm.
288 Zeligs, ibid.

energy to survive market forces or a five-year plan, depending on the culture we operate within; but we are alone in our struggle, and it is all short-lived. For whom are we toiling? Our children who will age us, replace us, and then join us in the grave. Solomon's wisdom gave him remarkable insight and the greatest of burdens. He was contemplating the demonic without God's support.

Living much later on and in the end times, we have additional burdens. These burdens do not replace the realities which the great king pondered. They add to them. We have a greater knowledge of time, place, space, and human history than ever before. These can add questions such as, "Why am I here and not there? Why am I living now and not then? And given the nature of space, what is my significance?" At present, the distance between Earth and the edge of the observable universe is forty-six billion light years, but the span of the universe is unknown. As for the Earth, young people, in particular, are being driven into a state of panic about global warming first and pollution second. Is an inhabitable Earth running out of time? Without being aware of eschatology—the destined end of things, God's will as revealed—these burdens must be great indeed.

Christ changes us. He is the best friend we can have, as David Robertson points out. He is a perfect friend and provides meaning. There is also more to it. To be born again is to experience a fundamental change in the nature of being. Solomon laments the state of the human being, even a lonely ruler, as an *individual*. As a solitary individual, he is cut off from others in a mysterious and fundamental way. He is also cut off from God. Hence the futility identified by Solomon and, much later, by philosophers such as the Existentialists. By being born again through Christ, however, accepting God and a relationship with Him, we are transformed from individuals into *persons*. The nature of our being has changed. It has been redeemed and transformed. We are still not (seemingly) as we will be at the last trump, but in God's economy and in an unseen but real way, we now are as we will be. As mere individuals, we were not. As persons, in and with Christ, we can engage rightly with others and with God. We can walk in love in this world.

INTERACTIONS WITH THE ELDERLY

In 2 Samuel 19:32-37, we have another description of old age in the story of Barzillai, who was a very aged and wealthy man who had helped King David for many years by providing him with supplies. David told Barzillai to come to Jerusalem to live, so that David could look after him. Barzillai refused, saying, "I *am* today eighty years old. Can I discern between the good and the bad? Can your servant taste what I eat or what I drink? Can I hear any longer the voice of singing men and singing women? Why then should your servant be a further burden to my lord the king?" (v. 35). Barzillai returned to his own city, where he chose to live out his last years.

As the physical body ages, the bone and muscle functions deteriorate; cognitive processes decline; and eyesight and hearing are less sharp. What Solomon wrote in Ecclesiastes 12 about old age and its limitations is very relevant for us today, at a time when far more people are living longer. Frailty is defined by the National Health Service in the U.K. as a long-term condition related to the aging process, in which multiple body systems gradually lose their in-built reserves. "Frailty is where someone is less able to recover from accidents, physical illness or other stressful events."[289]

---

289 National Health Service, *Ageing well and supporting people living with frailty*, 2019 https://www.england.nhs.uk/ourwork/clinical-policy/older-people/frailty/2019.

SUPPORTING ELDERLY PEOPLE

Is it important for Christians and churches to be aware of and to offer support to elderly people? I believe it is and that people of an advanced age have much to offer in church settings, even if they are housebound. Many elderly Christians are used by God in intercessory prayer. Old age and frailty can hinder participation in many activities, but older people can still pray for others and intercede for situations, especially because they have free time.

When we look at the number of elderly people currently alive in our nations, they are a group which we should not ignore. A report entitled "Later Life in the UK," shows that there are 5.4 million people aged seventy-five and over in the U.K..[290] And USA Population Statistics for 2017 show 50.9 million aged sixty-five and over.[291] Hong Kong and Japan are the two countries in the world where life expectancy is greatest. The increase in the number of elderly people is predicted to continue; however, nothing is completely certain in our changing world, especially following the global pandemic of the coronavirus in 2020 and 2021, which affects elderly people in particular very seriously.

HOW WE CAN SUPPORT ELDERLY PEOPLE

One of the best ways we can support the elderly is by visiting them. Try to find out if there are elderly people living alone who have no relatives nearby. If we each played a small part in our communities and churches by visiting elderly church members and neighbors, the whole of society would benefit. Despite the multiple digital connections which social media provides, society is becoming more disconnected because we are not spending enough time talking to others. It is also beneficial to visit nursing homes and retirement centers and hold short services or simply have times of singing to music.

Along these same lines, we need to make sure that the young are interacting with the elderly as well. I believe that older people have a wealth of experience and should be encouraged to share stories with young people of how God has

---

290 "Later Life in the United Kingdom 2019," AgeUK, 2019, https://www.ageuk.org.uk/
globalassets/age-uk/documents/reports-and-publications/later_life_uk_factsheet.pdf.
291 https://acl.gov/news-and-events/announcements/announcing-2017-profile-older-americans.

been faithful and brought them through trials and testing. Some have been missionaries in their younger days. Often, young people only have their separate gatherings and never get the opportunity to hear older church members share experiences and bring encouragement.

In Titus 2, we read instructions for wholesome interactions between old and young within the local church. The older men are to exhort the younger men to be sober-minded, and the older women are to admonish the younger women to love their husbands. Older men and women are both instructed to set an example in behavior, patience, and other qualities to the younger people.

Peter wrote similar instructions in his first epistle. All ages, old and young, are meant to meet and fellowship together, the one complementing the other. Solomon wrote in Proverbs 20:29, "The glory of young men *is* their strength, And the splendor of old men *is* their gray head." One local church decided to pair a young person with each elderly person in the congregation, with the purpose of getting to know and encourage one another. Both groups of people have found the bonding very uplifting. In Proverbs 17:6, Solomon writes, "Children's children are the crown of old men, And the glory of children *is* their father." He also encourages, "Listen to your father who begot you, And do not despise your mother when she is old" (Prov. 23:22).

The most important way we can support the elderly is to share the Gospel with those who are still unbelievers. There are people of advanced age who do not yet believe in Jesus Christ and His offer of salvation. They still need to hear the Gospel message, and it is never too late for someone to believe and accept Christ as their Savior, even on their deathbed. God's love can reach out to them in their last hours.

PREPARING FOR OLD AGE

Most people prepare for old age by organizing their finances, making a will, and ensuring that their family will live securely after they have passed on. With our human survival instinct to the fore, nobody likes to think about growing old and becoming physically weaker. But one of the ways in which Christians should prepare for old age is to deal with any sinful habits and attitudes within them and seek to become as emotionally whole as possible by allowing God to heal any wounds and hurts which have come in life, both in childhood and later. Habits and behaviors are often accentuated in old age if they haven't been brought before God and repented of previously. If these deep, inner issues are not dealt with, they will remain untouched and will still affect the person in old age. Inner healing and renewal can still be accomplished by God in an elderly person, but I think it is more difficult.

Why not let God do His healing work within you while you are still young or middle-aged? Then you will know true peace and be able to bless your family members, caregivers, and friends when you reach old age. Psalm 92:14 says, "They shall still bear fruit in old age." Solomon wrote in Proverbs 16:31, "The silver-haired head *is* a crown of glory, if it is found in the way of righteousness." We are to show His glory in our latter years, and we can do so if we walk in the way of righteousness.

Finally, David cried out to God in Psalm 71:9, "Do not cast me off in the time of old age; Do not forsake me when my strength fails." This can be our prayer, too.

MORE ABOUT DEATH

All the organs and physiological functions of the human body work properly and in order during most of a person's lifespan; but eventually, the parts wear out and can no longer sustain the physical body, and the body dies. In Ecclesiastes 9:2, Solomon reminds us, "All things *come* alike to all: One event *happens* to the righteous and the wicked; To the good, the clean, and the unclean, To him who sacrifices and him who does not sacrifice."

Death comes at some point for every person born. In death, a person has nothing left and takes nothing with him, no matter what riches he may have had. Ecclesiastes 5:15 confirms this: "As he came from his mother's womb, naked shall he return. To go as he came; And he shall take nothing from his labor; Which he may carry away in his hand."

However, in Ecclesiastes 9:4-10, Solomon writes about the hope which the living have and ensures us that life is worth living. He tells us to "live life joyfully with the wife whom you love all the days of your vain life which He has given you under the sun" (9:9). "Vain" means futile or pointless. He encourages righteous living: "Let your garments be always white, And let your head lack no oil" (9:8). In addition, it is worthwhile to work hard and to excel in the practical jobs of life: "Whatever your hand finds to do, do *it* with your might" (9:10).

Solomon also wrote about death in Ecclesiastes 7. "The day of death [is better] than the day of one's birth" (7:1), and it is "better to go to the house of mourning Than the house of feasting, For that *is* the end of all men And the living will take *it* to heart" (7:2). Solomon sounds very melancholic here, but many commentators think that he is saying that death and mourning cause us to be thoughtful, to face reality, and to be aware of the plain facts about our existence, unlike times of festivity and excitement when we think life will go on forever. He wrote, "For by a sad countenance the heart is made better" (7:3).

Derek Kidner writes, "The day of death has more to teach us than the day of birth."[292] The apostle Peter spoke about his forthcoming death at the hand of his persecutors, which Christ had showed him was going to happen. "Knowing that shortly I *must* put off my tent" is how he describes it in 2 Peter 1:13-15, as he urged his disciples to remember the truth of the Gospel after his demise.

---

292 Derek Kidner, ibid.

REFERENCES

Alexander, Pat, ed. *Lion Encyclopedia of the Bible.* Colorado Springs: Chariot Victor Pub, 1986.

Ballentine, Debra Scoggins. *The Conflict Myth and the Biblical Tradition.* Oxford, England: Oxford University Press, 2015.

Barker, Margaret. *The Gate of Heaven: The History and Symbolism of the Temple in Jerusalem.* Sheffield, England: Sheffield Phoenix Press, 2008.

Begg, C. T. "Solomon's Apostasy According to Josephus." *Journal for the Study of Judaism in the Persian, Hellenistic, and Roman Period.* Vol. 28, No. 3, 294-313. 1997. https://www.jstor.org/stable/24668405.

Bentley, Ray. *God's Pursuing Love: The Passion, Wisdom and Redemption of King Solomon.* Santa Ana, CA: Calvary Chapel Publishing, 2003.

Bergman, Ronen. *Rise and Kill First: The Secret History of Israel's Targeted Assassinations.* London, England: John Murray, 2018.

Berkowitz, Adam Eliyahu. "Recently Discovered Rock-eating Worm Could Be Key to Building Third Temple." Israel365News. com. June 30, 2019. https://www.israel365news.com/132404/recently-discovered-rock-eating-worm-key-third-temple.

Biltz, Mark. *Decoding the Antichrist and the End Times.* Lake Mary, FL: Charisma House, 2019.

Brill, A. A. *The Basic Writings of Sigmund Freud.* New York, NY: Modern Library, 1995.

Budge, E. A. W. *The Kebra Nagast: The Glory of Kings*. New York, NY: Cosimo Classics, 1922.

Bullivant, Stephen. "Europe's Young Adults and Religion: Findings From the European Social Survey (2014-16) to inform the 2018 Synod of Bishops." Distributed by St. Mary's University Twickenham London: Benedict XVI Centre for Religion and Society, 2018. https://www.stmarys.ac.uk/research/centres/benedict-xvi/docs/2018-mar-europe-young-people-report-eng.pdf.

Carlisle, Nate. "The Mormon polygamists who believe Missouri is the 'promised land.'" The Guardian.com. January 7, 2019. https://www.theguardian.com/world/2019/jan/07/the-mormon-polygamists-who-believe-missouri-is-the-promised-land.

Chavalas, Mark W. "Inland Syria and the East-of-Jordan Region in the First Millennium BCE Before the Assyrian Intrusions." *The Age of Solomon: Scholarship at the Turn of the Millennium*. Lowell K. Handy, ed. Leiden, The Netherlands: Brill, 1997.

Chavel, Charles B. "David's War against the Ammonites: A Note in Biblical Exegesis," *The Jewish Quarterly Review*, New Series 30, No. 3, 257-261, 1940, doi: https://doi.org/10.2307/1452367.

Cook, Brady. *King of Hearts: Exploring King Solomon Through His Life and Writings*. Greenville, TX: Reedsy, 2019.

Cornuke, Robert. *Temple: Amazing New Discoveries that Change Everything About the Location of Solomon's Temple*. Charlotte, NC: LifeBridge Books, 2014.

Cowan, Douglas E. and David G. Bromley. *Cults and New Religions: A Brief History*. Oxford, England: Wiley Blackwell, 2015.

Davis, Dale Ralph. *1 Kings: The Wisdom and the Folly*. Fearn, Scotland: Christian Focus Publications, 2000.

Davis, Deborah. *The Children of God: The Inside Story by the Daughter of the Founder, Moses David Berg*. Basingstoke, England: Marshalls, 1984.

Dolezal, Mary-Lyon and Maria Mavroudi. "Theodore Hyrtakenos' Description of the Garden of St. Anna and the Ekphrasis of Gardens." *Byzantine Garden Culture*.

A. Littlewood, H. Maguire, and J. Wolschke-Bulhman, eds. Washington DC: Harvard University, 2002.

Drazin, Israel. *The Authentic King Solomon.* Jerusalem, Israel: Gefen Publishing, 2018.

Duling, Dennis C. "The Eleazar Miracle and Solomon's Magical Wisdom in Flavius Josephus's *Antiquitates Judaicae* 8.42-49." *Harvard Theological Review.* Vol. 78. No. 1-2. Jan-April, 1-25, 1985.

Eareckson Tada, Joni. *When Is It Right to Die?: Suicide, Euthanasia, Suffering, Mercy.* Grand Rapids, MI: Zondervan, 1992.

Eareckson Tada, Joni. *When is it Right to Die?* Grand Rapids, MI: Zondervan. 2017.

Eareckson Tada, Joni. "Why Suicide is Everybody's Business." Christianity Today. com March 14, 2018. https://www.christianitytoday.com/ct/2018/march-web-only/joni-eareckson-tada-suicide-everybodys-business-euthanasia.html.

Eareckson Tada, Joni and Ken Eareckson Tada. *Joni and Ken: An Untold Love Story.* Grand Rapids, MI: Zondervan, 2013.

Edrey, Meir. "Towards a Definition of the pre-Classical Phoenician Temple." In *Palestine Exploration Journal.* Vol. 150. No. 3. 184-205, 2018. doi: https://doi.org/10 .1080/00310328.2018.1471652.

Erman, Adolf. *Life in Ancient Egypt.* New York, NY: Dover Publications, 1971.

Esteban, César and Daniel Iborra Pellín. "Temples of Astarte Across the Mediterranean." *Mediterranean Archaeology and Archaeometry.* Vol. 16. No. 4. 161–166, 2016.

Fenichel, Otto. *The Psychoanalytic Theory of Neurosis.* New York, NY: W. W. Norton and Co., 1996.

Foster, Lawrence. *Women, Family, and Utopia: Communal Experiments of the Shakers, the Oneida Community, and the Mormons.* Syracuse, NY: Syracuse University Press, 1991.

Foster, Lawrence. *Free Love in Utopia: John Humphrey Noyes and the Origin of the Oneida Community*. Urbana and Chicago, IL: University of Illinois Press, 2001.

Foster, Lawrence. "Free Love and Community: John Humphrey Noyes and the Oneida Perfectionists." In *America's Communal Utopias*. Donald E. Pitzer, ed. Chapel Hill, NC: The University of North Carolina Press, 1997.

Garfinkel, Yosef and Madeleine Mumcuoglu. *Solomon's Temple and Palace: New Archaeological Discoveries*. Jerusalem, Israel: Bible Lands Museum and the Biblical Archaeology Society, 2016.

Gaubert, Henri. *Solomon The Magnificent*. New York, NY: Hastings House, 1970.

Ginzberg, Louis and Boaz Cohen. *The Legends of the Jews Volume 4*. Charleston, SC: Nabu Press, 2010.

Glanville, S. R. K. *The Legacy of Egypt*. Oxford, England: Oxford University Press, 1942.

Glickman, S. Craig. *A Song for Lovers*. Downers Grove, IL: InterVarsity Press, 1976.

Green, Garrett. "Imagining the Future." In *The Future as God's Gift: Explorations in Christian Eschatology*. David Fergusson and Marcel Sarot, eds. Edinburgh, Scotland: T & T Clark, 2000.

Grossman, Igor and Ethan Kross. "Exploring Solomon's Paradox: Self-Distancing Eliminates the Self-Other Asymmetry in Wise Reasoning About Close Relationships in Younger and Older Adults." *Psychological Science*. Vol. 25. No. 8, 1571-1580, 2014. https://doi.org/10.1177/0956797614535400.

Hinn, Costi W. *God, Greed and the (Prosperity) Gospel*. Grand Rapids, MI: Zondervan, 2019.

Holloway, Steven W. "Assyria and Babylonia in the Tenth Century BCE." In Lowell K. Handy, ed. *The Age of Solomon: Scholarship at the Turn of the Millennium*. Leiden: The Netherlands: Brill, 1997.

Ikeda, Yutaka. "Solomon's Trade in Horses and Chariots in Its International Setting." In Tomoo Ishida, ed. *Studies in the Period of David and Solomon and Other Essays*. Tokyo, Japan: Yamakawa-Shuppansha, 1982.

Jacq, Christian. *The Living Wisdom of Ancient Egypt.* New York, NY: Pocket Books, 1999.

Josephus, Flavius. *The Complete Works of Flavius Josephus.* Green Forest, AR: New Leaf Publishing Group, 2008.

Jung, Carl G. *Memories, Dreams, Reflections.* London, England: Collins and Routledge & Kegan Paul, 1963.

Kalimi, Isaac. "Love of God and *Apologia* for a King." *Journal of Ancient Near Eastern Religions.* Vol. 17. No. 1. 2017. 28-63. doi: https://doi.org/10.1163/15692124-12341285.

Karpin, Michael. *The Bomb in the Basement: How Israel Went Nuclear and What That Means for the World.* New York, NY: Simon and Schuster, 2007.

Keller, Timothy and Kathy Keller. *The Meaning of Marriage.* New York, NY: Riverhead Books, 2011.

Kidner, Derek. *The Message of Ecclesiastes: A Time to Mourn and a Time to Dance.* Nottingham, England: InterVarsity Press, 1976.

Kitchen, Kenneth A. "Sheba and Arabia." *The Age of Solomon: Scholarship at the Turn of the Millennium.* Lowell K. Handy, ed. Leiden, The Netherlands: Brill, 1997.

Konkel, August H. *1 and 2 Kings, the NIV Application Commentary.* Grand Rapids, MI: Zondervan, 2010.

Kosmin, Barry A. and Ariela Keysar. *Religion in a Free Market: Religious and Non-Religious Americans.* Ithaca, NY: Paramount Market Publishing, 2006.

Lifshitz, Joseph Isaac. "Welfare, Property and the Divine Image in Jewish Law and Thought." *Markets, Morals and Religion.* Jonathan B. Imber, ed. New Brunswick, NJ: Transaction Publishers, 2008.

Maimonides, Moses. *The Guide for the Perplexed.* New York, NY: Cosimo Books, 2007.

Malamat, Abraham. "The Kingdom of David & Solomon in Its Contact with Egypt and Aram Naharaim." *The Biblical Archaeologist.* Vol. 21. No. 4. 1958. 96-102, doi: https://doi.org/10.2307/3209177.

McCluskey, Christopher and Rachel McCluskey. *When Two Become One: Enhancing Sexual Intimacy in Marriage*. Grand Rapids, MI: Fleming H. Revell, 2004.

McLean, Clay. "Real God and Real Me." *Nightlight Newsletters*. No. 306. November 1, 2018. Hickory: McLean Ministries. https://www.mcleanministries.org/uploads/nightlight_newsletters/nov_2018_reg_layout.pdf.

McLean, Clay. "The Soul in Prayer." *Nightlight Newsletters*. No. 312. May 1, 2019. Hickory: McLean Ministries. https://www.mcleanministries.org/uploads/nightlight_newsletters/may_2019_reg_layout.pdf.

Mettinger, T. N. D. "YHWH Sabaoth – The Heavenly King on the cherubim throne." *Studies in the Period of David and Solomon and Other Essays*. Tomoo Ishida, ed. Tokyo, Japan: Yamakawa-Shuppansha, 1982.

Meyers, Carol. "Israelite Empire: In Defense of King Solomon." *Michigan Quarterly Review*. Vol. 22. No. 3. 1983. http://hdl.handle.net/2027/spo.act2080.0022.003:45.

Millard, Alan. "King Solomon in his Ancient Context." *Bible and Spade*. Vol. 15. No. 3. Summer, 2002.

Morris, Henry M. *The Remarkable Wisdom of Solomon*. Green Forest, AR: Master Books, 2001.

Nelson, Shawn. "David's Magnificent Temple Built in the Flesh." GeekyChristian.com. December, 2013. http://geekychristian.com/evidence-the-temple-was-not-gods-will.

National Health Service (NHS). *Ageing well and supporting people living with frailty*. 2019 https://www.england.nhs.uk/ourwork/clinical-policy/older-people/frailty.

Parker, K.I. "Solomon as Philosopher King? The Nexus of Law and Wisdom in 1 Kings 1-11." *Journal for the Study of the Old Testament*. Vol. 17. No. 53, 75-91, 1992. https://doi.org/10.1177/030908929201705305.

Patterson, James, John Connolly, and Tim Malloy. *Filthy Rich*. New York, NY: Grand Central Publishing, 2017.

Patterson, Roger. "Mormonism." *World Religions and Cults: Counterfeits of Christianity.* Bodie Hodge and Roger Patterson, eds. Green Forest, AR: Master Books, 2015.

Pawson, David. "Song of Solomon—the Royal Wedding." IHOPKC. YouTube video. October 4, 2017. 58:54. https://www.youtube.com/watch?v=F9ELivh0v1A.

Perrota, Cosimo. *Consumption as an Investment (Routledge Studies in the History of Economics).* Abingdon, England: Routledge, 2004.

Pontz, Zach. "Richard Dawkins Perplexed by Number of Jewish Nobel Prize Winners." TheAlgemeiner.com. October 29, 2013. https://www.algemeiner.com/2013/10/29/richard-dawkins-perplexed-by-high-number-of-jewish-nobel-prize-winners/.

Prince, Derek and Ruth Prince. *God is a Matchmaker.* Tarrytown, NY: Chosen Books, 1986.

Prince, Derek. *Foundations for Righteous Living.* Harpenden, England: Derek Prince Ministries, 1998.

Prince, Derek. *Marriage Covenant: The Biblical Secret for a Love That Lasts.* Baldock, England: Derek Prince Ministries, 2012.

Rice, Michael. *Who's Who in Ancient Egypt.* London, England: Routledge, 1999.

Ritner, Robert K. *The Libyan Anarchy: Inscriptions from Egypt's Third Intermediate Period.* Atlanta, GA: Society of Biblical Literature, 2009.

Robertson, David. "Ecclesiastes 4 and the cure for loneliness: the cord of three strands." Christian Today online. February 2, 2018. https://christiantoday.com/article/ecclesiastes-4-and-the-cure-for-loneliness-the-cord-of-three-strands/125282.htm.

Rosenau, Douglas E. *A Celebration of Sex.* Nashville, TN: Thomas Nelson, 2002.

Roy, Archie W. N. *The God of Dreams: Understanding the Meaning and Significance of Dreaming.* Sisters, OR: Deep River Books, 2017.

Rudolph, Ariel. "The Agricultural Language of the Bible." *Israel Today.* December, Vol. 35, 2019.

Sacks, Deana Pollard. *The Godfathers of Sex Abuse Book 1: Jeffrey Epstein*. Saint Louis, MO: Stonebrook Publishing, 2019.

Salter, Anna C. *Transforming Trauma: A Guide to Understanding and Treating Adult Survivors of Child Sexual Abuse*. Thousand Oaks, CA: Sage, 1995.

Sauter, Megan. "The Doorways of Solomon's Temple." Bible History Daily online. October 27, 2020. https://www.biblicalarchaeology.org/daily/biblical-artifacts/artifacts-and-the-bible/the-doorways-of-solomons-temple.

Scott, R.B.Y. "The Pillars Jachin and Boaz." *Journal of Biblical Literature*. Vol. 58. No. 2. June, 1939, 143-149. doi:10.2307/3259857.

Shapiro, Rami M. *The Divine Feminine in Biblical Wisdom Literature*. Woodstock, VT: SkyLight Paths, 2013.

Shear, T. Leslie. *Trophies of Victory: Public Building in Periklean Athens*. Princeton, NJ: Princeton University Press, 2016.

Sittser, Jerry. *The Will of God as a Way of Life*. Grand Rapids, MI: Zondervan, 2004.

Schuster, Ruth. "Why Do Jews Win So Many Nobels?" Haaretz.com, 2013. https://www.haaretz.com/jewish/why-do-jews-win-so-many-nobels-1.5347671.

Stone, Michael E. "Concerning the Penitence of Solomon." *Journal of Theological Studies*. Vol 29. No. 1. 1-19, 1978.

Thieberger, Frederic. *King Solomon*. Oxford, England: East and West Library, 1947.

Thompson, Richard. "Who was Asaph?" HFBCBibleStudy.org. May 30, 2005. www.hfbcbiblestudy.org/index2.php?option=com_content&do_pdf=1&id=482.

TOI Staff. "5 Jews make Forbes' list of top 10 wealthiest Americans." The Times of Israel.com. October 6, 2018. https://www.timesofisrael.com/5-jews-make-forbes-list-of-top-10-wealthiest-americans/.

Van Blerk, N.J. "The Concept of Law and Justice in Ancient Egypt, With Specific Reference to the *Tale of the Eloquent Peasant*." M.A. Dissertation. University of South Africa. 2006.

Ward, Vicky. *The Talented Mr Epstein*. Vanity Fair, March, 2003.

Weitzman, Steven. *Solomon: The Lure of Wisdom*. New Haven, CT: Yale University Press, 2011.

Wheat, Ed and Gaye Wheat. *Intended for Pleasure*. Bletchley, England: Scripture Union, 1977.

Wight, Fred H. *Manners and Customs of Bible Lands*. Chicago, IL: Moody Publishers, 1953.

Wurmbrand, Richard. *Tortured for Christ the Complete Story*. Eastbourne, England: David C. Cook, 2018.

Zeligs, D. F. "Solomon: Man and Myth." *Psychoanalysis and the Psychoanalytic Review*. Vol. 48. No. 1. 77-103, Spring; and Vol. 48. No. 2. 91-110, Summer, 1961.

Zimmermann, F. "The book of Ecclesiastes in the light of some psychoanalytic observations." *American Imago: A Psychoanalytic Journal for the Arts and Sciences*. Vol. 5. No. 4. 301-305. December, 1948.

For more information about

Archie W. N. and Margaret P. Roy
and
King Solomon's Empire
please visit:

www.godofourdreams.com

For more information about
AMBASSADOR INTERNATIONAL
please visit:

www.ambassador-international.com

Thank you for reading this book. Please consider leaving us a review on your social media, favorite retailer's website, Goodreads or Bookbub, or our website.

More from Ambassador International

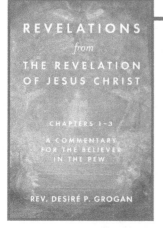

For the believer in the pew, the Book of the Revelation of Jesus Christ needs no other introduction than that it is the most avoided Book of Scripture that few feel capable of navigating and understanding on their own. The dense amount of imagery and the horrific scenes of judgment are mind-boggling and remain a mystery for many. The purpose of this volume is to empower you—the believer in the pew—with the most accessible tool to navigate and understand this last Book of Scripture, and that tool is the Bible itself, the Bible in your hand!

To some people, saying David had a godly heart is almost offensive. How do you apply that description to a man whose legacy includes neglecting responsibilities, lust, adultery, murder, deception, hypocrisy, and callous indifference? *David: The Godly Heart of a Sinful Man* examines David's heart, identifying specific character qualities that influenced his response when confronted with his sin.

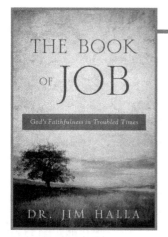

Job, the book and the man, is well-known even in the public arena. However, the main character of the book is the Triune God. Moreover, some have suggested that the book of Job focuses on the larger problem of evil in a good God's world. By definition that would include the concept of victimhood. However, Dr. Jim Halla thinks that approach misses major issues in the book. *The Book of Job: God's Faithfulness in Troubled Times* presents Dr. Halla's understanding of the book and how it applies to the New Testament, Jesus, and us.